CAN'T DENY IT

An Unlikely Wall Street Career and the Calls that Reshaped an Industry

DOUG TERRESON

Disclaimer

The information contained in this book is for educational and informational purposes only and is not intended as investment, financial, or legal advice. All opinions expressed herein are those of the author and are subject to change without notice. They are not to be imputed to any other person or organization with whom I may be affiliated at any time.

While the author has made every effort to ensure the accuracy and completeness of the information contained in this book, no guarantee is given regarding the reliability, accuracy, or completeness of any content. Any performance data represents past performance and does not guarantee future results. The reader is strongly encouraged to conduct their own research and consult with a qualified professional before making any investment or financial decisions.

The examples of securities purchases and sales, as well as the investment strategies discussed in this book, are for illustrative purposes only and based solely on the experience of a single individual. Nothing contained herein should be interpreted as providing information that is sufficient to make an informed investment decision. This book does not constitute a recommendation for any person to adopt or refrain from adopting a specific investment strategy, or to purchase, sell, or refrain from transacting in any particular security, class of securities, index, or other asset or asset class.

No investment decisions should be made based on the contents of this book. The author's past experience does not guarantee the future success of the investment strategies or concepts described herein. All investment decisions involve risk of loss and may not be suitable for everyone in all circumstances. Readers considering investments are encouraged to conduct independent due diligence to determine if a particular investment is appropriate for their unique circumstances, including but not limited to their investment objectives, investment experience, risk tolerance, and investment time horizon.

The author, publisher, distributor, and their affiliates do not assume, and specifically disclaim, any liability for any loss or damage resulting from any act or omission, directly or indirectly, in whole or in part, based on any information, description, suggestion, methodology, or explanation contained in this book. Any reference to a specific company, class of securities, index of securities, asset, or asset class does not imply that the author, at any particular time, held those securities or that they were part of a portfolio managed by the author. Furthermore, such references do not constitute an investment recommendation regarding those securities or assets.

By reading this book, you acknowledge and agree that the author is not responsible for any decisions you make regarding your financial or investment strategies and that you assume full responsibility for your actions and decisions.

Copyright

CAN'T DENY IT Copyright © 2024 by Doug Terreson. All rights reserved.

Printed in the United States of America. No part of this book may be used or reproduced in any manner whatsoever without written permission except in the case of brief quotations embodied in critical articles and reviews. For information, address Seminole LLC, 18042 Woodland Drive, Point Clear, AL.

FIRST EDITION

Dust Jacket Design & Interior Layout by Michael J. Williams

ISBN - 979-8-9916810-0-1

In the world of finance, your track record is your resume. Every trade, every recommendation is documented and scrutinized.

Stanley Druckenmiller

CONTENTS

Foreword   7

1. A Shocking Call, A Stunning Exit   11
2. Cutting My Teeth in the Oil Patch   21
3. Both Sides of "The Street" and My Road to Morgan Stanley   35
4. The Era of the Super-Major   45
5. Privatizations   89
6. The Golden Age of Refining   121
7. Crude Oil and the Chaos of 2008   145
8. The Pledge   165
9. Can't Deny It   217
10. What About the Future?   231

Acknowledgments   247
About the Author   249

FOREWORD

The role of an equity analyst on Wall Street is one of immense challenge and scrutiny. It demands a rare combination of analytical prowess, market insight, impeccable timing, emotional resilience, extensive industry connections, and exceptional communication skills. While many analysts achieve success, truly distinguished careers in this field are few and far between.

Names like Mary Meeker, Mike Mayo, and Dana Telsey come to mind as exemplars in their field. However, Doug Terreson stands out not just for his analytical acumen, but for the transformative impact he has had on the global oil and gas industry. Doug's ability to convince investors, management teams, and boards of directors that the fundamental structure of the energy industry needed an overhaul is unprecedented. "Can't Deny It" is not just a retelling of how this change occurred; it's a vital piece of oil industry history that deserves to stand alongside the works of Daniel Yergin and Matthew Simmons.

Doug and I share remarkably similar backgrounds. Both hailing from the Gulf Coast with engineering backgrounds, we spent countless hours offshore on drilling rigs and production platforms. These experiences laid the foundation for our careers in the financial services industry. I transitioned into my portfolio manager role at Barrow Hanley in Dallas several years after Doug was already recognized as one of the country's top analysts.

Doug's gentlemanly nature and willingness to mentor others, including myself, speaks volumes about his character. To this day, every conversation with Doug yields new insights, and I believe readers of "Can't Deny It" will experience the same enlightenment with each turn of the page.

The book offers a front-row seat to some of the most pivotal moments in recent oil industry history. From Doug's "Era of the Super-Major" call in 1998 that reshaped the entire industry, to his prescient "Golden Age of Refining" prediction in 2003, and his controversial but ultimately correct oil price forecast during the tumultuous period of 2008, readers will gain unprecedented insight into the inner workings of Wall Street and the global energy sector.

Doug also details his "Pledger" movement from 2015 to the present which challenged energy companies to prioritize capital discipline and shareholder returns, fundamentally altering the industry's approach to financial management and shareholder alignment. Through Doug's narrative, readers will understand how this movement not only reshaped corporate strategies but also helped the energy industry "get back on track again in the current era," marking yet another instance where his foresight and influence have left an indelible mark on the industry.

Doug's story is not just about making accurate predictions; it's about having the courage to stand by one's convictions in the face of immense pressure. His ability to see beyond short-term market dynamics and identify long-term trends is truly remarkable. The book also offers a glimpse into the personal side of being a top Wall Street analyst, including the challenges of balancing a high-pressure career with family life and personal fulfillment.

"Can't Deny It" is more than just a memoir; it's a master class in energy market analysis, a chronicle of industry transformation, and a testament to the power of independent thinking. Whether you're an industry professional, an investor, or simply someone interested in the forces that shape our global economy, this book offers invaluable insights and lessons.

As someone who has witnessed Doug's career firsthand, I can attest to the accuracy and importance of the stories and insights shared in this book. It's a mustread for anyone looking to understand the complexities of the energy industry and the role of visionary analysts in shaping its future.

– Lewis Ropp
Senior Managing Director, Portfolio Manager at Barrow Hanley Global Investors

1

A Shocking Call, A Stunning Exit

Houston, Texas | 2008

My lifeline to my internal network had been blinking red for weeks. Colleagues were warning me that an internal coup was underway—and I was the target.

Though I recently made what many dubbed "the call of the decade" on Wall Street,[1] I was under pressure to change my low oil price forecast which, admittedly, appeared dead wrong at the time, and seemed to go against the current and conviction of the entire energy industry.

On top of that, my firm, Morgan Stanley, had become a marginal fit for me by 2008. The culture in research seemed to be shifting from a meritocracy to a bureaucracy in my area, with what I viewed as mediocre talent increasingly taking positions of power. While I didn't mind as long as they didn't bother me on a day-to-day basis and my compensation wasn't affected, I knew my days at Morgan Stanley were probably numbered. The job no longer aligned with my ambitions, and it wasn't bringing me the enjoyment and fulfillment it once had. With my house

---

1. The "Golden Age of Refining," was dubbed the "call of the decade" because it resulted in a 1,700% rise in refining stocks during 2003-2007.

in Houston already on the market, I had one foot out the proverbial door, just waiting to see who would make the final move in this corporate chess match.

While every analyst misses from time to time, even at the highest level of Wall Street, this was different. This was early 2008 when investment banks like Bear Stearns were going under, the housing market was teetering on collapse, crude oil prices were surging, and nothing less than the global economy was hanging in the balance. Remember the Great Recession?

Oil had just breached $110 per barrel (bbl) for the first time ever, blowing past my closely watched projections. As one of the leading global experts on the oil market, my methodology indicated that fundamental conditions surrounding the price of crude oil did not justify the strength in the market (instead suggesting only modest gains in prices by the end of the year).

Armchair forecasters came out of the woodwork to beat the drum on crude oil, much like amateur epidemiologists did during the COVID-19 pandemic. Key competitors lined up against me, forecasting that oil prices were headed for a shocking $200 and even $300/bbl.

And while the pressure grew daily for me to capitulate and align with consensus, I thought the oil bulls were not seeing the bigger picture and would eventually be exposed. My methodology suggested that oil prices would stay below $100/bbl throughout 2008, but as prices rose, my forecast seemed more wrong. The adage on Wall Street that "if you want a friend, you should get a dog," hit home as it seemed my chocolate Labrador Herschel was the only one who believed in me at the time.

Still, I held my ground. I knew it was a risky career move, but my research methodology had served me and my clients well in the past. As such, I was determined to persevere through the criticism and skepticism directed at me, patiently awaiting the vindication that would come when oil prices ultimately collapsed. If my forecast turned out to be correct, it would rival my other industry leading calls on Wall Street.

You see, in my 35-year career as a Wall Street energy research analyst, I seemed to have had the unique ability to make what some deemed to be shocking, contrary, industry-changing calls that other analysts, who were worried about things like their job security, would not risk. One of my clients even told me, "Doug, you had a success rate that was so improbable it bordered on creepy." Truth be told, there was nothing supernatural about it—it was just math (well, a lot of complex math), and an acute understanding of incentives and human nature.

The first call that made me a household name on Wall Street was titled the "Era of the Super-Major" where I suggested that the business models of all the largest oil companies—Amoco, ARCO, BP, Conoco, Chevron, Elf Aquitaine, Exxon, Mobil, Phillips, Shell, Texaco, and Total—had become obsolete.[2] It goes without saying this was a questionable career choice for any analyst in any sector. But in 1998, the oil industry was in a major slump[3] and I thought I had discovered a solution. In my report to investors, I suggested that the major oil companies should merge and become a group of powerful "Super-Majors" in order to deliver the scale needed to restore performance to past glory. Once the Super-Major mergers were complete, I was certain that CEOs would remain committed, and that returns and valuation would rise, and exceptional market performance would follow.

While my call was met with plenty of detractors, to my delight, BP and Amoco announced the first Super-Major merger six months after I predicted the merger phase (and as investor pressure grew) with ExxonMobil, Elf-Total, Chevron-Texaco, and ConocoPhillips following soon after. In the next three years, the entire petroleum industry would experience its most significant transformation since the break-up of the Standard Oil Trust in 1911—almost identical to the way I had indicated in my research.

---

2. My "Era of the Super Major" report from February 13, 1998, is the source of the term "Super-Major."

3. By 1998, S&P Energy had declined from 28% of S&P 500 in 1980 to 14% in 1990 to only 4%.

When the new Super-Majors remained committed to the value-based model that I espoused, S&P energy went on to rise from a mere 4% of S&P 500 to 14%, from 1998 to 2008. During that time, market value rose by a whopping $500 billion with the energy sector posting its best decadal performance ever.[4] The global oil industry was reshaped along the lines of my thesis, ultimately resulting in exceptional performance in the equity market.

In just 36 months, the "Super-Major" model became the prototype for the entire energy sector, and my life was forever changed.

Thanks to the success of the "Era of the Super-Major," my team at Morgan Stanley went on to win three of the highest-profile energy privatization mandates in the world. From 1996 to 2000, we were involved with almost every national oil company in Asia, Europe, and Latin America, completing Initial Public Offerings (IPOs) for Sinopec in China, Statoil in Norway, as well as Conoco in the U.S. I was thrilled when the market performance for the companies that we restructured or IPO'd was spectacular (with Sinopec and Statoil shares rising by 500% during their first five years in public markets).[5] During my globe-trotting era, I developed lasting relationships with the CEOs of the largest energy companies in the world, including those in North America, Europe, Asia, and the Middle East.[6] When my privatization world tour ended in 2000, I'd visited countless countries, and been the lead analyst on the largest energy IPOs in North America, Europe, and Asia—a nice hat trick.

Better yet was the "Golden Age of Refining" call in 2003 when my research methodology uncovered a hidden treasure in the market. In my report to my clients, I suggested, that "2003

---

4. Results surpassed that of every other major industry sector in S&P 500 during the period as well

5. An initial public offering (IPO) is the process by which a private company offers shares to the public for the first time. It marks the transition of a company from private to public ownership, providing it with access to capital markets to raise funds for expansion, debt repayment, or other corporate purposes.

6. My Middle East relationships gave me a unique window of insight into OPEC.

will be a good year to invest in global refining, but 2004 to 2006 will be the best three years of the past three decades, with 2006 being the best year of all." The Wall Street Journal quoted me saying "Buy them all, it won't matter which ones you own." At first, my competitors thought I was overreaching. "Global refining? You must be kidding." Indeed, Refining and Marketing (R&M) companies rarely earned their cost of capital in any year of the prior decade which justified Wall Street's broadly negative sentiment toward the sector. I doubted "The Street" had done the work in refining like I had and instead thought they were just coasting with the negative view that worked so well in the prior decade. While clustering around the negative thesis was surely more comfortable for them, it also created the perfect setup for a major market surprise if I was right.

And that's exactly what happened.

It took a few years, but by the time that I downgraded refining stocks in mid-2006, the stock prices of Holley, Tesoro, and Valero—all industry leading refiners—had risen by an otherworldly 1,700%, qualifying for the "call of the decade" across Wall Street.[7] During the success of the "Golden Age of Refining," I also was the lead analyst on almost every major equity offering in R&M with the assets purchased during this period forming the cornerstone positions held by the major players in the sector today.

If you want to learn about my biggest call, "The Pledge," where I helped the energy industry get back on track again in the current era, that and a lot more happens further down the road.

So, keep reading. I will talk about that later in the book.

Yet in early 2008, even with my proven track record, our research team was losing credibility every day that oil prices continued to rise. Although I was confident in my forecast and believed I would be proven right in the end, I knew the clock was ticking—not just on my call, but possibly on my Wall Street career as well.

I understood that investors were justified in questioning

---

7. For perspective, historical S&P 500 returns approximated 30% for the same period.

what was going on with my forecast: Was I just experiencing a temporary setback, or had the market evolved beyond my approach? If the latter was the case—and I had lost my "magic touch"—it would pose an even graver threat to my career. Time would tell.

The day after the collapse of Bear Stearns on March 14, 2008, as economic turmoil escalated, I published my highly anticipated update on the oil market. While I was widely expected to capitulate with my new oil market outlook and adopt the positive consensus view, I didn't. Instead, I doubled down. I indicated that oil market fundamentals deteriorated during the previous six months and that increased caution was warranted on future oil prices. Meaning, rather than turn positive, my new view was wholly against the grain and more negative.

In simpler terms, I predicted that the amount of oil being produced would soon be almost 2 million barrels per day (MMBPD) more than what consumers needed. This surplus would cause the total stored oil worldwide to jump significantly, reaching 55 days of global demand, which would be an all-time high. With such a significant surplus of oil, I thought the price of Brent crude oil (a major benchmark for oil prices) would drop a lot and would only be about $95/bbl in 2008.

My updated call did not sit well with oil bulls inside Morgan Stanley—or industry-wide—and spears began to fly. I was already fatigued by the carnival-like atmosphere on Wall Street at the time, and the daily barrage of criticism only added fuel to my burnout. As the stakes grew higher, I found myself at a crossroads and had to confront some hard questions. Was I ready to weather this storm indefinitely? Did I still find fulfillment in my work, or had the joy been overshadowed by the constant stress? As I waited patiently to see if my methodology—and the market—would come through for me as it had time and time again, I reflected on what kind of future I wanted for my career—and for my family—and contemplated my next move.

I continued to publish research and called clients to relay my investment view, and in the afternoons, I was at the ballpark coaching my son's Little League team. "The Frogs" had started slowly that year, going winless in their first two games. But the afternoon of our third game, they flipped a switch, and scrapped their way to a tie with the defending champions, "the Cavaliers." I was so proud of the boys that in my post-game speech, I challenged each of them. "Get your expectations up. If the mighty Cavaliers were the best, what does that make us?"

Though they were just kids, I was trying to encourage the boys to compete at the highest level, and to win. Believe it or not, I get as much satisfaction out of coaching youth sports as I did in my analyst career. I coached 24 teams in all. And, during the uncertainty of 2008, that bunch of rambunctious 9-year-olds helped to rally my spirits and encouraged me when I needed it most. Weekends with family were also a much-needed retreat from all the chaos that surrounded me at work.

July rolled around and what happened next can best be described in an article published by a New York media outlet later that year in September 2008:

> "Douglas Terreson, the Morgan Stanley analyst who said that independent refining and marketing companies were undervalued, was the bank's chief oil analyst. The award-winning, nationally recognized Terreson had fielded questions in relation to oil prices and futures since the mid-1990s. On March 14 of this year, he said that oil would settle at around $95/bbl for the remainder of 2008. Moreover, Terreson also concluded that oil would retreat to around $83/bbl for 2009. This would be Terreson's last forecast for Morgan Stanley. Two short months later, Dow Jones Newswires reported that Terreson had been ousted in a round of layoffs. Two weeks after that, Morgan Stanley issued a statement saying that crude oil could easily reach $150 a barrel. This speculation set off a round of speculative fervor never before seen in

the market. Goldman Sachs immediately followed suit by forecasting oil to roar beyond $150, saying it could hit $200 a barrel in the near future. Oil prices were off to the races, with the investment banks in full lobbying mode while pointing the finger at China and India. Terreson, once an integral part of the Houston community and a star in the financial sector, seemingly disappeared from the city altogether. His home phone has been disconnected. His former co-workers were unsure of his whereabouts. And almost no one from the firm at which he spent years as a superstar in his field wants to discuss why…"[8]

Although not as covert and mysterious as some suggested, I had been planning to move my family to Fairhope, Alabama, since early 2008, regardless of whether I remained at Morgan Stanley. After more than two decades on Wall Street and its relentless pace, I was looking forward to the peace and quiet of small town living and being close to the beautiful beaches of the Gulf Coast, near where I had grown up.

My departure from Morgan Stanley was amicable; they treated me with fairness, consistent with their solid reputation. They expressed gratitude for my leadership in building the highest-rated energy team ever on Wall Street, and we parted ways with a handshake. The firm and I had simply grown apart, and it was clear that it was the right time for both of us to pursue new opportunities.

And as for whose forecast was ultimately proven right? Shortly after my exit, oil prices plummeted from $147/bbl in July 2008 to $37/bbl by Christmas. Overall, oil prices averaged $98/bbl—within 3% of my projection of $95/bbl—for the year. In the end, I almost hit the bullseye—and bullseyes rarely happen on Wall Street. The market psychology turned on a dime, collapsing just as quickly. Oil bulls who had predicted prices of $200 to $300/bbl disappeared from the media spotlight, their credibility shattered.

---

[8]. Jerod Morey, The Long Island Press, September 25, 2008

As I packed up my family to move to Alabama, I contemplated what my next steps would be for me professionally. Oil companies, hedge funds, and private equity firms reached out in short order, but I remembered the advice that former ExxonMobil CEO Lee Raymond gave me, which was to say no to every job offer for one year. This sounded like a wise decision and would allow me some time to regain my perspective.

On the other hand, future Continental Oil CEO Bill Berry told me that, while taking a break was fine, I would not be the "fair-haired child" forever. His advice got my attention too.

I don't get recognized much living a world away from Wall Street here in Fairhope, but whenever people ask me how I made the right call so often, I just shrug and reply, "I just skated to where the puck was going, rather than where it already was."[9]

Looking back, it was a magical ride for me and my clients.

You occasionally see people in my profession given the Hollywood treatment in movies, so many assume that working on Wall Street must be a glamorous job. But the truth is, a research analyst's life can be intense, lonely, hyper-competitive, and not for those with thin skin or a faint heart. Forecasting commodities is complex and difficult. Only a handful of global firms provide credible energy calls, which is why the best forecasters are so closely watched.

Some may find it odd that an individual with my unusual background would have accomplished what I did. I'm not an Ivy Leaguer. I didn't grow up in the tri-state area, home to many of the major investment firms. Growing up in a small town in Mississippi, my family, my faith, and competing in sports consumed my time. I wasn't interested in the stock market—I didn't know Wall Street from Main Street back then—but I was fascinated by oil and gas and started working on offshore rigs when

---

9. I am paraphrasing Wayne Gretzky, arguably the greatest hockey player of all time.

I was in college. I didn't excel in high school like my brother, who went on to become a renowned heart surgeon. In fact, if you asked my teachers, they'd tell you I gave no indication that I would become a thought leader of any sort.[10] I was just a determined young man with a public-school education who came out of the oil patch looking to compete at the highest level. Now that I think about it, perhaps it was my sports background that gave me the confidence to enter one of the most competitive arenas in the world. I always felt comfortable taking the last shot, a skill that translates nicely to pressure packed Wall Street.

To be honest, a lot of it felt like an out-of-body experience. I still can't believe I was the person whose credibility was strong enough that my words moved U.S. and global energy stocks. I'm still a little stunned that so many people bought my uncomfortable theses for change over the conventional wisdom of the major oil companies and the consensus of Wall Street analysts.

> But, as the record shows, they were right to do it. Numbers don't lie on Wall Street.

---

10. I think most CEOs of the largest oil companies would say they were positively surprised by their path and destination as well.

2

Cutting My Teeth in the Oil Patch

While I never envisioned myself as a high-level energy sector analyst on Wall Street, a career in the oil business interested me from an early age. And growing up on the Mississippi Gulf Coast provided many opportunities for me to test the waters (quite literally) of what I thought could be a potential career path.

I was a student at Mississippi State University and on track to graduate with a degree in petroleum engineering when my father introduced me to Mr. Doyle Berry, co-owner of Berry Brothers, an oil field service company in Morgan City, Louisiana. I knew I would need hands-on experience in the oil field: first, to see if I had the skills and work ethic required, and second, to bolster my credentials when applying for jobs after graduation.

I vividly remember my first meeting with Doyle Berry and his brother Everett. They were kind and welcoming, but they made it clear the work would be arduous, and the other crew members would be rougher around the edges than I was used to. While most were "good ole boys" from Louisiana, Mississippi, or Texas, some had run-ins with the law and were on work-release from local jails or prison. Tales from Louisiana's notorious Angola Penitentiary, including stories of what had landed my co-workers in prison in the first place, quickly got my attention and added an element of risk and intrigue to the experience.

I started out working as a roustabout (like a deckhand on a boat) on one of Berry Brothers' dredge barges in the Louisiana swamp in 1982. Our barge was equipped with a drag line excavator—a large crane with a bucket for moving earth, and a box-like living quarters for the crew. The barge's main job was to create passage-ways for drilling rigs that led to drilling locations, that based on seismic data showed likely oil and gas reserves. It was also used in coastal restoration, and building levees, dams, and shell pads.

Our work schedule was demanding: two weeks on, one week off. Factoring in travel time from my home in Pascagoula, Mississippi, to the crew boat in Morgan City, Louisiana, it effectively became 15 days on and six off. With 12-hour shifts, operations ran continuously, making our time off highly valued.

Let me start by saying that I've never been afraid of hard work, even as a boy. But the heat and humidity on the bayou in South Louisiana is enough to send even the toughest guys hightailing it for the cool air of their college dorm room. The summer months are intense, with temperatures above 90 degrees most days, a heat index well into the 100s, and humidity above 80%. While frequent pop-up thunderstorms would cool things briefly, the "heat bursts" that followed as the sun reheated the moisture left behind by the storms would make it even more unbearable. Imagine 12-hour days of manual labor in a steam room, only made worse by the long-sleeved coveralls we wore to protect from the swarms of mosquitoes and horse flies prevalent on the Louisiana marsh.

My days started at 5:30 a.m., and breakfast was always substantial—eggs, grits, bacon, biscuits—the works. It was a hearty meal to fuel us for the strenuous day ahead. My primary job was to operate a large drum-style winch for lifting the spuds when we needed to move the barge, a task that came up only once or twice an hour. The rest of my time was spent cleaning the deck and mopping the entire 4,000 square foot space—a serious upper body workout in the hot and humid Louisiana climate.

Being the only one on our 10-person crew who didn't speak French, I initially felt like an outsider. Gradually, though, I started to grasp some of their Cajun French and began to develop a camaraderie with the crew. They appreciated my efforts, even if I was far from fluent.

After our shifts, we would typically unwind by watching the Astros or Braves, or occasionally, we'd go alligator hunting. While this might seem unusual, it was a common activity in South Louisiana, despite the snakes and other large reptiles that watched our every move. Alligator hides can be made into belts and boots, and the meat often found its way to our grill, and into delicious Cajun-style dishes served by my new friends.

Working in the oil field was hazardous, despite the industry's strong focus on safety. Traveling to the job site by crew boat, air boat, or helicopter at all hours of the day and night, added to the risks, and injury and death from electrical incidents, equipment accidents, explosions, and drownings were common.

The adage that "it doesn't rain, doesn't get cold and there aren't any holidays" in the oil field proved true, but I didn't mind. I was fascinated by the industry—its processes, its people, its culture—and it paid my way through college.

The experience pushed me out of my comfort zone and taught me how to connect with individuals whose backgrounds and perspectives differed greatly from my own. I learned the importance of balancing emotional and academic intelligence, a blend I found crucial for success in any business role, from entry-level positions to executive suites worldwide. This time was a formative chapter in my personal and professional growth, shaping me in ways I couldn't have imagined when I first stepped onto our barge in the Louisiana marsh.

While I've described how dangerous and daunting life in the oil field could be, it may come as a surprise that it was the safest and easiest of my summer jobs, compared to shrimping and commercial fishing. Looking back, I'm not sure what drew me to the jobs that my peers avoided, but it seems there's a connection to these industries that runs deep—maybe it's not just oil that's in my blood, but a bit of saltwater too. Or maybe it's that I've always loved a challenge. Whatever the deeper reason, it certainly helped that these jobs funded my school and my social calendar for the following year.

My first shrimping gig was on a 47-foot Biloxi-style boat called *The Pride of St. Tammany*. She had a shallow draft and a slight V-shaped bottom, allowing her to navigate in shallow waters where shrimp thrive. The boat was owned by my high school buddy Russell Bosarge and his dad Clyde, who were Pascagoula seafaring legends.

Shrimp are nocturnal creatures and sensitive to light, so our workday started around 4 p.m. We'd set our nets from dusk until dawn, wrapping up around 9 a.m. to rest. Out in the Gulf of Mexico, about 50 miles offshore, the conditions varied, and without air conditioning, sleep was often challenging, especially with the seafood smell and flies it attracted. As the newest crew member, I often slept on the kitchen floor or on deck under a sheet for protection from birds and insects.

To catch shrimp, we used a large net or trawl that allowed water to pass while capturing the shrimp. We'd drag the net for a few hours, then use winches to lift and empty our catch onto the deck for sorting. We would re-tie the net, throw it back in the water and repeat the process. Each round often left us with a 3-foot-tall mound of shrimp, crabs, fish, and other sea life to sort through before the next haul. Because we sorted our catch at night with limited visibility, we often sustained wounds from the spines of catfish and venomous stingrays, which we treated with ammonia, dubbed the "shrimper's friend."

After a week in the hot, humid Gulf, we'd return to Pascagoula for supplies and a brief two- to three-day break before heading out again. Despite the demanding schedule and tough work, I loved the adventure and the cash money. Shrimping demands strength, endurance, adaptability, and manual dexterity, often in harsh weather. It's a job that builds resilient, resourceful individuals—skills that would serve me well throughout my career.

Commercial fishing, while also adventurous and lucrative, was even more dangerous. It was an "every man for himself" environment so self-preservation was my goal. Our operation was managed by brothers Buck and Ott Guthrie from Albemarle, North Carolina, who were experienced and tough fishermen.

During the summers, we fished for pompano, black drum, and redfish in the Gulf, capitalizing on the demand fueled by the blackened redfish craze of the 1980s, made popular by New Orleans chef Paul Prudhomme. In the winter months, I returned to college and the crew shifted to fishing for king mackerel between Key West and North Carolina

Our operation used two large vessels manned by an eight to 10-person crew and an airplane to spot the fish. The *Sandra* served as the mothership with a large hold where we stored our catch, while the *Sue Ann*, a 50-foot speedster, held our nets. *Sue Ann* could reach speeds of near 50 miles per hour and was purportedly one of the fastest large boats in the Gulf of Mexico at the time.

Now, as you might imagine, using aircraft and fast boats with large cargo holds in marine operations tends to catch the eye of law enforcement. And especially so in our case, considering the widespread drug trade in the Gulf of Mexico and Caribbean during the early 1980s. As the Drug Enforcement Administration (DEA) ramped up its efforts in South Florida, drug traffickers started looking for alternative routes to transport products to different regions of the country. This led to the rise of a phenomenon known as the "balloon effect" or "spillover effect," where drug trafficking networks shifted their operations to new areas. States like Alabama, Mississippi, and Louisiana, with their closeness to Florida and established transportation networks, became attractive new hubs for drug trafficking.

Our pilot would take off from Pascagoula at sunrise, along with our two boats and their crews. Once the pilot spotted the fish, typically 50 to 70 miles out in the Gulf, *Sue Ann* would head to the location. We would encircle the fish with our "purse seine" net and hold them until *Sandra* arrived, often a few hours later. Transferring the fish to *Sandra's* hold usually took half a day, and if we had a full hold of fish, we would make the six- to seven-hour trip back home. Otherwise, we would stay offshore overnight and fish the next few days until our hold was full or our ice ran out.

When *Sandra* was loaded with fish and ice, she became heavy, compromising her stability, freeboard, and maneuverability. The shifting weight of the catch and ice caused changes in her center of gravity, once even loosening our exhaust pipe, causing an engine room flood and a rescue visit from the Coast Guard.

Being on a boat with 20 tons of fish in the shark-infested waters of the Gulf is the last place you want to be. Thankfully, most of our incidents happened in daylight, giving us more clarity on our potentially perilous situations.

While *Sue Ann* was usually nearby if we had to abandon ship, the effects to Sandra's structural integrity from the relentless battering in the Gulf was something I was taught to question in engineering school. And I did.

Commercial fishing paid well, but I was glad to head back to college at summer's end. And whether the Pascagoula fishing operation was linked to money laundering or covert activities around Key West, I couldn't say. I do know that our setup with aircraft spotters and fast, large-hold boats was ideal for smuggling. Despite my youth, I was smart enough to avoid the topic, wanting no part in that side of the business.

After those summer jobs, one thing became clear: I was set on a career in the oil and gas industry. I was captivated by its culture, collaborative spirit, processes, and the expansive scale of the sector. I was also drawn to the idea of being part of an industry that was making a substantial difference on a global scale. The immense power and influence wielded by the Big Oil companies, along with their role in delivering affordable energy to fuel economic growth and enhanced living standards worldwide, captivated my interest. Energy was indeed the lifeblood of the global economy and its effect on every individual's daily life was undeniable.

Drilling, production, or reservoir engineering were all areas of interest to me although it was hard to know where my engineering degree would take me or where I might fit best for an employer. I planned to start in the field to learn the business from the ground up and then move into some type of office position in Houston, Dallas, or New Orleans.

However, as graduation approached in May of 1984, dark clouds were gathering over the oil industry.

To give some context, back in the 1970s, the world's biggest players in the oil industry were famously known as the "Seven Sisters." These were BP, Shell, Chevron, Texaco, Gulf, Exxon, and Mobil. Their dominance in the market was so significant that they made up nearly 30% of the U.S. stock market in 1980, as indicated by the S&P Energy Index. This index is a subset of the broader S&P 500 and represents the energy industry, which includes businesses involved in the exploration, production, and distribution of energy sources like oil, natural gas, and renewable energy. This level of market share in the equity market was unprecedented, exceeding all other sectors except for technology during its peak years in 2000 and again in 2024. In simpler terms, if you imagined the entire U.S. stock market as a pie in 1980, then the slice representing the energy sector, including those major oil companies, would have been nearly a third of the whole pie. This shows how dominant the energy sector, especially oil and gas, was in the economy at that time. Their influence was not only in the energy market but across the entire spectrum of industries, reflecting their critical role in the global economy and their financial power.

These companies had larger revenues than many governments around the world and controlled a staggering 55% of the world's oil production, meaning they touched over half of the oil produced and sold around the globe every day. Even further, the money they made from this amounted to nearly 10% of the world's total economic output, or GDP. To put it in perspective, the Organization of Petroleum Exporting Countries (OPEC), a group of countries that collaborate on oil production and prices, controls about 35% of the world's oil supply today, and Russia was able to disrupt the global economy with oil supply of just 10% of the total in 2022. This shows just how dominant and influential the Seven Sisters were in their time.

So, why the dark clouds, you ask?

To answer that question, we need to go back to the 1970s when crude oil prices soared tenfold due to high demand and supply constraints from the Arab Oil Embargo.

The embargo was driven by OPEC's decision to suspend oil supply to the U.S. in retaliation for U.S. support of Israel during the 1973 Arab Israeli War. As oil prices surged, the U.S. found that it did not have enough extra oil capacity to deal with this crisis. As a response, the U.S. created the Strategic Petroleum Reserve (SPR), a huge stockpile of oil to use in emergencies. Other measures included setting a speed limit of 55 miles per hour to save fuel and letting the value of the U.S. dollar change freely in the global market, rather than being fixed to a specific value—all significant developments in our history.

Because the Seven Sisters were headquartered in the U.S. and Europe—the regions targeted by the embargo—they had to scramble to find alternative supply to feed their refineries and fuel distribution networks, negatively impacting financial results. Making matters worse, many oil-producing countries, particularly in the Middle East, nationalized their oil industries in the following years, further eroding the Seven Sisters control over oil production and pricing. This resulted in a steady loss of leverage in the global oil sector. While geopolitical instability such as the Iranian Revolution caused oil prices to rise further by 1980, it was a double-edged sword. Oil became increasingly expensive to other fuels like coal and natural gas leading to a decline in both oil demand and prices each year from 1980 to

1983. This also led to reduced profitability, industry cutbacks, and a weakening job market for petroleum engineers by the summer of 1984.

My job search started slowly as hiring freezes were widespread. I drove all over Louisiana and Texas, staying with friends along the way, looking for a job with Exploration and Production (E&P) and Oil Field Service companies.[11]

I was finally hired by Schlumberger in New Orleans in July of 1984. At the time, the company was the top oil field service entity in the world, so the opportunity excited me. Schlumberger had the leading market position in "wireline logging," a key oil field service technology. Wireline logging involves lowering special tools down the well on a cable to collect data to help companies understand if there's oil or gas in the ground and, more importantly, if it's enough to be worth extracting and selling. Schlumberger was also involved in a variety of other key businesses that were essential to the drilling and completion of wells.

I worked in the Anadrill division of the company, which specialized in three primary areas: Physical Formation Logging, Measurement While Drilling (MWD), and Directional Drilling Services. Formation Logging had been a basic part of oil field work for decades, but MWD, introduced in 1980, emerged as breakthrough technology. For the first time, MWD enabled operators to see borehole conditions, formation properties, and drilling parameters in real-time, enhancing the efficiency, safety, and accuracy of oil and gas drilling. It greatly improved drilling productivity when used in conjunction with Directional Drilling and Steerable Systems.

These technologies were the forerunners of the horizontal drilling techniques that powered the shale revolution in the U.S. a few decades later. I was fortunate to begin my career during one of the most significant technological transitions in the

---

11. Exploration and Production (E&P) refers to the processes involved in discovering, drilling, extracting, and bringing oil and natural gas to the surface from subsurface reservoirs. Oil Field Services companies provide specialized services and equipment to support the exploration, drilling, completion, and production phases of oil and gas operation.

industry. Not only was I seeing the cutting-edge technologies and methods firsthand, but I was also being trained to be an expert in their use. And, of course, to operate these complex technologies, especially in challenging, high-pressure geological conditions, it would take extensive training. Schlumberger's training programs for its engineers and geologists were top-notch. New recruits like me received rigorous classroom instruction and substantial hands-on field training as well. Once proficient in the key technologies and services, which typically took nine to 12 months, engineers were able to provide Schlumberger's services in the field on oil and gas drilling projects. Leveraging my petroleum engineering degree with the comprehensive training I received from Schlumberger accelerated my learning curve.

My firsthand experience with the evolving technologies and processes in the oil industry gave me a significant edge in my Wall Street career. Not only did I gain geological and technological expertise, but I also amassed extensive field experience—a rarity among my peers, who typically came from finance or economics backgrounds and worked in investment banks, asset management, or private equity.

Working at Schlumberger also gave me valuable exposure to every major player in the Big Oil, E&P, and Oil Field Service sectors. I gained direct insight into the competitive landscape, product lines, and corporate culture within these companies. Although stereotypes about each company weren't always spot-on, they came close in my experience. This specialized knowledge proved instrumental in developing and executing major industry-focused strategies on Wall Street from the 1990s to the present day.

In my oil field career, I worked on projects both onshore and offshore in and around the Gulf of Mexico in Alabama, Louisiana, Mississippi, Texas and even drilled some of the last offshore wells in Florida. At Schlumberger, like at Berry Brothers, my schedule was 14 days on, seven days off. But if someone were sick or quit, my stint could stretch to 20 to 25 days on an oil rig with 75 to 80 other guys which felt incredibly confining.

For onshore projects, we worked 12-hour shifts and stayed in nearby hotels, or in trailers on the drill site if our location was remote. Our per diem was for food, which sometimes meant stocking up on groceries or dining at the only local option, like the Dairy Queen in Goliad, Texas.

Offshore drilling is a whole different world, and it's not for everyone. It's a team effort involving drilling contractors, service companies, and consultants, all coordinated by an operating company that handles the funding and management. Deepwater drilling is particularly complex and risky, especially in places like the Gulf, where you're dealing with extremely deep waters and drilling depths, plus intense geological pressures.

The cost of drilling offshore in deep waters is huge, often running into hundreds of millions per well. The daily rate for just the drilling rig can be as high as $500,000. There's a lot of planning involved, using seismic data and information from other wells to make sure the drilling goes smoothly. On an offshore rig, you've got about 75 to 100 people working non-stop in various roles. Everyone needs special training, especially since each region is different.

The food on offshore drilling rigs is usually good, and the facilities are well-maintained, which is remarkable given how messy drilling can be. Crew members typically stay on the rig for either seven or 14 days at a time, depending on their company's schedule. Often, we'd be drilling 100-150 miles out in the Gulf, breaking new ground with some of the first deepwater wells there. In these uncharted areas, the drilling conditions and geology are not fully understood until you're drilling, which adds to the risk. Storms can be a big challenge too, sometimes making it impossible for boats or helicopters to evacuate the crew if the weather gets too rough. The rigs themselves are like floating steel fortresses, designed to withstand these conditions.

A crucial part of the drilling process involves balancing the weight of the drilling mud against the pressure exerted by the formation that is being drilled into. This balance prevents uncontrolled oil and gas flows, known as "kicks," or worse, "blowouts" if they can't be controlled. Blowouts can lead to explosions and fires, like what happened with the BP Macondo incident, the Deepwater Horizon spill, in 2010.

Our job at Schlumberger was to drill the well while carefully monitoring pressure to detect changes while drilling. This made our team the first line of defense against potential accidents. Imagine drilling two miles beneath a football stadium, then steering towards a fire station a mile away to hit a target the size of a few school buses. It's a high stakes endeavor that blends science, physics, math, and engineering, and you're constantly on alert for any small changes that could signal trouble.

After spending 14 intense days on the rig, time off was always a relief. Being out there, far from shore, the pressure was always on, as any mistake could have profound consequences. The experience would serve me well later in my Wall Street career.

In addition to my training for Gulf of Mexico operations, I also completed a specialized course in Lafayette, Louisiana, to work in the harsh North Atlantic. I was selected for Mobil's Hi-bernia project, located about 200 miles off the coast of St. John's, Newfoundland, in waters 300 feet deep. The conditions there were tough, with near-freezing water temperatures all year and waves reaching up to 35 feet during winter storms.

Just two years before I started, on February 15, 1982, the Ocean Ranger drilling rig tragically sank while heading to the Hibernia area, claiming the lives of all 84 crew members. The rig faced a brutal winter storm with hurricane-force winds, and a failure in its stability control system caused it to capsize and sink into the Atlantic. This disaster was one of the deadliest in offshore history and brought about major changes in safety rules for the industry.

Our safety training for the North Atlantic was intense and called Helicopter Underwater Escape Training (HUET). During HUET, we were blindfolded and submerged in a pool within a mock helicopter fuselage which was rotated to simulate a helicopter crash. The blindfold simulated the disorienting conditions of an actual crash, such as low visibility or complete darkness, with the goal being to exit the compartment and swim to the surface.

We learned that in an emergency in the icy North Atlantic, our survival suits could keep us alive, but only for about nine minutes—a very brief window for rescue, which explained the tragic fate of the Ocean Ranger crew.

I was fully aware of the risks of offshore drilling. As soon as I arrived at a rig, I'd always sign in, stow my gear, and figure out the quickest evacuation route in case of an emergency. I was probably not alone with this practice. Considering the possibilities of explosions or fires, knowing how to get to the lifeboats quickly was crucial—certainly better than hoping for rescue in shark-infested waters.

Teamwork among the operator, drilling contractor, and service companies like Schlumberger was key to maintaining safety. My role involved drilling the well, assessing risks and helping develop safety plans. Thankfully, in my time, we never faced an uncontrollable blowout like the BP Macondo incident. We managed "kicks" safely, but I was fortunate to never experience a major disaster on the job.

My years drilling oil and gas wells in a variety of locations and conditions fulfilled my need for travel, adventure, and intellectual stimulation. The oil patch had been a crucible, forging not only my technical skills but also my ability to connect with people from all walks of life. From the roughnecks on the drilling rigs to the PhD engineers at Schlumberger, I had learned to communicate, collaborate, and lead across a wide spectrum of personalities, backgrounds, and nationalities.

Yet, the lifestyle of an oil field nomad started to wear on me. Somewhere along the way, I grew interested in finance and the stock market. I was especially interested in how influential Wall Street analysts and strategists could sway markets with their insights and forecasts.

At the time, it seemed far-fetched to think that I might one day be among those influential figures in the energy sector, let alone be recognized as one of the top Big Oil analysts in Wall Street's history. Economist Ed Hyman of Evercore ISI and strategists Michael Wilson of Morgan Stanley and Henry McVey at KKR (all friends of mine) are analysts that fit the same bill on Wall Street today. That is, their credibility is so strong that their words can move the overall market in the U.S.—an impressive feat.

While I was fascinated by the oil and gas industry, I wanted to shift gears from engineering and the offshore life to the worlds of finance and investment. My engineering training had given me a strong foundation in quantitative analysis and problem-solving, skills that I thought could be applied to analyzing companies and markets. Moreover, my deep curiosity about the inner workings of the stock market and the influence of Wall Street analysts had been piqued. I wanted to understand this world on a deeper level and be part of shaping the conversation.

This was a significant leap from my position in the turbulent Gulf of Mexico. Lacking the traditional connections and educational pedigree often seen on Wall Street, I wasn't deterred. Instead, I was eager to embrace the challenge and compete in this new arena.

3

Both Sides of "The Street" and My Road to Morgan Stanley

In the world of investing, there are two sides of "The Street," so to speak—what's referred to as the "buy-side" and "sell-side," each representing a different facet of the market and its operations.

Imagine a group of people with a lot of money, like big companies or funds, looking to invest their money to make more money. They're like shoppers in a market, looking for the best advice and the best deals on products (in this case, investments like stocks or bonds) that will grow in value over time. These are the buy-side investors. They're trying to find good opportunities to invest their money.

On the other side, imagine the sellers in the market. These are the people who create and sell the investment products, like banks or stockbrokers. They're like the stalls in a market, offering various goods (stocks, bonds, etc.) for sale. Their job is to ensure investments look attractive, provide information, and help the buy-side make decisions. They also help make sure that there are enough buyers and sellers to keep the market moving smoothly.

The buy-side and sell-side need each other. The buy-side is

looking for good investments, and the sell-side provides them. The sell-side also helps the buy-side by giving them information and advice to make smart investment choices. It's like a dance between buyers and sellers in a marketplace, where each side has its role in keeping the market active and healthy.

My career began on the buy-side of investing when I landed an internship with Sun Bank Capital Management in Winter Park, Florida, just one semester into my MBA studies at Rollins College. One of the things that set Rollins apart at the time was its computer intensive MBA program, which was a cutting-edge feature for an MBA program back in the '80s. Additionally, Rollins had extensive connections in the Orlando business community, which I knew could serve me well as I transitioned from engineering to the world of finance and investing. And it probably goes without saying the idea of year-round golf and the beautiful beaches in sunny Florida played a part in helping to make my decision.

Rollins sits on the shores of Lake Virginia, which allowed students to take part in a number of water sports and leisure activities. There was a 25-yard, 8-lane swimming pool on campus that overlooked the lake where students would congregate to study and sunbathe, and we could even check out windsurfers with our student ID. I had brought my Mistral windsurfer with me from Pascagoula but used theirs on occasion.

While I felt fortunate, I didn't quite understand at the time just how lucky I was. Sun Bank was the investment arm of Sun Banks of Florida which became SunTrust and is now Truist.

After graduation, I chose to stay on with Sun Bank instead of accepting offers from AT&T, IBM, Humana, and the City of Orlando. The position paid less, but I believed that finding my passion would lead to more enjoyment of my work and greater success, and ultimately, financial rewards.

The investment side of Sun Bank was led by Tony Gray, who was an excellent investor and an institutional money management legend. He was lauded by the Wall Street Journal in 1990 as being the top stock picker in the U.S. during the previous decade. Indeed, his 10-year performance results of 22.8% per year were stronger than those of nationally renowned investor Peter Lynch of Fidelity at 21.3% per year. Peter managed the Fidelity Magellan fund in Boston and, like Tony, was a student of the game and was in his prime at the time. While both were regarded as growth stock managers, Tony focused on investing in large, established U.S. companies, which is generally seen as a safer, more straightforward approach. Peter, on the other hand, diversified his investments across companies of all sizes and from various countries, aiming to capture more growth opportunities at the cost of higher risk and complexity.

Tony was from Omaha, Nebraska, was disciplined, self-taught in many ways, and encouraged me to be the same. While he used Wall Street research, he always made major buy and sell decisions on his own through a disciplined approach to valuation. In Tony's book titled "A Thousand Miles from Wall Street" he advised "developing and having confidence in your abilities and your style and sticking to it." He was also adamant about doing your homework, waiting until you have good ideas, making checklists, and making your own decisions rather than relying on others. This framework became a staple of my approach as a high-profile Wall Street analyst down the road and was especially applicable to the deep-cyclical oil industry that would be the focus of my career. I tried to remain an independent thinker and not be swayed by consensus.

Tony also had a list of "deadly sins" for investing, warning against being timid, overconfident, stubborn, impatient, or disillusioned.

In my initial role at Sun Bank, I found myself in an ideal position to learn about promising sectors and stocks, and the dynamics of equity markets. I was clearly in the right place at the right time. My job involved conducting research and recommending stocks for Tony's growth investment funds and for Greg DePrince, a renowned value investor at Sun Trust with consistently strong results.

Not only was I working at Sun Bank and pursuing my MBA, but I also decided to undertake the Chartered Financial Analyst (CFA) studies at the same time. The CFA exams, offered annually in June, required passing three levels with a seven-year limit for completion. Given the high caliber of candidates—almost all held master's degrees or higher—and the low pass rates, extensive preparation was crucial. Balancing work at Sun Bank with my studies, I started preparing in January, aiming to go three up three down on the exams, which I eventually did. Achieving the CFA designation significantly bolstered my competitiveness in the investment industry.[12]

The knowledge I gained at Sun Bank, combined with my MBA and CFA studies, led to an exponential learning curve. My first year there, under the mentorship of Tony and Greg, laid the foundation for my three-decade career on Wall Street, as I shared years later in a speech at Rollins.

This blend of experience at Schlumberger in the oil industry, along with my MBA, CFA, and investment experience at Sun Bank, significantly enhanced my credentials as an energy analyst on either the buy-side or sell-side, aligning perfectly with my career plan. While almost all investment analysts held degrees in finance, mathematics, or accounting, fewer had technical or operating experience in their sector of expertise. This made me an attractive candidate for buy-side and sell-side firms, both of which began to reach out to me at an early stage in my career—almost overnight.

Though I was grateful for my time at Sun Bank, I made the decision to accept a position with Kemper Investments in Chicago in 1990. Kemper was one of the largest national investment managers at the time, which afforded me the opportunity to travel around the world in search of energy investment ideas for our portfolios—an appealing proposition to me in my early thirties.

---

12. The Chartered Financial Analyst program provides essential and advanced skills in investment analysis and portfolio management. Its comprehensive curriculum is regularly updated to mirror current financial practices, covering everything from Ethical and Professional Standards to Portfolio Management & Wealth Planning.

Arriving in Chicago during the summer, I was enthusiastic. I found the people to be welcoming, although the sheer size and intensity of the city left me feeling out of place at times. Once winter set in, the harsh cold and long, gray days came—something that I had not experienced before and required acclimation.

Most of my peer analysts at Kemper graduated either from Northwestern University or the University of Chicago so it was a relatively homogenous group. The running joke was that every firm needed an oil analyst, preferably one with the right accent, making me Kemper's token Southerner.

One of the memorable highlights of my years in Chicago was getting to experience the first three NBA championships for the Chicago Bulls led by Michael Jordan. Because of Kemper's position as one of the largest investment managers in the Midwest, it seemed that I was at the old Chicago Stadium for the Bulls, Wrigley Field for the Cubs, or White Sox Park a few times per week. These experiences not only enriched my time in Chicago but also shaped my approach to my work. They reinforced the importance of building strong relationships, seeking out diverse perspectives, and always striving for excellence.

I enjoyed my time in Chicago, but just three short years later in 1993, I was approached with an offer that would be a big career break for me.

Putnam was globally renowned as one of the oldest mutual fund companies in the U.S. They offered me the role of energy analyst and manager of their energy mutual fund, which was one of the largest in the world. This opportunity to become a portfolio manager in my early thirties, especially for such a prominent fund, marked a significant career milestone and I accepted the offer.

Boston is a great place to work if you're in the investment business. It's home to 20% of the Assets Under Management (AUM)—meaning, investment money managed—in the U.S. and 10% of the AUM managed worldwide. The city boasts top-notch investment firms like Fidelity, State Street, MFS, Putnam, Wellington, and big hedge funds like Adage and Baupost.

Consequently, Boston is a key meeting place for CEOs and investors, and despite the competitive atmosphere, there's a strong sense of community among investment professionals in the city.

I enjoyed Boston's proximity to Vermont, New Hampshire, Maine, and Cape Cod and the beautiful landscapes and seasonal changes of the New England area.

My role at Putnam enabled access to most sources of global investment information and positioned me to succeed in a big way as a professional investor. I was exactly where I wanted to be and planned to remain in Boston for the foreseeable future—or so I thought.

Not long after arriving in Boston, Brian Jacoboski, Wall Street's top integrated oil analyst, contacted me about succeeding him as head of the energy group at Paine Webber in New York City.[13] The role of the #1 Big Oil analyst is both high-profile and lucrative. Brian planned to transition to the buy-side (a natural transition for most) and start his own hedge fund, and he saw me as the ideal candidate to take over his position. While it was an honor to be considered for such a prominent position, I really enjoyed investing and preferred to stay on the buy-side. I had been with Putnam for just a few years and was hesitant about leaving. I told Brian I would consider his offer but was likely to stay at Putnam. He proposed we keep the conversation open as his departure date neared, and I agreed, valuing our friendship and his advice on Big Oil research.

Over the next six months, I frequently discussed the matter with Brian, David Bradshaw, and Jim Carroll, their E&P and Oil Service analysts. Regular communication between buy-side and sell-side analysts about market developments and changes in investment recommendations was common. However, I was still uncertain about becoming a sell-side analyst. Despite the

---

13. The "#1 integrated oil analyst" ranking is determined through industry surveys and evaluations focusing on the accuracy of earnings forecasts, the insightfulness of market analysis, and the influence of research on investor decisions. This recognition is a testament to an analyst's expertise and impact in the integrated oil sector.

appealing aspects of the role, the excellent position I held at Putnam and the significant differences between the two roles made me cautious about making the change.

In my former colleague Jim Valentine's book, "Best Practices for Equity Research Analysts," he outlines what makes a top equity research analyst. According to Jim, these analysts are intelligent, innately inquisitive, self-motivated, self-directed, resourceful, focused, risk takers, and influential. A key point in the book is that influential analysts have wide networks, leading to better analysis. This applies to analysts on both the buy-side and sell-side of investing.

However, there are big differences between buy-side and sell-side analysts. Buy-side analysts typically cover a broader range of three to five industries and focus on about 20 sub-industries within them. Sell-side analysts, on the other hand, specialize deeply in just one sub-industry. This specialization allows them to become experts with extensive knowledge and contacts. They often spot critical trends before buy-side analysts, have exclusive access to company management, and provide detailed financial forecasts. Their deep dives into companies include traveling globally to meet with management and operations teams, giving them and their investors a competitive edge. Sell-side analysts are also known for being readily available to share their insights with investors at any moment if market developments break—day, or night. Success requires organization, focus, and the ability to manage daily pressures effectively.

At Putnam, I was responsible for covering the energy sector, including Big Oils, Oil Service, E&P, and R&M, as well as the food sector and its sub-segments, although I can't say that I ever distinguished myself in the latter group.

In contrast, my sell-side counterparts, like Brian and David at the prominent Wall Street firms in New York, specialized in just one sub-segment each. They had an in-depth understanding of their industry, including companies and their management teams. Their expertise was highly valued, and their firm was well paid by Putnam and other large investors because they provided essential investment insights that contributed to the success of their multi-billion-dollar portfolios.

Although I appreciated my role at Putnam and the lifestyle in Boston, I was drawn to the challenge of working on Wall Street in New York. It's common for professionals to move from the sell-side to the buy-side for a better work-life balance, but I was intrigued by the prospect of making the opposite transition. Despite the perception that the buy-side offers less pressure, I found that both sides faced their own forms of stress, whether related to portfolio performance or the constant demands of sell-side research. I decided to cross sides of "The Street."

I was fortunate to be starting my career on the sell-side along-side David Bradshaw and Jim Carroll at Paine Webber. Both were top-ranked analysts in the Institutional Investor and Greenwich polls, making them household names in the energy investment sector.[14] Their expertise in both fundamental research and marketing set a high standard, complementing my skills in these areas and in commodities like crude oil and natural gas. They guided me in developing my research products and marketing strategy, teaching me effective marketing techniques—a crucial skill for someone with a quantitative orientation like mine.

Working as a team, we collaborated on investment calls, and they introduced me to leading investor clients in the U.S. and Europe. My career took off quickly, landing me in the top-five analyst rankings in the major investor polls during my first year—a rare achievement. Joining Jim and David in

---

14. The Institutional Investor and Greenwich polls are prestigious annual rankings in the financial industry. The Institutional Investor poll is conducted by "Institutional Investor" magazine, which surveys top money managers and investors to rank analysts based on their expertise, accuracy, and overall contribution to their sectors. Analysts who rank highly in these polls are recognized for their exceptional research, insight, and ability to guide investment decisions. Similarly, the Greenwich poll, conducted by Greenwich Associates, evaluates financial services firms and professionals on various criteria, including client service, strategic advice, and market knowledge. Being highly ranked in these polls signifies excellence and is a coveted honor among professionals in the finance sector, reflecting their reputation and influence in the investment community.

the rankings, our team gained a reputation as one of the firm's top research teams, catching the attention of our competitors and giving us significant momentum. This ascent in my career happened against the backdrop of a dynamic and competitive Wall Street environment.

The most prominent Wall Street firms in the early '90s were the "white shoe" investment banks, Morgan Stanley and Goldman Sachs.[15] These firms were active in most major global markets and were well positioned across all the major industry sectors. Energy was deemed to be an area of growth on Wall Street at the time, and both were in the market to enhance their competitive position in energy investment banking and energy research. I was at the top of the call list on the research side, only six years removed from drilling oil and gas wells as a Schlumberger engineer in the Gulf of Mexico. Looking back, it's still hard for me to believe that it happened that quickly.

Like my situation with Putnam in Boston, I was content at Paine Webber and had only been there for one year. However, many considered Morgan Stanley to be the most prestigious institutional securities firm in the history of American finance and it was probably the most coveted place on Wall Street at the time. When Research Director Mayree Clark called in 1994, I was told by peers, even those at Paine Webber, that I had to listen. And I did.

Leaving my colleagues at Paine Webber was a difficult choice, given the strong momentum our team had built together. Yet, opportunities at Morgan Stanley were rare, as the firm prioritized internal promotions to preserve its distinct corporate culture. This culture was upheld by fostering talent from within its own ranks, a practice that not only reflected Morgan Stanley's commitment to its values but also its reputation for excellence. The chance to join such a revered institution, known for its

---

15. The term "white shoe" was used to describe prestigious and elite financial firms that had a long-standing reputation for serving high-profile clients and conducting business with integrity.

selective and elite talent pool, was an opportunity too big to pass up. I joined Morgan Stanley in 1995, knowing this would be a defining moment in my career, but never imagining all that would unfold over the next 13 years.

4

The Era of the Super-Major

Stepping into New York City for the first time was both exhilarating and a bit overwhelming, especially for someone coming from a small town in the Deep South. The city buzzes non-stop with its stunning skyline, rich mix of cultures, countless sights and attractions, and eateries galore. While I'd visited many big cities before, NYC was in a league of its own, packed with endless possibilities, adventures, and challenges. I was eager to dive in and make my mark.

My new office was in Morgan Stanley's iconic headquarters right in the heart of Times Square. Once the epicenter of New York's prestigious theater district, the area had fallen into decline during the 1960s, until a clean-up and revitalization effort in the '90s aimed to reestablish Times Square as a major tourist destination and entertainment hub. Today, Times Square is one of the world's most visited tourist attractions, drawing an estimated 50 million visitors annually. Its rich history is a testament to New York City's ability to reinvent itself and remains a central part of the city's identity, reflecting its challenges and triumphs.

I arrived in Manhattan just as Times Square was bouncing

back. Walking into Morgan Stanley on day one, little did I know, not only was Big Oil on the verge of a major shakeup of its own, but I would be the one to light the fuse.

At Morgan Stanley, my energy team partners were John Lovoi and Phil Pace, who specialized in the Oil Service and E&P sectors. Both were not only top-quality individuals and professionals but also remain friends of mine today. Tasked by research management to become Wall Street's leading energy team, John, Phil, and I, despite my role as head of global energy, worked as equals with that shared goal in mind.

To broaden our coverage, we expanded our energy research globally, adding teams in London, Singapore, Sydney, Moscow, Tokyo, Mumbai, and Beijing. This expansion, which grew our team to over 80 members, allowed us to compete on a global market scale.

My early years at Morgan Stanley were a whirlwind and maybe the most fun years of my Wall Street career. This was a time when research and investment banking collaborated closely, often resulting in better financial outcomes for our corporate clients through comprehensive and tailored solutions.

Despite potential conflicts of interest highlighted by the "Global Settlement" in 2003, our firm maintained a strict legal and compliance framework that was effective.[16] Although the collaboration between research and banking raised concerns about the potential misuse of material non-public information (MNPI), our robust compliance procedures helped mitigate these risks and preserved the integrity of our services. I never encountered situations where I had access to MNPI without being under communication restrictions. In other words, I was never in a position where I knew sensitive, not-yet-public information about companies without also having strict rules

---

16. The Global Settlement was an agreement reached in 2003 between 10 of the largest investment firms and U.S. regulators to address conflicts of interest between investment banking and research departments. The settlement aimed to restore investor confidence by separating investment banking from research to prevent undue influence and ensure the objectivity of research reports.

about who I could talk to and what I could say.

The complex legal environment and stringent compliance structures enhanced our research efforts, ensuring we stayed well within ethical and legal boundaries. This was crucial, especially given the competitive landscape and the notorious actions of some Wall Street analysts who compromised their integrity for financial gain.

Coming from a buy-side background (where the focus is on buying and managing investments), I took my stock recommendations seriously, understanding that my investor clients relied on my insights for their financial success. I believed that sell-side analysts (the ones advising on which stocks to buy or sell) who allowed ulterior motives to influence their recommendations were harming their own careers. Poor investment advice, particularly if a conflict of interest is perceived, could lead to a loss of support from buy-side clients and, consequently, a significant decline in an analyst's value within their firm and the broader job market. And there's another layer to this: the investment banking side of things. Sometimes, the interests of investment banking (like advising companies on mergers or raising money) might tempt an analyst to give favorable reviews to certain stocks. However, investment banking deals come and go. When those deals dry up, as they inevitably do, analysts who relied on them instead of giving solid, unbiased advice might find themselves out of a job—or in free agency, looking for work elsewhere because their credibility has taken a hit.

The performance of sell-side analysts was closely monitored by major financial news services like the Wall Street Journal and Bloomberg. This meant investors knew which analysts had a knack for picking winning stocks. Analysts were also held accountable through internal commission votes from buy-side firms and external polls like the Institutional Investor (II) poll.

With my buy-side experience, specifically my orientation to quantitative and valuation factors, I felt stock-picking would be a natural ability for me. I leveraged this strength, raising the profile on my big calls and pressing my recommendations with clients.

Because I was probably overly confident on some investment ideas, no stage was big enough for my best research ideas—at least in my own mind.

But being a good stock-picker wasn't the only path to success for sell-side analysts. Other analysts thrived by offering value beyond stock-picking, such as deep industry knowledge, key contacts, prompt client responses, and organizing informative site visits and calls. Stock-picking was a critical skill though, and analysts who could consistently identify market inefficiencies and provide a structured, repeatable investment process were highly sought after by portfolio managers. Success in this area often led to fast recognition on Wall Street and significant financial rewards. Every analyst dreamed of picking the tops and bottoms of sectors and stocks and the professional acclaim that followed.

During my early years at Morgan Stanley, we focused on delivering high-quality research to investors through extensive marketing efforts. Our team was consistently ranked high in major research rankings. I adopted a traditional approach, and analyzed commodities like crude oil and refined products, as well as the stocks of major oil companies and refiners. Our research suite included in-depth reports, quarterly earnings updates, and insights from management meetings. We also took our major investor clients on field trips around the world and engaged with government intelligence groups to gain a deeper understanding of the global geopolitical factors affecting the energy market. Balancing personal and professional life was paramount to me, yet we were dedicated to providing an informed perspective in the energy sector and were driven to succeed.

While our energy team was positioned to prosper, a major economic phase was unfolding which would impact my career and my research strategy for years to come. This phenomenon was known as globalization, and it was set to reshape how countries and businesses around the world operated, including in the energy industry.

Globalization kicked off with two major events: the fall of the Soviet Union in 1989 and the end of the Cold War in 1991. These events led to countries becoming more connected than ever before. Countries that were once cut off from the rest of the world, particularly those under communist rule, started to join the global market. This meant they were now participating in international trade, attracting investments, and becoming part of a worldwide economy.

One of the biggest drivers of globalization was technology, particularly the rise of mobile phones and the internet. Suddenly, people all around the world could communicate easily, share ideas, and do business with each other. The World Wide Web, for instance, connected billions of people and devices, opening endless opportunities for trading goods and services, sharing cultural content, and spreading knowledge and ideas.

During this time, favorable financial conditions like lower interest rates and tax rates also helped the economy grow. This was good news for businesses and the stock market, as it meant more profit and investment opportunities.

Trade agreements played a crucial role in this new era of globalization too. For example, the North American Free Trade Agreement (NAFTA), signed by the United States, Canada, and Mexico in 1992, made it easier for people, goods, and services to move freely across these countries. This wasn't just happening in North America. Similar agreements and trade blocs were popping up all over the world, like the European Union (EU), which helped countries within these regions trade more easily with each other.

As globalization progressed, numerous government-owned businesses in nearly 100 countries transitioned to private ownership in a process known as privatization. The push for privatization was influenced by declining support for socialism and a growing belief in free enterprise, fueled by the rise of global trade. This shift aimed to improve business efficiency, encourage competition, and enhance financial performance. Proponents of privatization argued that private companies, driven by profit motives, are more likely to innovate and reduce costs. Despite concerns about potential drawbacks such as higher prices, reduced service accessibility, job losses, and diminished democratic control over public resources, governments rarely re-acquired privatized entities, suggesting that the advantages of privatization were superior.

In the energy sector, this evolution led to significant structural changes. Early leaders in oil industry privatization, like Norway (Statoil), the UK (BP), Canada (Petro-Canada), and Italy (ENI), showed that privatization could fill government coffers and allow companies to thrive both regionally and globally. As these privatized companies succeeded, other governments began to privatize their national oil companies, listing them on stock markets and changing the global competitive landscape. This shift meant that existing companies had to rethink their strategies to stay competitive. Their success would depend on how well they adapted to the new conditions created by globalization and eventually privatizations in their sector.

In 1997, my third year at Morgan Stanley, I was ranked as the top integrated oil analyst in the Institutional Investor (II) poll. This was a significant achievement, especially in the highly competitive field of Big Oils, where it's rare for someone with just three years of experience to outperform others who have been in the field for a decade or more.

The II poll is a major deal in the finance world akin to the Oscars for Wall Street analysts. It draws participation from nearly 4,000 analysts and portfolio managers from the biggest investment firms in the world which oversee about $30 trillion or two-thirds of global investments. While imperfect like every other poll, the II poll is the best independent way to recognize best-in-class research on Wall Street over the past few decades. Rankings are based on a points system that considers the size and influence of the voting firms, ensuring that the most respected firms have a larger say in the outcomes.

When the poll results are announced, the top analysts gain public recognition—a significant boost for their careers and their firms. Industry giants like J.P. Morgan and Evercore ISI often respond with press releases and even host parties to celebrate the victory. The validation from investors was immensely gratifying, even though I knew that competitors would soon be plotting to unseat me in next year's poll, and that maintaining my position would require continued strong performance.

I always took the II poll seriously, both during my time on the buy-side and when I moved to the sell-side. Participating in the poll on the buy-side was not only about showing appreciation for good research but also about maintaining strong professional relationships. However, on the sell-side, not everyone sees the value of the II poll. Some firms play it down, either because they're focusing on other areas like investment banking or they're trying to cut costs. But ignoring the poll can lead to the loss of top talent. The saying goes that 25% of research analysts bring in 75% of a department's revenue. So, if a star analyst leaves because they're not getting recognized, it can hurt the firm financially. Others view the II poll as just a popularity contest, although my experience is that it rewards genuine talent and hard work. Analysts who make bold, profitable recommendations always get noticed and rewarded by the investment community.

My career has shown me the power of teamwork, even in an industry often seen as cutthroat, highly individualistic, and mercenary-like. By collaborating closely with colleagues across different specialties, like E&P or Oil Services, we could offer richer, more accurate analyses. This approach not only helped us stand out as individuals and as a team but also fostered a healthier work-life balance, reducing burnout and turnover.

Becoming the top Big Oil analyst on Wall Street, especially for the first time at age 36, was a proud moment for me, but it also came with pressure to keep up the high standard of my research. Being voted to the top spot by the most influential investors across North America, Europe, Asia, and Oceania in the highly competitive Big Oil category was both an honor and a hefty responsibility. I knew I had to deliver the best analysis on crude oil and other energy commodities, as well as on major stocks such as BP, Chevron, Shell, and Exxon to maintain my status. I was determined to meet and exceed these expectations.

With the win confirming the value of my work and the reach of my platform, I saw an opportunity to effect change in the oil and gas industry. My plan was twofold. First, I would continue to compete with peers on energy commodities and company specific content just in case my new strategy was unsuccessful. In other words, I wanted to be able to keep my day job. Next, I planned to introduce a major strategic research theme to investors over the coming year. My concept was going to challenge the value propositions and business model of the entire oil and gas industry and every major company and stir controversy between energy CEOs and their board of directors. Investors who held stocks in the energy sector weren't going to be too pleased with me either since I planned to say that the value of energy stocks would deteriorate unless there were major changes in how things were done. I knew I was about to ruffle some feathers by challenging the long-held status quo.

But even though I knew my opinion would be unpopular, I was just as sure that the energy sector wouldn't do well without significant changes. I also felt that this might be my only chance to push for a new direction, and I felt certain that I was right about this. Even if things didn't go as planned, I figured I was still young enough at age 36 to bounce back from a major setback. I was ready to take on the challenge, fueled by the belief that my research could help shape the future of the energy industry.

My plan was to take on the giants of the energy sector by publicly critiquing the Big Oils. These companies, successors to the Seven Sisters of the 1970s—names like BP, Shell, Chevron, Texaco, Gulf, Exxon, and Mobil—were about to hear my argument that their business models were outdated and maybe even obsolete. I was convinced they needed to radically change their ways, which had been set in stone for decades, to stay relevant. If things went as I predicted, we could see huge, unexpected gains in the stock values across the entire energy sector and in commodities like crude oil, natural gas, and refined products too. Of course, it's not like my idea alone would be the magic key to prosperity for the industry over the next decade—there are a lot of factors that influence the markets. Still, I believed that embracing the changes I suggested was essential to kickstart the engine for success and for the gains to be sustained.

Knowing full well that my suggestions might stir controversy and attract criticism from the corporate world, I decided to take the risk. And it would be risky—the opinions of industry CEOs carry a lot of weight with investors who rely on them for insights on a range of topics including the quality and value of research from sector analysts.

I also expected pushback from my analyst competitors on the sell-side—especially because I was at the top of the game. But if they were short-sighted and outright dismissed me just to under-cut a rival, they could end up damaging their own reputation.

Still, I was prepared for the backlash; it was part of the territory. My focus was to ensure that my thesis was sound both strategically and financially, and that it could stand up to scrutiny from a wide, highly intelligent audience. If I couldn't defend my position effectively, it would not only damage my reputation but could also jeopardize my career.

By early 1998, after a year of diligent work on my thesis, I was prepared to present what I believed to be the blueprint for success over the coming decade. I titled my report "The Era of the Super-Major," a name designed to seize attention and challenge industry stakeholders to engage with the report, especially since I kept it deliberately short at just eight pages. My aim was to craft a document that was not only succinct but also easily understandable for every management team, board member, and investor with an interest in the global energy industry. Effectively, it was an open letter to every board and management team under the guise of sell-side research. I wanted to open the floor for debate and for the oil industry or investors to tell me why I was wrong.

At the time, the term "Super-Major" wasn't even a phrase in common use; however, I envisioned it becoming a key part of the industry's vocabulary and, eventually, its history, as my thesis gained recognition. I wanted "Super-Major" to become synonymous with the strategic transformation I was advocating for, and for both investors and corporations to link this concept directly to me and the outcomes I predicted.

My report began by highlighting the industry's record of poor capital management,[17] both on an absolute basis and as compared to other sectors in the S&P 500. I argued that the global oil and gas industry's decision-making was leading to unsatisfactory financial results and continued market underperformance. In the 1980s, the energy sector was a powerhouse, making up 28% of the S&P 500. By the end of that decade, its share had halved to 14%, and it continued to plummet to just 3% by 1998. This wasn't just a minor fluctuation; it was the most significant decline of any sector in global markets, signaling deep-rooted problems within the industry. Despite energy companies' efforts to cut costs and sharpen their focus, these measures were not enough. They were facing a much bigger problem that couldn't be solved with cost-cutting alone. As a result, their financial performance suffered, dragging down their market value.

I attributed part of the problem to a worsening competitive structure, marked by the rise of smaller domestic companies

---

17. Capital management refers to the strategic planning and control of a company's financial resources to achieve its objectives. This includes budgeting, investing, financing, and managing the overall capital structure to maximize profitability and ensure long-term sustainability.

specializing in exploration, production, and refining who started to take a bigger piece of the pie. Internationally, with so many national oil companies becoming privatized, the market would see the emergence of what amounted to eight "new Texacos."[18] These new players meant that companies would have to share the spotlight and possibly miss out on investments they used to dominate. This called for a change in how they did business if they wanted to keep their competitive edge and profitability.

The solution that I proposed was for companies to become what we referred to as a "Super-Major." This term, coined at Morgan Stanley in the late 1990s, was given to an elite class of large oil companies that would dominate the competitive arena in energy for years to come. Prototypes included Exxon and Shell, which were managed for superior returns on capital, which usually led to higher valuation and better stock market performance. These companies didn't just throw money at random opportunities but instead were selective and disciplined, choosing investments that would pay off even when the industry was going through tough times. Their geographical diversity also positioned them well for international opportunities which were expected to become even more important in the future.

We advocated for mergers of equals (MOEs) between companies with similar quality assets, corporate cultures, and functional and geographical scopes as the optimal path forward. This would enhance competitive advantages and broaden opportunities for investment and efficiency. This strategy was about more than just expansion; it was about optimizing value creation[19] leading to outstanding equity market performance. The playbook would be that larger companies would leverage economies of scale, access to capital, and technological resources to outcompete smaller players, allowing them to undertake

---

18. The Era of the Super-Major, February 13,1998

19. Value creation is defined as the increase in shareholder value achieved by earning a return on capital employed (ROCE) that exceeds the weighted average cost of capital (WACC). This differential represents the surplus value generated for shareholders or economic value added (EVA).

more ambitious, capital-intensive projects and weather market volatility more effectively. This would further their lead over competitors and solidify their status as industry leaders, providing significant strategic advantages that smaller, more regionally focused companies would struggle to match. Along the way, the enhanced industry framework we envisioned, a holy grail of sorts, would be realized.

Some experts thought big oil companies merging with smaller ones, or "Mini-Majors," was likely. However, we didn't think so. Companies like Marathon, Occidental, and Unocal—these Mini-Majors—had most of their operations in North America where competitive advantage and returns began to level off. The real potential for growth and enhanced market presence lay in the union of larger entities with international exposure. Our expectation was that companies matching the criteria for successful consolidation, like BP, Chevron, Amoco, and Texaco, would pursue these strategic mergers, enhancing their competitive stance. Bigger and more international was better, in our view.

While the last major merger in the sector was almost 15 years earlier, the Chevron and Gulf merger was a case in point. Chevron not only expanded its portfolio—one standout asset being the Tengiz field in Kazakhstan—but significantly improved its competitive stance, particularly in international exploration and chemicals. The merger was a financial success, boosting the market value of the combined entity by 40% and setting Chevron on a path of growth and high performance for the next decade.

We also made the case that financial conditions were perfect for big oil companies to join forces to create our proposed Super-Majors and that "combinations would be cheered in the equity market." While the profits these major oil companies were making on their investments (as indicated by returns on capital or ROCE) had declined significantly in recent years, returns were still higher than what you could get from very safe investments, like long-term government bonds. These bonds are seen as risk-free, so if oil companies are doing better than these, it's a good sign.

This difference between corporate returns and the cost of equity and borrowing money is important because it makes the idea of merging more attractive. When there's a bigger gap between what companies can earn from their operations compared to the cost of money, it's a sign that merging could lead to more value being created for the companies and their shareholders.

It was also important that companies were "tiered" based on their price/earnings ratio, which is a way of measuring how expensive a company's stock is compared to its earnings. Companies that were well positioned globally and had greater scale were in higher tiers, meaning their stocks were valued more by investors. These companies stood to use their highly valued stock kind of like money to merge with or acquire other companies, which would be a good deal for their shareholders.

So that was the thesis of "The Era of the Super-Major." Companies that merged to combine high-quality assets and expand their operations internationally would reward their shareholders in superior fashion. The ones that moved first to merge would grab the best opportunities and, as their profits increased, they would become the top performers in the stock market over the next 10 years. On the other hand, companies that failed to recognize the changing competitive landscape and the optimal solution for their entities would fall behind. They would lose their competitive edge and their stocks would not do as well as those that followed our proposal. We urged investors to avoid investing in these companies.

Effectively, our plan was to intellectually bring all the major players in the industry to an island and burn the ships—no one was leaving until we all agreed on the best way forward. The status quo was no longer viable. After that, we would start fresh and head down the path to prosperity.

Coming up with a new investment strategy for an old, slow-moving and established industry wasn't easy, especially when it meant breaking away from the well-worn path followed by its constituents which were still some of the largest companies in the world. But the real challenge would be in making this new idea gain traction in the market. And if it didn't, all that effort, time, and my own reputation could go down the drain, making for a serious setback in my career.

For the plan to succeed, three groups needed to be convinced that my thesis was the best path forward for all stakeholders: large institutional investors, oil company CEOs and their boards, and the Federal Trade Commission (FTC).

Let's start with the low hanging fruit: the investors. They were the ones who would eventually vote for or against mergers. They were fatigued by poor performance, a sentiment echoed in "The Decade's Worst Stocks" article in The Economist. I believed investors would agree with me on the necessity for change and the effectiveness of my proposed solution, especially once they grasped how it could significantly enhance the value of their investment portfolios. We spoke the same language as I had been part of their world both as an analyst and a portfolio manager at one of the leading buy-side investment firms in the U.S. just a few years prior.

While I anticipated some investor pushback to my unwavering emphasis on ROCE as the primary yardstick for evaluating Big Oil companies, resistance was negligible. Investors aligned with me because ROCE signals competitive advantage, astute capital management, and the ability to innovate, all of which serve shareholders. "ROCE gives insight into how well a company is deploying its capital. It's a powerful tool for identifying potential compounding machines—businesses that can reinvest their profits at high rates of return," according to renowned investor Howard Marks of Oaktree Capital. Since it was the predominant performance measure by which companies in other major sectors were evaluated, energy companies needed to emphasize it to regain competitiveness with S&P 500.

The main points of resistance and dissent were summarized by the Harvard Business Review in a report called "The Dubious Logic of Global Megamergers," which questioned the reasoning behind large-scale international mergers.

They reasoned that:

"Pushing these huge—and pricey—cross-border deals is the almost universal belief that industries will inevitably become more concentrated as the world's markets become more globalized. The spoils of the market are supposed to go to a select few in each industry. And companies believe that if they are going to be among the winners, they will have to shore up economies of scale in manufacturing, branding, and research and development. That's how they hope to scare off potential competitors and sew up new markets. From this perspective, cross-border mergers are a do-or-die proposition. If you want to survive, let alone thrive, you must be one of the world's biggest players.

"The assumption that the global economy is a winner-take-all economy has become common wisdom—but there's no evidence to support this premise. The theoretical links between the globalization of an industry and the concentration of that industry are weak. Empirical research indicates that global—or globalizing—industries have been marked by steady decreases in concentration in the post-World War II period. Executives, then, need to break free of the biases that lead them to pursue larger and larger cross-border deals. There are better, more profitable strategies for dealing with globalization than relentless expansion." While the Harvard study made some valid points, others not so much. First, the mergers that we proposed were not "pricey" and instead would create economic value from cost savings alone. We also thought that companies that merged and became some of the largest in the world would thrive because they'd have more and better options for investing money, leading to better returns compared to other companies. As these merged companies became more diversified both in terms of what they do and where they operated, the distribution of risks would be more balanced, leading to a decline in their cost of equity and to borrow money. Lastly, we weren't advocating for unrestrained expansion or that companies grow without a plan. Instead, we were advocating for carefully chosen mergers between companies that we thought were "optimal partners" and ones that upheld our proposed value proposition and met our stringent criteria for value creation.

My client Stan Majcher at Hotchkis & Wiley in Los Angeles who brought the article to my attention said that one of us was "not only going to be wrong but dead wrong, and in a high-profile way." He said he'd be watching closely with his popcorn! I agreed with him but indicated that it would be the team from Harvard and not me that would be wrong. Time would tell.

Convincing the second group would pose a greater challenge. The Big Oil CEOs were inherently conservative, prone to move slowly and deliberately, and reluctant to heed external advice or stray from the long-established routes laid down by decades of tradition. While I had positive relationships with each of the major oil company CEOs—including Amoco, BP, Chevron, Conoco, Exxon, Mobil, Phillips, and Texaco—and being a former member of their ranks from my days at Schlumberger, my thesis publicly repudiated the value propositions and business models that they had proposed to their boards and were actively implementing at their companies.

However, the best CEOs understood that my push for change wasn't personal and that I wanted all of us to succeed. At the same time, they also knew that the status quo wasn't going to work out for their company, or for them personally, in the long run, especially if continued deterioration in financial performance placed "sacrosanct" dividends at risk.[20] I knew it would take time to convince this group and that most CEOs would not publicly support my view until the day that they announced mergers. Their steady opposition would provide

---

20. Because dividends represented most of the total return for Big Oil stocks, they were considered "sacrosanct" or untouchable. Reductions in dividends were often regarded as failures by senior management teams and changes to these teams often followed.

fodder for my Wall Street competitors in the meantime though.

In retrospect, this group of CEOs were among the smartest and most innovative people in the energy industry in recent decades. I learned that leaders who were open to change when presented with a better path forward often ended up being the most successful ones, and this group fit the bill. Within this group though were CEOs who were content with the way things were, highly resistant to change, and did not grasp the seriousness of the situation. And they pushed back hard. While jabs were thrown my way during analyst day presentations, I didn't mind the public criticism. I saw it as good publicity and even welcomed it in a strange way.

My trump card was that I was driving the narrative and interacting with the largest investors in the energy sector on the topic every day, so I had the advantage of having my finger on the pulse of the debate. Investors were more candid with me as their meetings with CEOs were often bound by the need to maintain harmony to secure future access to management teams and company information. This often relegated more important but difficult conversations about business model obsolescence and mediocre corporate performance to the sideline, if at all.

The third group that needed convincing was the FTC, which would rule whether the Super-Majors proposal violated anti-trust laws, or the rules against forming monopolies. These laws were set in 1911 when the Standard Oil Trust was ordered to be broken up into 34 different companies per the Sherman Anti-Trust Act after being deemed too powerful.

The FTC looks at mergers to see if they make the industry too concentrated using something called the Herfindahl-Hirschman Index (HHI). The HHI is a way to measure how competitive an industry is. The score is calculated by summing the squares of the market shares of all firms in a particular industry. The resulting number can range between 0 and 1, with higher numbers indicating greater market concentration and lower levels of competition. For instance, three companies splitting the market evenly translates into a Herfindahl index of .99. Ten companies splitting a market evenly translate into a

Herfindahl index of .10.

Or look at it this way: Imagine if in a race, instead of many runners, you only have a few, and one of them is significantly faster than the others. That race wouldn't be very competitive, right? HHI helps figure out something similar for businesses in a market. Take each company's market share (think of this as how much of the race they're winning), squaring those numbers (as if making sure the differences stand out more), and then adding them all up. If the total score is low, it means there are many companies competing against each other, like a race with lots of runners closely matched in speed. A high score means fewer companies hold most of the market, like a race with only a few runners where one is much faster than the rest. So, a high HHI points to less competition among companies, and a low HHI means a healthy level of competition.

Because the HHI had fallen by half in recent decades for oil production and refining, the timing of my call for consolidation seemed prescient. That is, because my proposed combinations scored well on HHI calculations, and the FTC previously allowed combinations between the R&M units of BP, Mobil, Texaco, and Shell, I thought that success was higher than most people thought. But only if the FTC was basing it on economic and non-political factors. Because the FTC was not prone to provide insight, especially to Wall Street types like me, it was hard to know exactly how they would rule on this critical issue.

So, I needed the okay from three distinct groups and the path was likely to be rocky. However, besides the positive tailwind from globalization, other significant changes were unfolding that would increase my chances of success, even though I didn't see them coming or understand how much they could help me. It was a stroke of luck that happened at just the right time for my Super-Major thesis.

The changes related to the Asian Economic Miracle, which

was a period of rapid growth in countries like South Korea, Taiwan, Hong Kong, and Singapore, often called the "Asian Tigers." Following them were the "new tigers," including Malaysia, Indonesia, Thailand, and the Philippines, which also started to grow quickly in the 1990s.

These countries opened their capital accounts and liberalized their financial systems and were experiencing strong economic growth and rising standards of living. This growth was accompanied by significant reductions in poverty and improvements in healthcare, education, and other social indicators. Between 1990 and 1996, the amount of money flowing into these economies from other countries dramatically increased from $42 billion to a massive $329 billion. During this time, the overall size of these economies, measured by GDP, grew at an astonishing rate of 8% every year, and stock markets boomed.

The economic boom led to a surge in oil demand, with Asian countries accounting for over 40% of the increase in global oil demand from 1995 to 1997. While the International Energy Agency (IEA) projected continued growth in oil demand, concerns were rising beneath the surface due to speculative bubbles in real estate and stock markets. These underlying risks suggested that reductions in OPEC output might eventually be needed to balance the market, but the prevailing optimism made such measures harder to consider.

Given these economic cross currents in Asia, OPEC faced a complex decision when it gathered in Jakarta, Indonesia, in November 1997 to develop oil market strategy. Tensions were high leading up to the meeting because Saudi Arabia, OPEC's biggest producer, was upset that Venezuela and others were not sticking to their production limits. The Saudis feared a loss of market share—a concern given their unfavorable experience in the 1980s.

After four days of intense deliberation, OPEC was unable to reach agreement on production cuts, and instead decided to increase oil production by 2 MMBPD. Doing so allowed member countries to pump at their maximum—responding to Venezuela's high production rates. The Saudis felt that if Venezuela would have unbridled production, they would too.

Our analysis suggested that OPEC's decision to ramp up production would lead to a rise in oil inventories and that oil prices would decline. Despite our concerns, OPEC remained optimistic, with Kuwait's oil minister expressing confidence in the stability of prices, stating, "The rise is a very reasonable one."

Under a normal economic scenario, he may have been right. However, the economic situation in Asia had already started to deteriorate due to overborrowing and weak financial systems, and oil demand plummeted. This made major imbalances in the oil markets and a drop in oil prices highly likely. And that is exactly what happened.

This downturn started with a financial crisis in Thailand's property sector, which caused the Thai Baht currency to collapse as developers defaulted on loans.

Morgan Stanley's Barton Biggs, one of the foremost global investment strategists of my lifetime, was among the first to predict this economic disaster, its contagion, and its widespread impact. Barton's call was one of the most remarkable non-consensus calls that I ever witnessed on Wall Street, and I admired it. He was a true student of the game, and it was beneficial for me to be at Morgan Stanley and to watch him develop and deliver the call. Barton and his contemporary Byron Wein had a knack for making bold, unconventional forecasts seem like a blend of science and art. This one was a master class in global investing, and I hoped to apply what I learned in my own analyses in the energy sector.

Following Thailand's currency devaluation, several East Asian countries also saw their currencies and economies falter, leading to massive financial instability. The International Monetary Fund (IMF) eventually intervened with restrictive financial measures, but the damage was severe, with the Association of Southeast Asian Nations (ASEAN) economies shrinking by 32% in 1998.

In the energy sector, oil demand and prices were extremely weak. Ongoing disagreements between Saudi Arabia and Venezuela further complicated matters, revolving around questions of which nation should curtail supply and to what extent, as well as whether the responsibility for cutbacks should extend to non-OPEC countries. This led to record-high global oil inventories and a significant drop in oil prices, from $20/bbl before the Jakarta meeting to $9/bbl by the end of 1998.

The collapse in oil prices put immense financial strain on energy companies around the world. Many faced the threat of bankruptcy, especially those heavily in debt. This dire situation was highlighted by an Economist cover story declaring the world was "drowning in oil," where I discussed the need for industry restructuring regardless of a potential recovery in oil prices.

Although I hadn't anticipated the economic downturn in Asia or the steep drop in oil prices related to it and due to OPEC's actions, the timing suggested that the strategic shift toward "The Era of the Super-Major" would gain momentum if key stakeholders agreed. As oil prices fell, this concept emerged as the possible lifeline for the struggling energy sector.

Amid plunging oil prices and growing financial turmoil, I ramped up my marketing campaign to promote the Super-Major concept. I met with major investor groups in cities across the U.S. and Europe, including New York, Boston, Philadelphia, Los Angeles, San Francisco, Seattle, Chicago, London, Paris, Geneva and others too. Initially, I had medium-sized investor audiences, but as my idea gained footing, my meetings grew larger.

I was careful about my interactions with the media but had built trusted connections with major publications like the Wall Street Journal, the Financial Times, and the Economist. I also appeared on the popular TV show "Wall Street Week" with Louis Rukeyser, reaching a national audience of millions of viewers.

I met with management teams from Arco, BP, Exxon,

Chevron, Conoco, Hess, Mobil, Phillips, and Texaco, which sparked a lot of discussion and debate.

During my meetings with investors, there was plenty to discuss given the drop in oil prices and energy stocks following the OPEC meeting. I said that low oil prices would boost oil demand and that financial strains on OPEC countries would lead to a supply agreement, eventually resulting in higher oil prices.

Indeed, the former Saudi Arabian Oil Minister, Ali al-Naimi, indicated in his book that Saudi Arabia had expressed interest in coordinating a production cut with OPEC to American officials, who were cautious about appearing to support higher prices at the gas pump. However, they comprehended the sustainability issues posed by the situation, impacting both Saudi Arabia and major American oil companies amidst such depressed oil prices. My own discussions in Saudi Arabia during the period led me to believe that positive changes in the oil market were on the horizon although the exact timing was difficult to predict.

I advised investors that while there would be a profitable short-term trade in energy stocks as oil prices rose, the more substantial investment opportunity would come from the long-term gains in value creation if the industry consolidated as I suggested. In simpler terms, while oil prices would inevitably rise given wide-spread financial distress in the energy industry, the real game-changer would be the transformation of the energy sector if my Super-Major plan was adopted.

By spring of 1998, the conversations I had with CEOs of the major oil companies started to shift in a positive direction. In every meeting with investors, CEOs were questioned about why they thought my concept was incorrect and why they believed their existing strategies—which hadn't been successful over the past decade—would suddenly start working. It was difficult for CEOs to make their case, especially with sophisticated institutional investors, who by now understood the economic potential of the model that I espoused. In short order, "The Era of the Super-Major" theme had taken on a life of its own, and while I had marketed the concept heavily, the buy-side and the media increasingly did the work for me, especially at the Wall Street Journal, the Financial Times, and the Economist.

Overall, though, skepticism remained healthy for a few reasons. First, I was calling for the most far-reaching reshaping of the structure of the petroleum industry since the breakup of the Standard Oil Trust in 1911. Second, when every major oil company CEO was asked publicly at analyst meetings about my thesis—which had become the prominent topic in the sector—their response was clear: They planned to continue with their current approach. A big fat public "no," in other words.

Platts Oilgram reported in April of 1998:

"Officially, CEOs of Big Oil have given Terreson's mega merger scenario short shrift. Exxon Chief Lee Raymond dismissed Terreson's theory at a recent analyst meeting, declaring that Exxon for its part has no present interest in paying top dollar for some other company or someone else's assets. Exxon has plenty of firepower in house.

"Likewise, BP CEO John Browne parried a question about merger prospects from Terreson at a New York analysts meeting on April 8, 1998. Given the huge size of existing companies, Browne said, 'By adding up any two, you immediately see possible cost savings, at least on paper. We are inundated with proposals, laterally bound and covered in blue.' But Browne insisted cost savings are not sufficient reasons for a big merger. Instead, Browne told analysts that it's the growth potential. In the end, it requires a cultural takeover combined with a financial merger. There are many opportunities and theories but few deals that can be delivered."

The responses from the CEOs, while pleasing my competitors since they seemed to publicly question my credibility, were entirely expected. CEOs would predictably disagree with my views publicly—that is, until they didn't and announced a merger. As Platts put it, "the mere fact that CEOs would even publicly entertain talks of outright combinations is enlightening and grist for Terreson's mill."

At the time, I didn't know that investment bankers were also pitching my big idea to major oil companies worldwide, alongside my efforts to convince the investment community. According to Dan Yergin's book "The Quest," famed Morgan Stanley bankers Joseph Perella and Robert McGuire shared insights that really got the attention of executives during a meeting with Norwegian government and oil companies in February 1998.

Joe and Bob pointed out in their presentation that "the roster of the top publicly traded firms in the oil industry is largely the same as it has been since the breakup of the Standard Oil Trust. Were he alive today, John D. Rockefeller would recognize most of the list, but Carnegie, Vanderbilt, and Morgan on the other hand, would have difficulty with similar lists for their industries."

I presumed other bankers must be discussing similar ideas with their clients, given the buzz around the topic in the energy sector. If we were indeed at the brink of a historic merger wave in the oil industry, the bankers that provided the best advice to their companies could make a huge impact on their careers. Success in this area could also place their firms in a premier league of strategic advisors and set them up for a windfall from the expected privatization of energy companies in the future.

I also suspected that CEOs must be talking among themselves about my thesis, even though I was cut off from these conversations due to my separation from the investment banking division. While it seemed that the ball had to be rolling, I had no way of knowing if my ideas were being taken seriously by key constituencies.

Still, I kept pushing forward. When investors asked me how the merger wave would play out, I told them that one merger would lead to five, as the positive reaction from the market to the first would trigger a chain reaction. I believed that these mergers would significantly alter the competitive hierarchy, return profiles, and stock market performance for the foreseeable future, and company boards and CEOs knew it. They also knew that missing out on this merger wave could disadvantage their company for decades.

Whenever someone asked me about which companies would merge first, I told every investor and corporate executive that I was sure Amoco and Chevron would be the first combination. My reasoning was that both companies had high-quality assets which overlapped nicely and similar corporate cultures, making them a great match. Although Amoco's Larry Fuller and Chevron's Ken Derr played golf together and knew each other well, the merger that I was so sure about didn't happen.

While most CEOs doubted my thesis, BP's John Browne[21] was an exception. John and I had many discussions about the best strategic direction for energy companies and the industry. I really enjoyed the time I spent with the BP team with him as lead as it always stretched my mind. Whenever John came to the U.S., I arranged small group meetings with investors, which was the type he preferred, and which also suited my biggest investor clients.

Before one of our meetings, Betsy Griffith, a charming Southern belle from South Carolina and salesperson from Morgan Stanley, and one of my closest friends at the firm, suggested I invite her client Edie to a lunch meeting with the BP CEO. Edie was a sharp equity analyst from Delaware Management in Philadel-phia, a leading value investment firm. Betsy was convinced that Edie and I would hit it off, eventually get married, and have the perfect family life, complete with a house in the suburbs and a white picket fence.

Despite Betsy's detailed vision for us, Edie hinted she might prefer someone with a more interesting personality, rather than just a numbers guy. I wasn't keen on a blind date but decided to invite her since I was intrigued, and Delaware was an important

---

21. BP CEO John Browne was granted the title Baron Browne of Madingley in the County of Cambridgeshire, England on January 21, 2001. Since then, he has been known as "Lord Browne" or "Lord Browne of Madingley."

client. Edie, who had a strong background with a finance degree from Florida State and an MBA from NYU, was temporarily focusing on the energy sector. We met before the BP CEO meeting to brief her on BP and the sector, and then attended the lunch I had organized.

Within six months, we were engaged, and a year later, we were married. Now, over 25 years and three wonderful children later, it turns out Betsy was spot on!

BP's John Browne was extremely interested in the details of my ideas about the Super-Majors during our meetings, which made me think I was on the right track. This was different from my talks with other company leaders. Some were simply curious, while others doubted the necessity or feasibility of mergers due to regulatory constraints. A few were offended because they felt I was saying their business models had become obsolete under their leadership.

What I didn't know at the time was that John Browne was already looking into merging BP with another company. Behind the scenes, he had told his board that without acquiring another company, BP could risk being taken over itself. He believed BP needed to grow to compete effectively, especially against state-owned oil companies that were becoming big players on the global stage. In other words, Browne and I were on the same page; I just wasn't aware of it.

In 1997, Browne and the CEO of Mobil, Lou Noto, started talking about merging their companies, just a few months before "The Era of the Super-Major" was published. They made some headway but couldn't agree on the financial terms. BP couldn't offer enough money to satisfy Mobil, and so, their negotiations ended without a deal during a meeting at the Carlyle Hotel in New York City in May 1998.

After returning to London, Brown reached out to Larry Fuller, the CEO of Amoco which was headquartered in Chicago. They decided to meet the very next day at the British Airways Concorde Lounge at JFK Airport in New York where they began their merger discussions. Both CEOs believed that the tough competition in their industry meant they needed to take significant strategic steps.

To keep their talks private, they used code names: "Bear" for BP and "Eagle" for Amoco and called their discussion "Project Belgium." A breakthrough happened on Sunday, August 2, at an office in London, when the CEOs overcame a common deal-breaking issue: deciding who would lead the merged company. Age played a role in the decision, with Browne at 50 and Fuller at 59. Their boards approved the merger on August 10, making it a record-setting $48.2 billion deal on Wall Street. The announcement came the next day on August 11, 1998.

The new company would be called BP Amoco. It would vie with Exxon and Shell for industry leadership, ranking second in the industry in terms of oil and gas reserves and production. The merger stood to be a game changer for BP. I hoped it would start the domino effect that I envisioned for the industry.

In CEO Browne's words: "Being at the top of the second division is fine but there are limits to what you can do. The whole point of this deal is that it allows us to do more. This is not an end game for a declining industry, but instead a renewal, the making of a new industry. International competition in the industry is already fierce and will grow more acute as new players emerge. In such a climate, the best investment opportunity will increasingly go to the companies that have the size and financial strength to take on those large-scale projects that offer a truly distinctive return. In the 32 years I've been working with BP, this is the most exciting of them all. Many executives have been talking about the restructuring of the industry, but it didn't happen until now."

Let me point out that, if the stock prices of BP and Amoco had fallen after their merger was announced, it would have been bad news for my concept and my career. However, the opposite happened: the shares of both companies rose significantly. In the three months following the announcement, BP's stock price increased by about 20%, which was 13 percentage points better than the stock price increases of Chevron, Exxon, Shell, and

Total. These companies also saw their stocks go up because the market expected them to benefit from strategic moves as well.

This jump in BP's stock was a big deal, especially in such a short period of time. According to the Wall Street Journal, BP was aiming to reach the size of major players like Royal Dutch/Shell or Exxon, companies who were more highly valued by investors, as shown by their price-earnings (P/E) ratios. The P/E ratio is a measure that compares a company's stock price to its per-share earnings, indicating how much investors are willing to pay for each dollar of earnings. A higher P/E ratio means that investors have a higher valuation of the company's future growth and earnings. At the time, Exxon's earnings were valued at 21 times, meaning investors were willing to pay $21 for every dollar of Exxon's earnings, showing high confidence in Exxon's returns profile and growth prospects. In contrast, BP's earnings were valued at 16.6 times, indicating that investors were less willing to pay as much for BP's earnings compared to Exxon's. BP's goal in the Amoco merger was to increase its financial performance and its valuation to levels similar to those of Royal Dutch/Shell or Exxon, which would increase its stock price further.

The Wall Street Journal's commentary on this situation sounded a lot like my published research, possibly because I was regularly talking to their energy reporters, sharing my ideas with them to both publicly promote and test my concept. Even though they were independent and didn't agree with everything I said, they supported my view that the industry needed to change and that my specific plan was ideal. Some of my investor clients noted that the newspaper's articles sounded quite a bit like my own research—which of course was my objective.

BP Amoco indicated that the rationale for its merger involved: "1.) scale, financial strength, and distinctive assets, 2.) strategic and geographic fit, 3.) synergies and 4.) complementary management" in its proxy filing with the SEC.

Daniel Yergin, author of the Pulitzer prize winning oil-industry history "The Prize," supported their position by saying that "this merger clearly has a very strong and compelling strategic vision," and that "the companies are really quite complementary."

To my delight, BP laid out a clear plan to increase its value, which included cutting costs by $4 billion or 20%, selling off $10 billion worth of assets that didn't fit their strategic vision, and planning to spend less money than the predecessor companies did for the next three years. Their aim was to improve their ROCE, my recommended financial measure, by six percentage points, representing a huge 50% increase. They also planned to keep a healthy balance sheet with only 35% of their capital in debt. On top of all this, BP committed to give shareholders 50% of its regular earnings as dividends. This meant that BP was following every key tenet of the Super-Major value proposition to the letter. I was elated about the historic changes taking place.

That first merger changed everything. In Yergin's "The Quest" he put it this way: "The taboo against large-scale mergers had been broken, or so it appeared." The stock market showed that investors believed the financial prospects of the Super-Major model were better than other options. This quick and positive reaction changed the conversation almost immediately. Instead of discussing whether the Super-Major idea was the right path forward, the conversation shifted to which companies would be the best partners.

In "The Era of the Super-Major Begins,"[22] which I published shortly after the BP-Amoco merger, I indicated that "the combination of industry powers BP and Amoco will be the first of several in the integrated oil industry, with our Era of The Super-Major consolidation thesis in its early stages."

Further, "We question how returns for the 'non-Super-Majors' will keep pace with that of the Super-Majors, with the wealth of productivity and global investment opportunities more readily available to the latter. The answer, in our view, is that without consolidation, returns are unlikely to keep pace over the longer term, and with lower risk due to superior

---

22. The Era of the Super-Major Begins, August 19, 1998

financial and geo-graphical diversification (higher earnings quality), risk-adjusted returns will be superior for the Super-Majors. While status-quo strategies are possible, companies that are not involved in the industry's consolidation phase are likely to become disadvantaged in coming years. We believe the activity will dictate competitive placement, returns, and equity market performance for years to come. Integrated oil companies are at a critical historical juncture, in our opinion, with upcoming strategic actions expected to separate the leaders from the followers in the new millennium."

The Financial Times underscored my views by indicating that "BP Amoco will put intense pressure on some of the mediumsized U.S. integrated oil companies, such as Texaco and ARCO, which are struggling to build foreign businesses to offset declines in U.S. production. Continental European companies like Elf-Aquitaine and Total of France, and ENI of Italy also face tough choices in the wake of the BP Amoco deal. No longer will Exxon and Shell be able to take for granted that the biggest projects will automatically come their way. In the past, other companies had neither the management expertise nor the money to consider them. That will now change."

I was pleased to see the market react positively to the consolidation thesis, which confirmed my ideas that some had dismissed as "harebrained" only a few months before. Even though I believed the stars were aligned for success, there was no guarantee. The kind of movement that I was leading was unprecedented. CEO Browne hinted at this during the BP Amoco merger press conference, mentioning that nothing like this had happened in his 32 years with the company.

As mergers began to show more benefits than Wall Street and the companies expected, I believed that entities that embraced the Super-Major model would perform better than others. This success would push more companies to consider consolidation. Of course, companies needed to work hard to make the most of these mergers, but from my experience working with Big Oil and energy companies as an engineer at Schlumberger, I saw a lot of easy wins that could make these mergers very successful.

My background gave me confidence that the outcomes of these mergers would exceed Wall Street's expectations, as I thought I had insight that others did not.

After the success of the BP-Amoco merger, everyone wanted to know which companies would merge next, leading to a lot of interest and questions directed to me at my office. The most likely pairs seemed to be Exxon and Mobil, Chevron and Texaco, Chevron and Conoco, Chevron and Phillips, or Elf and Total. However, there were also other possible combinations that seemed likely too.

Mobil was a prize in the sweepstakes. The company was strong in E&P and R&M with a robust international presence in Australia, Kazakhstan, Nigeria, Saudi Arabia and Qatar.

Exxon was the envy of the industry as during CEO Lee Raymond's leadership from 1999 to 2005, the company led the oil industry by almost tripling its economic value added (EVA)[23]—one of the most impressive records of value creation across all industries.

Under CEO Raymond, Exxon was known for its disciplined approach to managing shareholder capital and it set the financial performance standard for the rest of the industry. With a ROCE of over 15% during his time, Exxon's market valuation was the highest in the industry, earning Raymond a "legendary" reputation. Despite his reputation as a tough businessman, I personally found Lee and his wife to be kind, humble, and respectful, making them some of my wife's and my favorite people to spend time with during my career.

Exxon, alongside Shell, effectively formed a powerful duo

---

23. EVA, or Economic Value Added, is a financial metric that measures the profitability of a company based on the returns generated above its cost of capital i.e. its cost of equity and debt. It is calculated as net operating profit after tax (NOPAT) minus the cost of capital, which is the minimum return expected by investors. A company has positive that has positive EVA is deemed to be creating economic value which typically drives market value.

in the industry, with a superior position in the current industry structure. I advised investors that neither company was likely to make the first move toward merging or acquiring other companies because the existing industry structure was already in their favor. However, the merger between BP and Amoco posed a potential threat to their dominant position, especially if other companies with valuable assets started merging with their competitors.

On February 2, 1998, I was invited to speak to Mobil's top 150 executives in Fairfax, Virginia. I shared my views on the outlook for the industry, making Mobil the first major oil company to hear my proposal in detail and to have the opportunity to scrutinize its tenets in a public forum. And scrutinize the tenets they did. The discussion was lively, and after my talk, I was surprised to hear from senior management that my views were in line with their own thoughts, even if I hadn't been upbeat. This hinted to me that they might be considering the kind of big merger I was suggesting.

By June 16, CEO Raymond and Mobil's CEO, Lou Noto, were discussing a possible merger at the same Mobil headquarters. They agreed that any deal would need to: 1.) be satisfactory to both sides, 2.) get approval from regulatory bodies in the U.S. and Europe, and 3.) blend the two companies effectively, which would be the most daunting of the requirements.

While several conversations followed, the companies were unable to agree on valuation and especially the premium to be paid to Mobil shareholders. On August 6, Noto told the Mobil board that he and Raymond had "mutually agreed to discontinue discussions." Just five days later, BP and Amoco announced their merger, setting a benchmark for these kinds of deals.

When Raymond heard the details of the merger, he called Noto. They now had a basis to resolve their disagreement on the value of their companies' shares. Notably, BP's stock had gone up even after they paid a 25% premium for Amoco, as investors recognized the benefits of the merger.

Three months after the BP-Amoco merger announcement,

the Wall Street Journal cleared the air by reporting that Exxon and Mobil were in merger discussions in November of 1998.

Originally, the two companies were the largest parts of the 34-part Standard Oil Trust. Exxon was about half of the original Standard Oil entity with Mobil representing another 9%.

On December 1, before regulatory approval for the BP-Amoco merger was even finalized, Exxon and Mobil announced their own merger. Valued at $230 billion, it was the biggest merger Wall Street had ever seen, dramatically changing the global oil industry. The announced combination of Exxon and Mobil further validated my Super-Major thesis, ending any doubts about its viability.

"The New Oil Behemoth" headlined the New York Times. The new company would be called ExxonMobil, and the merger was set to create the largest company in the world.

CEO Raymond stated: "This is a case of the whole being greater than the sum of the parts. As many of you know, I have never been in favor of bigness for bigness' sake alone. I have always had the view that the objective is to be best. If in being best you also have to be biggest, that's fine. The merger will significantly enhance shareholder value by enabling us to manage the combined assets of Exxon and Mobil to produce a higher return on capital employed (ROCE) than either company could achieve on a standalone basis."[24]

CEO Noto, who was set to become the vice chair of the new company that Raymond would chair, said, "This is not a combination based on desperation. It is one based on opportunity. But we need to face some facts. The world has changed. The easy things are behind us. The easy oil, the easy cost savings, they're done. So, all of us are now looking for some

---

24. ROCE stands for Return on Capital Employed. It measures the profitability and efficiency of capital investments. It is calculated by dividing the company's earnings before interest and taxes (EBIT) by its total capital employed (which includes equity and debt). ROCE indicates how well a company generates profits from its capital investments and is used to evaluate management's ability to deploy capital effectively to generate returns for shareholders.

way to make a jump, to make a quantum leap, to be able to deliver more value to our shareholders and our employees and customers."

Oil and Gas Investor quoted me as saying: "Fasten your seatbelts because the Energy business in 2000 and beyond will bear little resemblance to the one that we know today. We're going to see major consolidation among Integrated Oils, E&P companies, Oil Field Service providers and Downstream players. The best way for companies to respond to the changed competitive condition is to combine forces to create larger entities with superior scale and globalization as this will translate into superior risk adjusted returns. That is the basis on which more mergers are going to occur."

Similarly, Business Week quoted me saying: "BP-Amoco was a shock to the system and ExxonMobil was a seismic shift. There are going to be several more to follow."

The Economist supported the theme by indicating: "After all, Exxon and BP, two of the sharpest as well as the biggest firms in the oil game, have shown the way. The rest of the industry has little choice but to follow."

And follow they did, with French oil giants Elf Aquitaine and Total next in line. Thierry Desmarest, the CEO of Total, and Philippe Jaffre, the CEO of Elf, led companies of similar size. I considered Total the better investment. My meetings with Elf's management in Paris made me think their strategy of growing at all costs could lead to problems, as this "empire building" approach often does poorly in the energy sector and other industries too.

Total started expanding by buying the Belgian oil company Petrofina, announced on the same day as the ExxonMobil merger. This acquisition fit well with Total's operations, but it made people wonder how much bigger Total wanted to get. The big question was whether Total would aim to merge with its French counterpart, Elf Aquitaine.

Elf Aquitaine had been privatized in 1986, and by 1996, the French government had sold more shares to the public but kept a "golden share," giving it the right to block any takeovers. After the BP-Amoco merger, Desmarest felt a push to merge with Elf, seeing it as beneficial for France. He said that the BP-Amoco deal made it clear they needed to grow through combinations.

After discussions with French Prime Minister Lionel Jospin, who eventually agreed, Total made a move.

On July 5, 1999, Total launched a hostile bid to take over Elf, the only such bid in that period of oil industry consolidation. After some back-and-forth and negotiations, the deal was finalized in September, creating TotalFinaElf. This new company crossed the $100 billion threshold, my criteria for being deemed a Super-Major. Desmarest took the lead of the new group as chairman, while Jaffre from Elf stepped down.

CEO Desmarest indicated: "About two-thirds of the world's top 15 oil companies have been involved in a merger in the past year. Our groups could not ignore this situation. Through a friendly agreement, we are constituting a powerful group that will be a major actor in the oil industry. I believe that it is necessary today to join forces to assure continued solid growth and to take our place as an oil major of the first rank at a time when the industry is restructuring on a global scale." Mr. Jaffree indicated: "This deal creates a major French champion in both oil and chemicals. It assures a great future for a company that holds a very great place in the history of France."

Their commentary was entirely consistent with my Super-Major doctrine for the global oil industry and was music to my ears. I was happy to have the giant European company under my tent.

While BP had already made a big splash and attained first-mover advantage, another move was in the works. Following the closure of the BP-Amoco transaction and the positive response in the equity market, CEO Browne sought to double-down on the Super-Major concept. U.S. major oil ARCO was a compelling target given strong strategic overlap with BP positions in Alaska and the North Sea.

ARCO had higher debt and more oil production per share than other companies, and with oil prices lower by almost half during 1998, ARCO's financials were stressed and CEO Mike Bowlin started to study potential combinations. By January of 1999 with oil prices near $10 /bbl, CEO Bowlin concluded that BP was the best fit. Bowlin reached out to CEO Browne, suggesting they meet to discuss a merger. Browne later reflected on the proposal, saying it seemed "too good to be true." So, talks about a merger began to move forward between the two companies.

In February of 1999, Browne, who was set to be the Tuesday keynote speaker at the Cambridge Energy Research Associates or CERA Conference in Houston, canceled his appearance. Bowlin was set to keynote on Wednesday, but with talks at an advanced stage between the two companies, Browne was concerned that it was too risky to be in the same arena with the ARCO CEO at that time.

The cancellation by the BP CEO was suspicious at a minimum. That same day, I had a private meeting with Bowlin and buy-side investment colleagues David Ginther from Waddell and Reed, Michael Kerr from Capital Research, and Lewis Ropp from Barrow Hanley. We all noticed that Bowlin seemed nervous during our meeting, making the whole encounter feel strange. Over dinner, we debated whether this was a sign of something bigger happening between BP and ARCO. Looking back, we should have made that connection.

On April 1, 1999, BP announced plans to buy ARCO for $27 billion, stating that merging with ARCO would create a more competitive energy and petrochemical company than either BP or Amoco could achieve alone, and would open significant opportunities for value creation.

The merger seemed like a perfect strategic match, especially because both companies had major operations in the North Sea and Alaska. However, the FTC came to the same conclusion. Alaska's laws prevented a single company from leasing more than 500,000 acres, and the merged company would have owned 860,000 acres.

Ultimately, BP-Amoco underestimated Alaska's interest in

changing the law, and as a result, they had to sell off ARCO's oil production assets in Alaska's North Slope (ANS) to Phillips Petroleum or another buyer approved by the FTC. Even though selling these assets diminished the overall value the merger would have added, BP went ahead and completed the deal in April 2000. After the merger, the combined company was valued at $185 billion in market capitalization, making it the 11th largest company in the world.

Chevron and Texaco were always viewed as a likely combination, and it seemed to only be a matter of time before the two entities merged. The two companies had a long-standing and successful partnership in Asia through a joint venture called Caltex, which had been around for 50 years.

In February of 1999, Texaco CEO Peter Bijur approached Chevron CEO Ken Derr about a potential merger and a confidentiality agreement was signed. The strategic fit between Chevron and Texaco seemed very strong, but the personalities of the two CEOs struck me as mismatched, and I anticipated that "social issues" might complicate the deal. In the end the two sides were unable to settle on price even though other similar mergers were successfully completed, and their valuations were clear in the stock market every day. The discussions ended in June of 1999 with CEO Bijur stating, "We have contingency plans to restructure our business that will allow us to grow. We will not rush into anything. We don't feel the urge to merge."

In the fall of the same year, CEO Derr retired, and David O'Reilly took over as the new CEO. O'Reilly also embraced the idea of creating economic value through corporate consolidation. Despite being careful in his public statements, O'Reilly made it clear that companies not participating in mergers would become less relevant and be "marginalized relative to the competition."

The merger conversations between Chevron and Texaco resumed under the leadership of CEOs O'Reilly and Bijur on May 19, 2000. After several months of negotiation, they reached a merger agreement on October 15, 2000, forming a new company named ChevronTexaco. O'Reilly would lead the merged entity. In the merger documents filed with the SEC, Chevron stated that the $87 billion merger would create a U.S.-based global enterprise. This new company would be among the world's largest and most competitive international energy companies, competitive across all energy sectors, and capable of creating greater value for shareholders than either company could on its own. Further, they stated that "investors believe that the so-called 'Super-Majors,' Royal Dutch/Shell, ExxonMobil and BP, deserve a higher relative valuation, as measured by price to earnings (P/E) ratios and other measures. This is due in part to the larger companies' ability to achieve higher return on capital employed or ROCE through improved capital efficiency by funding the best growth opportunities of both companies. Merger synergies will help ChevronTexaco to better compete with its competitors in earnings growth, ROCE, and total stockholder return."

This was a clear, concise synopsis of my Super-Majors concept. I was pleased to see that my thesis had become the central investment theme during the peak of the consolidation phase and was echoed in the communications around corporate mergers. Because I believed that the Chevron and Texaco merger would transform the company, which it did, I applauded their merger on behalf of all stakeholders in my published research.

The requirement by the FTC for BP-Amoco to divest ARCOs operations in Alaska's North Slope paved the way for the last significant merger of that period between Conoco and Phillips.

Conoco, then owned by DuPont, was being prepped for independence by its CEO, Archie Dunham, through an initial public offering (IPO) led by Morgan Stanley, with me as the lead analyst. It was the largest IPO in U.S. history at that time, raising $4.9 billion in October 1998, and set us up to be a leading player in the wave of international privatizations ahead.

Phillips Petroleum, under the leadership of James Mulva in Bartlesville, Oklahoma, had strategically positioned itself for success through significant acquisitions, including ARCO's

Alaska assets and the R&M entity TOSCO. This aggressive expansion made Phillips larger than Conoco, giving it the upper hand in any future merger discussions.

I had a strong personal and professional relationship with Jim, and I valued his wisdom and willingness to take calculated risks and his commitment to shareholders, the latter of which led to strong performance as CEO during his tenure. Jim and I often discussed key strategic issues both inside and outside the office over the years. We were both keen to solve these complex puzzles in the industry, and to do so before anyone else did.

Because Conoco CEO Dunham shared the same strategic outlook for the industry as Jim and I did, a combination always seemed likely during the Super-Major phase.

Despite initial slow progress in negotiations, the companies announced their merger in 2001, creating ConocoPhillips. The blend of assets was strategically complementary, held growth potential, and management's plan emphasized shareholder value. Pro forma equity ownership was set to be 43% Conoco and 57% Phillips.

ConocoPhillips emerged as the third-largest oil company in the U.S. when the merger was finalized in 2002. Jim's ambition was for the company to compete with the largest oil firms, a goal significantly advanced by the subsequent $36 billion acquisition of U.S. E&P company Burlington Resources, which was led by highly regarded CEO and friend Bobby Shackouls a few years later.

The ConocoPhillips merger and subsequent acquisition activity underscored that major strategic moves were necessary to thrive in the more challenging competitive landscape envisioned in "Super-Major World." This merger, along with the others that preceded it, marked a seismic shift in the oil industry, as companies scrambled to reposition themselves for the new era. The rapid succession of these mergers, each one seeming to spur the next, created a sense of momentum and inevitability around the Super-Major concept. It was becoming clear that the future of the industry would be defined by these mega-companies, and those that failed to adapt risked being left behind.

From beginning to end, the oil industry saw nine major mergers involving 14 of the world's biggest oil companies, all happening within just three years. This period marked the most significant transformation of the petroleum industry since the Standard Oil Trust was broken up in 1911. Right after these mergers were announced, the companies involved saw their total market value increase by over $50 billion within just 10 days—a massive amount of money, both then and now.

This trend of mega mergers wasn't just limited to the oil sector. It also took off in other industries, including automotive—with notable mergers like Daimler-Benz and Chrysler, Ford and Volvo, and Renault and Nissan. Similar moves were seen in telecommunications, entertainment, financial services, soft drinks, and cement, with the same strategic reasoning behind these mergers as was seen in the oil industry.

I expected a positive market reaction in the stock market to mergers because I expected returns on capital to rise significantly in the aftermath of combinations leading to higher market valuations.

In my final report of the Super-Major Trilogy, "Super-Major World,"[25] I indicated that the immediate benefits from the mergers in the energy sector were just the tip of the iceberg. The real value, I argued, would emerge over the medium term. Based on this, we advised buying energy stocks, predicting that their value would climb as the market began to appreciate the long-term positive impacts of these mergers.

The rationale behind this optimism wasn't just about cutting costs. It also involved strategically selling off less important assets and adopting a more disciplined approach to spending capital. This shift was partly motivated by the crisis many companies faced in 1998, when oil prices plummeted to $10/bbl and the evolving competitive condition. With a more focused investment strategy and sensible capital expenditure, companies

---

25. Super-Major World, February 24, 1999

were expected to see improved returns on investment. This was a key tenet of the Super-Major thesis, and one that was requisite for gains in value to be sustained. Now, these companies would be able to embark on projects that were out of reach before, when they were smaller and limited by their regional focus and lesser financial capabilities. In essence, by merging, these entities weren't just adding their values together; they were creating even greater value. Or, as I put it in my report, we expected the best of both worlds with "one plus one was set to equal three."

Though investors were excited about the new direction the energy industry was taking, many worried the good times might not last, and that the misguided investment policy would return once entities became flush with cash. I, however, felt confident about my positive outlook. Knowing the CEOs personally, I believed they remembered the mistakes that were previously made and were committed to the new, more disciplined approach promised by the Super-Major value proposition.

I expected CEOs to follow the new doctrine which espoused balance between spending and shareholder distributions and, if so, financial profiles in energy would become competitive with other sectors of the market. This outcome unfolded with capital expenditure in relation to shareholder payouts dropping by half from 1999 to 2007. This shift was significant, highlighting a real commitment to financial discipline. This was reflected in the numbers: ROCE in the energy sector jumped from 13 to 25% over the same period. The energy sector's share of the S&P 500 grew from 4 to 14%, and profits, cash flow, and dividends all saw a fourfold increase. This led to a $500 billion increase in market value by 2008, on top of the initial $50 billion boost following merger announcements. Energy performance was superior to every other major sector of the market during the phase. The industry giants had indeed come together, burned their ships of outdated practices, and emerged stronger.

Critics pointed out that this success wasn't solely because of the Super-Major model, and instead, that the global economy, especially China's growth, played a big role by driving up oil prices.

While true, I argued that without the new capital management policies, oil prices may not have risen, and even if they had, surplus funds may not have been used productively. Instead, the companies were well-positioned to capitalize on these economic tailwinds.

Before this era, the energy sector often fell into a trap where higher oil prices led to more cash flow and spending but not necessarily better returns, harming stock price performance. The Super-Major model, with its focus on smarter spending and value over volume, helped avoid this pitfall. It seemed CEOs were on the same page, believing in mergers for efficiency and better returns, regardless of oil prices. This was the sweet spot. BP CEO Browne and Exxon CEO Raymond indicated to The Economist they would have pushed ahead with their mergers even with higher oil prices because combinations led to substantially lower costs and improved returns in other ways as well.

Overall, my experience advocating for the Super-Major model was rewarding but at times, lonely and challenging. While some colleagues at Morgan Stanley saw it as a major career risk, I saw it as a crucial step to avoid the sector's decline. I was convinced that without a significant shake-up, the companies I was focusing on—and my career alongside them—would quickly fade into obscurity, ignored by investors. With the market pessimistic at the outset about the outlook for energy companies and investor expectations low, I saw an opportunity: a low-risk, high-reward scenario that went against the grain of popular opinion.

The strategy paid off, marking a turning point in the energy sector's fortunes, and writing a remarkable chapter in corporate history. "The Era of the Super-Major" isn't just a case study in value creation—it's a reminder that the biggest risks, when rooted in discipline and vision, can lead to seismic shifts in market leadership. The ride for my companies and investors was profitable. And for me, it validated a conviction I refused to abandon when it mattered most. Looking back, I'm grateful that I stood firm in my beliefs, even when they were unpopular. The rewards of taking that calculated risk have been immense, both professionally and personally. As The Wall Street Journal put it, "*Mr. Terreson came awfully close to perfect.*"

5

Privatizations

The Era of the Super-Major was like a dream come true for me. Even though I had spent an entire year working on my thesis and was convinced I had cracked the code that would lead to prosperity in the industry, it was tough at times and even made me question if I was wasting my time or, worse, jeopardizing my career.

But despite having doubts about how this would affect my future, I was convinced of my findings. So, when things began to play out just like I had envisioned, it wasn't just a win; it felt like a giant stamp of approval on everything I'd worked so hard for. That validation gave me a confidence boost that has served me well throughout my career. As one by one, the major oil companies started to adopt my model of the Super-Major, I felt a sense of influence in the industry that was incredibly fulfilling. The recognition and respect for what was considered prescient and innovative thinking reaffirmed by dedication to my work—and to what I felt was my purpose.

Don't misunderstand me. It wasn't just about being right; it felt like I was helping to lead the industry forward, which was immensely rewarding. In a way, it was a vindication of all the international travel, meetings with boards, management teams and investors, and the late nights I spent buried in research. It drove home how much perseverance matters, especially in the complex worlds of energy and finance.

Thanks to Morgan Stanley's strong client relationships and my role in shaping the most significant strategic shift in almost a century, the firm was an adviser on every major merger of the era, except for ExxonMobil. This success built tremendous goodwill with investors and corporates worldwide, cementing our global equity research and investment banking franchises in the top-tier. This would be a crucial distinction as we prepared for the upcoming wave of energy privatizations.

The move toward privatization started in the 1970s with Great Britain's partial sale of BP. This trend spread globally, with countries like Argentina (YPF), Austria (OMV), and Canada (Petro-Canada), among others, following suit.[26] By 1995, these companies were publicly traded, marking a significant shift toward efficiency and attracting foreign investment.

Despite the move toward privatization, national governments and their National Oil Companies (NOCs) still controlled over 90% of the world's oil and gas reserves. While the Middle East, home to a large portion of these reserves, had yet to embrace privatization, other countries were exploring it. The most promising opportunities for privatization were expected to involve the NOCs in countries like India (ONGC), Norway (Statoil), China (Sinopec, PetroChina, CNOOC), and Venezuela (PDVSA).

Government-run companies often didn't perform well due to their focus on social and political goals over profitability. In other words, they focused on job creation or supporting politically advantageous projects rather than maximizing profits. These goals, though well-intended, didn't always line up with the

---

26. In all, Argentina (YPF), Austria (OMV), Canada (Petro-Canada), France (Elf Aquitaine), Italy (ENI), Hungary (MOL), Sweden (Fortum), Philippines (Petron), Poland (PKN), Spain (Repsol) and Thailand (PTT).

aim that private businesses had for value creation. The transition to privatization, despite its challenges and public opposition, led to more efficient, productive, and financially stable entities. This shift not only strengthened national economies but also allowed governments to redirect focus to other sectors, enhancing overall prosperity.

The aim was to transform these state-owned entities, which often enjoyed strong local and regional market positions and favorable regulations, into companies driven by market-oriented business strategies, management, and modern corporate governance. This approach would create strong competitive edges and sustainable financial performance, opening doors for international expansion. This transformation was especially important as global competition was expected to heat up with more countries joining the World Trade Organization (WTO).

For investors, this shift promised rising share prices as companies transitioned from inefficient government-run entities to formidable national, regional, and global competitors. With substantial cost-cutting opportunities likely boosting financial results in the first few years, investors saw a chance for more substantial growth as investment policies were modernized over time. The move to public ownership also meant that the management's decisions would now be in the spotlight, directly impacting the company's market value. This visibility would push governments and management teams to perform better.

With Morgan Stanley's leading track record in advisory services and initial public offerings or IPOs, we were well-positioned to lead the wave of privatizations. Notably, we secured the mandates to privatize Sinopec in China and Statoil in Norway, marking them as the biggest energy IPOs in Asia and Europe respectively. These were the most prestigious opportunities in the energy privatization phase.

SINOPEC

Privatizing Sinopec was a massive undertaking and quite possibly one of the most complex projects Wall Street had ever seen. In 1997, we at Morgan Stanley joined forces with China International Capital Corporation Limited (CICC) for China's very first investment banking joint venture. This partnership wasn't just another entry in our portfolio; it was the cornerstone of what would become China's blueprint for privatizing its state-owned enterprises (SOEs). Success here mattered not just for us but for China and CICC too.

At the time, China was modernizing its economy and placed top priority on the privatization of SOEs, particularly its oil companies. Sinopec was particularly important, not just because it was China's largest company but also because, in 1993, China started importing oil after being self-sufficient for nearly 30 years. Privatizing China's oil sector would involve the wholesale restructuring of an entire industry, including transferring assets like oil fields, refineries, petrochemical plants, and retail distribution companies—a daunting task.

Thomas Langford, Carlos Oyarbide, Wei Christenson, and I led the Morgan Stanley team. Tom was the Head of Investment Banking in Asia, Carlos was Chief Operating Officer in Asia, and Wei was dual hatted as Co-CIO of China and Co-CEO of Asia Pacific at Morgan Stanley. While Tom and Carlos had impressive careers, Wei was named in Fortune Magazine's Most Powerful Women International list every year for more than a decade.

The CICC team was led by Levin Zhu, who eventually became CEO of CICC. Levin was the son of Zhu Rongji, China's Premier from 1998-2003. Zhu senior was deeply committed to China's economic development, and his leadership came just three leaders before the current Premier, Xi Jinping.

Our roles were clear: Tom, Carlos, and I focused on strategy and execution, from restructuring to the sale of shares through Sinopec's IPO. Wei played a crucial part too, especially as the liaison between Morgan Stanley, CICC, and the Chinese government. Our base was in Singapore and Beijing, where we would be close to the action and able to meet the government's goals promptly. I would continue to operate out of Houston, simultaneously managing my energy research franchise.

We started the initial Sinopec privatization process in 1996. We flew into the Beijing Capital International Airport which had only one terminal at the time. The airport was adjacent to the Nanyuan Military Base, an important military airfield for the People's Liberation Army Air Force. Military aircraft and personnel significantly outnumbered commercial ones at the time, and this stark military presence was a vivid reminder of the unique challenges ahead.

After clearing customs, we headed to lunch to meet other members of the CICC and Morgan Stanley team. The restaurant was owned by Sinopec and offered a culinary experience I'll never forget. From the outside, it looked like a typical restaurant. The inside, however, looked more like a pet store. Cages housing a mix of different kinds of animals—birds, reptiles, small mammals, fish swimming in aquariums, and insects—lined the walls. The menu featured a variety of live animals and was an unusual concept to say the least: select your desired live animal for lunch, anything from poultry and seafood to snakes, turtles, frogs, rabbits, guinea pigs, and even hamsters.

At the recommendation of one of my Chinese colleagues, I ordered a brown snake. As soon as I pointed to it, two men in rubber aprons quickly butchered it and asked me to wait for a liquid that they would extract from the snake's organs. My Chinese associate assured me it was a delicacy, and so I braced myself for what was to come. For the first course, I was served a shot of spleen juice, followed by the snake itself and an assortment of vegetables and potatoes, and what I think was a jellyfish.

While the food tasted good, the awful smell of duck and pig intestines coming from the table next to us somewhat neutralized my experience. I washed my lunch down with a Tsingtao beer and after lunch, Morgan Stanley banker Dan Ward led us to our meetings at Sinopec headquarters. We were off to an interesting start in a fascinating country.

Sinopec was a global powerhouse, ranking fourth in refining and fifth in petrochemicals production worldwide. Our meetings with the company revealed strong competitive advantages in China—one of the world's fastest-growing energy markets at the time. This edge stemmed from the government's decision to restructure the Chinese oil industry into a duopoly, aiming to mimic the vertically integrated model of Big Oils like BP Amoco, ExxonMobil, and Shell.

Fortunately for Sinopec, the government had awarded it the lucrative refined products markets of southern and eastern China, which contained 75% of the country's oil demand. Its market shares in refining, wholesale, and retail were an impressive 94%, 80%, and 60%, respectively—unparalleled globally.

While Sinopec excelled in downstream operations, its counterpart PetroChina, which had gone public the previous year through Goldman Sachs, held a superior position in E&P. Despite receiving less favorable upstream assets during the restructuring, our team aimed to enhance Sinopec's E&P capabilities to create a more balanced portfolio.

With China entering the WTO and into a more competitive landscape led by the Big Oils, it would take significant restructuring for Sinopec to thrive and be considered a viable investment compared to its publicly traded counterparts like BP and Shell. We would need to improve comparability to increase valuation and share price—an ambitious yet crucial objective.

As the lead analyst charged with selling the offering to investors around the world, I was deeply committed to the process, and eager to influence the final structure of China's largest company. But there were several significant challenges. One was Sinopec's diverse portfolio of 80 to 90 loosely connected companies, including non-energy related businesses like hotels, restaurants, zoos, firing ranges, and even a CD manufacturing company with surprisingly high returns on investment.

While it wasn't unusual for a state-owned entity to provide employment, housing, schools, hospitals, and even fire and police department, separating the core oil businesses from these ancillary entities was a monumental task and would require a team of over a thousand professionals.

Even though some of the businesses were profitable, our strategy focused on aligning Sinopec's business mix with that of the Big Oils to enhance its market comparability and investor appeal.

Another issue complicating matters was the five subsidiaries that had already been listed on the Hong Kong Stock Exchange: Beijing Yanghua Petrochemical, Shanghai Petrochemical, Sinopec Kanton, Yizhen Chemical, and Zhenhai Refinery. Although we had the option of removing them from the exchange or selling off their assets, that would have to initially take a backseat to more pressing restructuring challenges.

Sinopec's size also posed a problem; it was the government's largest employer with more than one million employees. To put that in perspective, industry leader ExxonMobil only employed 125,000 people. Even though Sinopec paid its employees less than many other companies, it still spent a lot of money on staff salaries and office-related expenses compared to its total earnings. The company would need to find ways to work more efficiently to stay competitive and attractive to investors.

Sinopec's capital management policy was also flawed, with money allocated to businesses in proportion to their size without a clear focus on creating value or returns. Most of the inefficiencies were in downstream operations where over a hundred plants were deemed uncompetitive, which would only get worse with the increasing competition and expansion of industry giants.

Compounding these operational challenges was Sinopec's high debt level, a considerable concern given the cyclical nature of the industry. High debt in cyclical industries can be a toxic combination, as it exacerbates financial instability during market downturns, limiting a company's ability to invest and grow. However, given the government's major stake in Sinopec and its role as a leading employer, a certain level of state-backed security was assumed, reinforcing the perception that the company was too big to fail.

But the biggest hurdle was the regulatory environment in China's oil and gas industry. Unlike other companies, Sinopec was in a tough situation. While the prices it paid for refinery inputs like crude oil fluctuated daily with the global market, the prices it could charge for refinery outputs like gasoline and diesel were set by the National Development and Reform Commission (NDRC) and changed infrequently, often over a year or so. This meant that Sinopec could suddenly find itself paying a lot more for the oil that went into its refineries without the ability to charge more for the fuel that came out of them, which could lead to significant losses. Given that 60% of Sinopec's profits came from R&M, predicting Sinopec's total corporate profits would be near impossible. We explained to top Chinese officials that this would be a non-starter for investors.

And the challenge was bigger than just investor concerns. The government had set a strict deadline for Sinopec to restructure and go public, but changing oil policies takes years—time we didn't have. But knowing how important a successful Sinopec IPO was for the government, and especially for Premier Zhu, I thought there would be incentive to speed up the necessary policy changes. I knew that even with Sinopec's strong market position and growth potential, without reliable financial projections, investors would likely stay away from the IPO.

Identifying the problem was straightforward; finding a solution was the hard part. After several sets of meetings in Beijing over a period of a year or so, I headed back to Houston tasked with figuring out how to overcome these hurdles for Sinopec's IPO.

In January of 2000, I made a day trip from Houston to Beijing to present my proposal to Sinopec's board of directors and management team. Our meeting was set to last for three hours but usually took longer because the translator often needed assistance understanding my thick Southern accent, and because my presentation and questions and answers required translation from English to Mandarin and back again.

My presentation expanded on a report I had shared with management ahead of the meeting, titled "Seven Steps to Privatization Success," outlining the specific steps for the company's successful IPO per the government's timeline. I wrote the report in English, which was then translated into Mandarin for the company's leadership. Highlights of this report were later included in a broader analysis for investors, "China's Pure Petroleum Growth Story," with contributions from my colleague, Jing-Feng You, and released in the public domain worldwide in 2000.

The first recommendation was to divest the non-energy related businesses and to focus solely on core sectors like E&P, R&M, petrochemicals, and transportation. We believed that streamlining the business mix would render efficiency, accountability, and attract top talent, positioning the company as a dedicated player in the energy sector. This approach was expected to improve decision-making and increase transparency and make the company more comparable to the other oil majors in the eyes of investors.

The second step involved deploying a Western-style management information system, linking all major business segments within the country. This upgrade, undertaken with the assistance of KPMG and other firms, would improve financial reporting and decision-making, benefiting the company, the investors, and the regulatory agencies.

The third step required Sinopec to cut costs by reducing its workforce drastically, from approximately 1.2 million to 400,000 employees, again signaling the government's dedication to efficiency and productivity to investors.

Fourthly, we needed to take a hard look at Sinopec's assets and determine what was worth keeping. Its smaller, higher-cost plants would not be able to keep up with the cheaper, more cost-competitive petroleum products coming in from places like Singapore and South Korea.

We recommended shutting down 170 of these underperforming refining and chemical plants, which together processed 600,000 barrels a day—or about the equivalent of what large American companies like Texaco handled. These facilities were operating at half speed, eating into the profits and resources that could have gone to more competitive parts of the business. Even the plants with stronger competitive positioning were asked to cut costs and curtail investments until economic viability could be shown over a defined period. We also thought it would be smart for Sinopec to create strategic clusters among its plants that were better positioned to be successful. Because Sinopec's facilities had superior access to arguably the best petroleum market in the world, we recommended that these strategic clusters be the focus of investment capital in the future, like what industry leaders like ExxonMobil and Shell were doing.

Then, looking at Sinopec's E&P business, it was clear they could do better. We suggested bringing in some high-quality assets from another Chinese company, CNOOC, to give Sinopec a much-needed boost. With CNOOC's assets, Sinopec could look forward to more growth and new opportunities for investment. Since large integrated oil companies often achieved higher returns on their investments compared to standalone E&P operations, we reasoned that merging CNOOC with Sinopec would increase the overall value of the business.

Considering the R&M sector's poor performance and Sinopec's R&M division generating only a 2% return on investment, the addition of CNOOC would strengthen Sinopec's returns profile. The goal was to make Sinopec more vertically integrated, achieving a balance between upstream activities (E&P) and downstream operations (R&M). This would position Sinopec to compete with international companies, especially as more players looked to enter the Chinese market in coming years as it joined the WTO.

Step six of my presentation involved the balance sheet. Sinopec's debt load was heavy, and its debt-to-capitalization ratios were high compared to similar companies in the energy sector and other industries. Although this level of debt might have been manageable because the government was the major shareholder and could potentially change regulations or offer a bailout, if necessary, such government intervention was frowned upon by investors. We proposed that $10 billion in debt be removed from the company's balance sheet.

The final step was the most critical one and involved changes to China's petroleum policy. Without a change, it would be challenging for investors to forecast the company's profits accurately. We recommended that the Chinese government change how gasoline and diesel prices were set in the country.

Our proposal was to adopt an import parity pricing mechanism for fuel prices in China, a method we anticipated would be necessary in the new era. This method would calculate prices based on the cost of refining in Singapore, plus transportation expenses and an import tariff to temporarily protect local interests. We also recommended that the prices of refined products be updated more frequently to better reflect changes in regional market conditions. In other words, we asked the government to use our formula to set prices for gasoline, diesel, jet fuel and all other major petroleum products in China.

With these changes, it would become possible to make more accurate financial projections for Sinopec's R&M business, as well as for the company overall. Investors could then assess Sinopec's profitability and develop a clearer outlook for its stock.

These "Seven Steps to Privatization Success" were ambitious, especially considering the tight timeframe and how rare foreign involvement in high-level privatization efforts were with the Chinese government. I had no idea what to expect because few had come before us, but I knew the steps were crucial for Sinopec's successful transition to a privatized entity.

While some of the changes I suggested for the IPO were

up for discussion, others were non-negotiable. I wasn't sure if any of my proposals would be accepted, but I was hopeful we'd end up with a company that would be appealing to investors. Personally, I had a lot riding on making the company as attractive as possible to investors since I would be the one promoting it globally. My connection to the company was deep, and I knew investors would hold me accountable if things didn't go well.

If the most important of my recommendations weren't acted on, neither Morgan Stanley nor any other investment bank could successfully carry out the IPO. In other words, the Chinese government had a choice: implement these changes now with our team's guidance—especially the adoption of a market-based petroleum policy—or do it later, possibly with another firm. I hoped they would choose to keep working with us, considering how much effort our team had put in—and the progress we had made.

A few weeks after our discussions, investment banker Michael Dickman and I were invited back to Beijing to provide more insight into our plan for the company. The Sinopec management team also wanted me to teach a half-day workshop for the top 200 leaders in their finance division. The workshop was about capital management policy and the financial metrics that matter most to the company's value in the stock market—essentially, what they should focus on internally. The CFO and other finance leaders started calling me the "professor" on these matters, which I took as a compliment.

Even though Mike and I were worn out from all our trips to Beijing, we were not over the proverbial goal line yet. We met up in London and boarded a British Air 747 for our next trip to China. Since it was a quiet Wednesday in February, first class was almost empty. We half-joked with the flight attendants about expecting fantastic service because of this, and cheekily suggested that Mike should be able to sit in the cockpit for takeoff and that I would do the same for landing.

To our surprise, they said yes. Both experiences were amazing. When it was my turn to be in the cockpit for the landing, the sky over China was perfectly clear. I was really struck by how relaxed the pilots were, even as they let the autopilot handle most of the flight. Only when we got close to the ground, about 1,000 feet up, did they switch off the autopilot and take over for a smooth landing. Watching them work was incredible. It was such an unexpected and memorable experience.

In Beijing, our meetings were spread out over two half-days within a three-day span. On the last day, after wrapping up our morning meetings, we found ourselves with some free time before our flight back to the U.S. later that night.

We decided to visit the People's Liberation Army's weapons testing range. Yes, you read that correctly. The process of getting into the facility felt like something straight out of the "Get Smart" television series from the 1960s, which, for those of you too young to remember, was a parody of the secret agent genre of that decade. We'd enter one door into a lobby, and after it closed behind us, another door would open. This happened three times before we finally got into the secure area where they kept the firearms.

Inside the gun room, a government official in a lab coat greeted us and, speaking in Mandarin, pointed us toward some single-shot rifles to try out. We quickly let our translator know that we weren't interested in those and instead were eager to try the more exciting stuff—like their collection of automatic firearms and other advanced weaponry on display in a glass case or set up outside on the range. We specifically mentioned wanting to fire an Uzi, then an AK-47, and a 57-millimeter anti-tank gun. After some back-and-forth through our translator, the official reluctantly agreed.

It was an unbelievable experience. I was amazed at the engineering and efficiency of both the Uzi and the AK-47. And after firing the anti-tank gun, I remember Mike saying, "tracer bullets... this is good!" It was a needed break from our usual routine, and we left for the airport with smiles on our faces and a little less stress in tow.

A month later, I was called back to Beijing for our final meeting with the board of directors and management team. They had reviewed my seven proposals and were ready to respond. While we had invested years and countless hours in the project, there was no guarantee our requests would be met. The Chinese officials, always friendly, were hard to gauge, maybe because of my limited knowledge of Mandarin. Either way, we had reached a pivotal juncture in the Sinopec IPO process.

On the day of our meeting, I strolled around Tiananmen Square at daybreak, pondering whether we had included all essential elements for government approval and contemplated the risk of failure if we did not. Gazing at Mao's mural in the Forbidden City heightened my awareness of the stakes involved. The weight of history and gravity of our situation made me feel both significant and insignificant at the same time.

The government's response was overwhelmingly positive. They agreed to transfer the non-traditional energy businesses to a state-owned holding company, streamlining Sinopec's operations to better match those of our desired peer group. They also undertook an ambitious cost-cutting plan, reducing general and administrative expenses, and lowered headcount from 1.2 million to 500,000 employees.

A rationalization effort led to the shutdown of over 100 sub-scale refineries, cutting refining capacity by 220,000 barrels per day, or 4%. This move was expected to boost industry utilization rates from 69% in 1999 to nearly 90% by the time we went to market in 2000. Capital investments were also scaled back and refocused on strategic refinery upgrades.

However, the government decided against including CNOOC in Sinopec's upstream operations, opting to privatize it separately.

I had been told this request would be a long shot, but I went for it anyway. This was a smart move by the government, and when CNOOC went public its shares rose 500% and 1,700% in the five- and 10-year periods following its IPO.

As a consolation prize, Sinopec acquired National Star from the government, the fourth largest oil and gas company in China, strengthening its position in E&P, even though it was lower quality than CNOOC.

They also agreed to address the balance sheet problem by placing the debt of the non-strategic companies and their assets in a state holding company and executing a substantial debt-to-equity swap. This would reduce Sinopec's debt-to-capital ratio from near 50% to about 30% within three years after the IPO. Sinopec's credit rating was expected to be BBB-, closely following China's sovereign rating of BBB.

Most importantly, the largest hurdle was overcome as well, with China agreeing to change its petroleum policy. Retail fuel prices would now be based on a formula that would consider several factors: the cost of importing fuel (using prices from Singapore as a reference), shipping costs (whether by sea or land), insurance, customs taxes (9% for gasoline and 6% for diesel), and a set profit margin ($9.82/bbl for gasoline and $8.93/bbl for diesel). On top of these, a consumption tax and value added tax were added, which consumers end up paying.

The updated regulations also sped up how quickly fuel prices could change. Instead of taking years to adjust prices, it could now be done in months, and eventually even weeks and days. In other words, they agreed to use our proposed formula for setting fuel prices in China for the foreseeable future. This connection between prices of crude oil, refined products, and the market meant investors could better understand and evaluate the company's financial outlook and how it compared to other major oil companies.

The deal was finalized in a meeting between members of

the Morgan Stanley and CICC team, Morgan Stanley President John Mack and Chinese Premier Zhu in Beijing. Although there was concern about the impact of higher fuel prices on consumers and especially on sectors like transportation and agriculture, Premier Zhu recognized the importance of modernizing petroleum policy and approved our request after a call with 34 provincial governors the very next day.

While we were highly encouraged by the government's concessions, market concerns remained, partly due to turmoil in Asian markets in previous years. However, Sinopec and Petro-China held a monopoly over resources and markets in China, along with labor cost advantages and deep market knowledge—factors that gave them a competitive edge and strong investment appeal.

We reached out to BP-Amoco, ExxonMobil, and Shell to gauge their interest in acquiring part of the IPO, and the companies ended up purchasing 60% of Sinopec's offering. In return, they received preferential access to the expanding Chinese energy market over the next decade.

Once the changes were in place and the management team was coached for interaction with investors, we launched the Sinopec IPO roadshow, spanning over 100 meetings worldwide. The backing of the three Super-Majors was an important selling point to investors. That three of the largest, most experienced energy investors in the world were buying stock, made my job significantly easier.

On October 19, 2000, Sinopec's shares were listed on the Hong Kong, London, and New York stock exchanges, raising $3.5 billion and surpassing Petro-China's $2.9 billion to become the largest IPO in Asian and Chinese history. The stock's value skyrocketed in the following years—by 300% during the first three years and over 1,000% by the end of 2007—marking Sinopec as one of the world's best-performing energy stocks and delighting the government, the company, and investors alike. Today Sinopec is the fourth largest company in the world. My teammate Howard Wong jokingly dubbed me as an "honorary

Chinese" in light of our success.

CONOCO

Conoco, now known as ConocoPhillips, was founded in 1917. Originally the Continental Oil and Transportation Company, the company was based in Ogden, Utah, and initially focused on producing and refining petroleum products before expanding its operations to midstream and petrochemicals. In a big move in 1981, DuPont, a company that was mainly into chemicals, bought Conoco as part of its plan to diversify into the energy sector. Conoco was a blue-chip company with an established presence, diversified operations, strong financial performance, a resilient business model, and a global footprint.

By the late 1990s, the business world was changing, especially with the expected rise of Super-Major companies. DuPont saw this as the right time to take Conoco public—a move meant to cash in on their investment in Conoco and generate funds to boost their core chemicals business.

Every major U.S. investment bank wanted the opportunity to lead this IPO because Conoco was set to be the largest the U.S. had ever seen in any sector. It would be the sixth largest publicly traded oil and gas company worldwide.

Morgan Stanley won the mandate for the IPO, and I would be lead analyst. Investment bankers Michael Dickman and Dan Ward had strong relationships with Conoco, and on the research side I had interacted with the company while it was inside of DuPont.

Thanks to Conoco's top-notch business model, astute capital management policies, leadership, and positive governance, we expected a smoother process compared to other advisory projects in countries like Argentina, Brazil, China, India, Malaysia, Thailand, and Venezuela.

Nevertheless, because it was such a large and high profile offering, the Conoco roadshow was a massive undertaking. CEO Archie Dunham and his team traveled to 10 countries and 47 cities to make 120 presentations to hundreds of portfolio managers and analysts.

During the Conoco IPO process, Conoco's Tom Henkel wrote an insightful book which covered not only the grueling roadshow experience but also food critiques and an interview with Archie about the seven key factors that led to the success of the IPO.

In New York, Tom gave world renowned Spark's Steak House only a five out of 10 because it didn't have T-bone or ribeye steaks which he felt was a cardinal sin for steak houses. At Café des Artistes, Tom indicated that the beef cheeks appetizer was exceptional especially in the rich, dark wine sauce that accompanied them. The filet of sole came with a wonderful meuniere sauce and, along with a good crisp Chardonay, made for a wonderful meal. While there were many other critiques in Tom's book, he was excited to see that he was the only non-local when he entered the Old Swiss Inn in Zurich which may have been the most memorable. Tom indicated that "weiner schnitzel was prepared lovingly – but with finicky exactitude at their table and the filet of venison with a duck and liver sauce" was superb as well.

In highlighting the most important factors for IPO success, Archie advised: putting your ego aside, keeping the gold ring in clear view, playing the passion card, keeping the spin factor in check, maintaining faith, communicating effectively, and sharing the right values. These factors helped Conoco achieve positive performance on the offering and in the years that followed as well.

Investors were impressed with Conoco and indicated interest in buying shares worth over $12 billion, even though the company was looking to sell only $3.6 billion worth of stock. Because the offering was three times oversubscribed, we decided to increase the number of shares available for sale by nearly a third and increased the price too, selling $4.4 billion in shares to investors. While the financial success of Conoco's shares wasn't quite as massive as Sinopec's—where investors saw their investment increase tenfold—the shares still did quite well in the market following their IPO on October 21, 1998. Today, the company is the largest E&P entity in the world.

STATOIL

Norway and its national oil company Statoil were up next. Norway is beautiful with breathtaking natural landscapes, stunning fjords, picturesque villages, and vibrant cities. While some stereotype Norwegians as reserved and introverted, I found them resilient, adventurous, and deeply engaging, with distinctive egalitarian principles and cultural values that make the country and its people truly interesting.

The origin of the country of Norway, as well as that of its petroleum industry, traces back to the Karlstad Treaty of 1905, which separated the country from Sweden. The land division process was peaceful and in a spirit of cooperation and was aimed at establishing clear borders and ensuring a smooth transition to independent nationhood for both countries. While the economies of Norway and Sweden were driven by forestry, mining, textiles, and agriculture at the time, Norway also had oil—and lots of it. They just didn't know it yet.

Petroleum was discovered at Ekofisk by Phillips Petroleum and Norwegian entity Norsk Hydro in the North Sea in 1969. To manage this newfound resource, Norway established Statoil in 1972, a 100% state-owned entity, to oversee the country's petroleum endowment. Statoil quickly became a dominant force in Norway's oil sector, building significant stakes in many offshore fields. While Norsk Hydro and Saga held petroleum positions too, most oil reserves and the state's direct investment in the fields were controlled by Statoil.

Following the discovery, oil production in Norway surged from zero in 1970 to almost 3.5 MMBPD by 2000—the fastest growth rate globally during that period. By 2001, Norway had become the seventh largest producer of oil and the nineth largest producer of natural gas in the world. Today, the country remains one of the largest exporters of oil and gas and is a vital supply element in global markets.

Proposals to partially privatize Statoil gained momentum in the Norwegian Parliament during the Super-Major merger phase as industry emphasis shifted to scale and globalization which we regarded as key to prosperity. While some in Norway saw privatization as selling off the nation's "crown jewels," the government and Statoil contended that partial privatization would give the company greater flexibility to compete in the new environment.

After extensive discussions, the Norwegian Parliament approved a plan that would allow Statoil to sell up to 20% of its shares. This move was strategic, enabling Statoil to raise funds by selling stock and possibly exchange its shares for those of other oil companies, which could help in forming international partnerships.

The Norwegian government stood to benefit from the privatization because revenues from petroleum activities—dividends and share offerings from Statoil—funded the non-oil budget deficit in the country. This allowed the government to maintain and enhance public services, invest in infrastructure, and support social welfare programs without resorting to high levels of public debt. This fiscal stability ensured sustainable economic growth and a high quality of life for Norwegians. Surplus funds were then allocated to the Government Pension Fund of Norway, established in 1990, benefitting citizens too.

The race to win the IPO mandate was intense and drawn out, with every top investment bank in the mix—big names like Goldman Sachs, J.P. Morgan, Citigroup, Deutsche Bank, Credit Suisse, and UBS. While Statoil was headquartered on the outskirts of Oslo, the "bake-off" meetings where we would give our pitch presentations were held in the downtown offices. Oslo was suddenly inundated with the crème de la crème of investment bankers, all decked out in dark suits, sleek Italian loafers, Hermes ties, and meticulously styled haircuts.

Renowned investment banker Bob Maguire and I made the pitch for Morgan Stanley. Honestly, I wasn't at my best that day, maybe a B+ performance from me, but Bob hit it out of the park. He had a solid relationship with the company, and we both really connected with CEO Olav Fjell and CFO Inge Hansen. Because of our major international successes with Sinopec and Conoco, Morgan Stanley was regarded as a favorite even though we had limited experience in Norway before Statoil. We left the meeting feeling confident about our chances.

Following our pitch, Bob and I braved a snowstorm to grab lunch at Engebret Café, the oldest restaurant in Oslo, dating back to 1857. Bob ordered lutefisk, while I went with a reindeer filet. Lutefisk, a dish with centuries of history, is dried whitefish (usually cod) rehydrated in water and lye, making it gelatinous and translucent after cooking. Originally, developed for food preservation during harsh winters, lutefisk now holds deep symbolic and cultural significance. It's traditionally served with boiled potatoes, peas, bacon, and various sauces. While I was fascinated by the Viking culture and went to every museum of the type in my spare time, lutefisk never won me over. Having grown up on the Gulf Coast, where delicious seafood like red snapper and tuna is abundant, my seafood standards are high. However, Engebret's reindeer steak quickly became my go-to dish in Norway.

A few weeks later, we learned that Morgan Stanley was selected as co-lead book-runners along with UBS.

The Wall Street Journal reported:

"The coveted international mandate was sought by at least eight banks, at least four of which were asked to make their final presentations in the last week of 2000. While UBS Warburg has been advising the oil ministry on Statoil, this is the first major appointment that Morgan Stanley has received from Norway.

"Morgan Stanley played a leading role in two other major IPOs for Chinese Petroleum & Chemical Corp or Sinopec, and for Conoco, at the time the biggest U.S. IPO ever.

"The Statoil offering is expected to be among the biggest

in Europe. The ministry said that other domestic and international institutions participating in the public placement of the shares would be chosen later."

While we were initially aiming for a sole lead, having both U.S. and European investment banks in lead roles was probably best for Statoil. Despite the competitive nature of investment banking, I was particularly struck by the dedication and expertise UBS brought to the table. This was a high-profile transaction for them. As co-lead analyst for Statoil's offering, I became the lead on the largest energy IPOs ever across Europe, Asia, and North America—a nice hat trick.

Statoil's value proposition was strong, and the offering process was straightforward. The company was in excellent competitive shape, with well-managed assets, strong financials, modern corporate governance, and robust leadership under CEO Olav Fjell.

The roadshow for Statoil kicked off in June 2001, and the offering quickly became four times oversubscribed, raising $2.9 billion for the Norwegian government. Over the following five years, Statoil's shares surged by 500%, significantly outperforming the S&P energy sector by 250 percentage points. In 2018, the company rebranded to Equinor.

As of today, the Government Pension Fund of Norway, or the "Oil Fund," primarily fueled by oil revenues, is overseen by Norges Bank Investment Management (NBIM). It stands out as the world's leading sovereign wealth fund with assets exceeding $1.4 trillion, surpassing those in China, Abu Dhabi, Saudi Arabia, and Kuwait. The fund's strategy focuses on diversifying wealth across generations, fostering social and economic stability and making responsible investments in equities, fixed income securities, real estate, and other asset classes. With ownership stakes in about 1.4% of all global listed companies, Norway's visionary management of its petroleum wealth has thrived, ensuring long-term benefits for future generations. The fund's value is near an impressive $250,000 per Norwegian citizen.

PDVSA

Our final—and potentially largest—venture was with Venezuela's national energy company, PDVSA. At the time, PDVSA ranked among the world's largest oil and gas companies, with 74 billion barrels of proven oil reserves and 146 trillion cubic feet of gas. That made Venezuela the the seventh-largest holder of oil reserves globally, not even counting an estimated 250 billion barrels of extra-heavy crude in the Orinoco Belt. By that measure, Venezuela could potentially hold the world's largest petroleum endowment.

PDVSA was founded when the Venezuelan oil industry was nationalized on January 1, 1976. This move transformed the landscape of oil operations in Venezuela, as PDVSA took over from multinational corporations like Exxon, Mobil, Shell, and others by forming a national holding company with several subsidiaries to operate the assets.

After nationalizing the industry, the government was faced with a significant concern: the risk of political influence and meddling in the company given its high cash flows. This concern stemmed from a history of public entities mismanaging funds, government and political interference, and appointing unqualified individuals to high-ranking positions due to personal connections. In other words, the same factors commonly associated with the consistently poor performance seen in other emerging markets over the past few decades.

The law establishing PDVSA was written to minimize political influence over its complex technocratic structure. That meant, by law, the Venezuelan government, and indirectly political parties, would be limited to a presence on the board of the parent company. As the sole shareholder, the state, represented by the head of the Ministry of Energy and Mines, presided over shareholder meetings. The Venezuelan government therefore played a key role in defining strategies, but the law insulated the company's management and day-to-day operations from political interference, positioning PDVSA primarily as a commercial entity governed by corporate principles. This setup aimed to prevent the company from engaging in ineffective social employment initiatives common in other state-owned enterprises. While initially effective, this concept alone was not enough to allow PDVSA to be competitive in the increasingly globalized economy, particularly in the context of our "Super-Major World" scenario.

By the late 1990s, Venezuela was transitioning toward a market-oriented economy, having already privatized its telephone services, airlines, and several banks. However, the oil industry, with PDVSA at the center, was the kingpin. PDVSA accounted for 75-80% of the government's exports and 50% of its revenue, and GDP.[27] The oil and gas sector was the backbone of the Venezuelan economy.

The privatization of PDVSA was set to be a landmark event for the country, particularly because of the significant capital it was expected to raise in comparison to Venezuela's relatively small population. We estimated that selling just 20-25% of the company could bring in around $25 billion, which had the potential to either wipe out Venezuela's national debt entirely, fund top-tier social and infrastructure programs and/or built a large sovereign wealth fund. That is, the process stood to enhance the standard of living for everyday Venezuelans and for generations to come, as was the case with Statoil and Norway. We jokingly remarked that Venezuela stood to be like Norway, but on steroids, given the even larger petroleum potential in Venezuela.

---

27. "La Apertura": The Opening of Venezuela's Oil Industry, Luis E. Giusti, Journal of International Affairs, Fall 1999.

In 1997, acknowledging the need to adapt to the new competitive environment, PDVSA CEO Luis Giusti announced his plan to improve the company's performance by restructuring it along the lines of the Big Oils. The program eliminated the three competing integrated oil companies within PDVSA and replaced them with three functional units: E&P, R&M, and Oil Field Services. The reforms proposed to generate economic value of around $12 billion over the span of a decade, setting an ambitious target for the company's future growth and efficiency. The program modernized business process and would redefine the roles of the different companies under the PDVSA umbrella.

The goal of the plan was to cut costs and boost how effectively capital was used by bringing in better technology and a new pay system that would both demand and reward high performance. This push toward modernization needed the backing of Venezuela's political landscape, and fortunately, President Caldera's administration was all for the positive change.

The U.S. also supported progress in the country, eager to bolster Venezuelan oil production to diversify supply options away from the politically volatile Middle East. The trend towards greater energy self-sufficiency in the Western Hemisphere was welcomed in other consuming countries too. Mr. Giusti is helping create "an energy supply backbone from the Rocky Mountains to the Andes" according to U.S. officials.[28]

At the same time, Venezuela was experiencing a shift in its national energy policy, a move toward opening up—or "apertura"—the oil industry's upstream (E&P) and downstream (R&M) sectors. This groundbreaking shift was designed to attract foreign investment and strengthen PDVSA's international market presence.

The apertura strategy involved partially privatizing some of PDVSA's operations. This meant private companies and individuals could now form strategic partnerships (kind of like joint ventures that need Congress's approval) and sign

---

28. David Vogel, "Venezuela Expands Oil Industry Rapidly, Irking Others in OPEC," The Wall Street Journal, August 17, 1997

operational deals with PDVSA. The plan included outsourcing jobs that weren't central to PDVSA's core mission and starting to privatize the domestic sale and distribution of oil products. Thanks to these reforms, PDVSA saw a rise in upstream joint ventures, particularly those based on sharing profits and operational agreements, and made strides into new markets, primarily in the United States.

These efforts paid off, and from 1994 to 1999—right up to the privatization phase—PDVSA reinvented itself. It updated all its main business areas to face the global energy market's challenges head-on. Moreover, it reshaped the role of oil in Venezuela's economy while positively transforming Venezuelan society.

Thanks to new developments in the oil sector, particularly the move toward outsourcing, there was a significant increase in the number of companies, establishments, and corporations engaged in oil-related activities. This shift provided new opportunities for the country's largely rural and unskilled labor force, which before had limited prospects in industrial sectors. Now, these workers were finding roles in highly productive activities, integrating them into more dynamic parts of the economy.

This expanded the sector's constituent base in the country beyond just the state, giving Venezuelan citizens an increasingly important role to play while reducing state control. The latter being the critical element to successful energy privatizations in other countries. Fueled by the booming energy sector, Venezuela's GDP skyrocketed by 40% from 1995 to 1997, leading to a rapid improvement in the standard of living for many Venezuelans, with further improvements seemingly on the horizon.

Despite the momentum, Venezuela's relationship with oil and politics has always been complex, given oil's critical importance to the national economy. The country has a long-standing ideology that favors nationalization and significant state involvement over free-market policies. This belief is deeply ingrained in many Venezuelans, including those in academic and political circles, which made the discourse surrounding privatization highly contentious and polarizing.

PDVSA CEO Giusti argued that with proper state policies, enforced accountability, and the right structure of royalties and taxes, national sovereignty could still be preserved. Giusti indicated that "the discussion of the privatization of PDVSA shouldn't be seen as taboo."[29] However, because PDVSA was deeply ingrained in the national consciousness as a valuable asset, any approach to privatization was bound to face opposition.

Our recommendation to the Venezuelan government and PD-VSA's Board of Directors was to sell a small portion of PDVSA, perhaps 10 to 15%, to the public. This approach, already tested in other countries, would not threaten state control and had been successfully applied with PDVSA's petrochemicals arm, PEQUIVEN.

We furthered this proposal in Caracas during our numerous visits, most of which were quite eventful. When we would arrive at Caracas airport, our team, led by Doug MacKenzie and Tom Langford, would receive VIP treatment from our local handlers. They whisked us through a special immigration and customs process arranged by the government. Outside, six black 1985 Chevy Impalas with tinted windows and engines idling were waiting for us. Our five-person team was directed to two specific cars, which then sped off in a convoy, bypassing all traffic signals to reach the Tamanaca hotel.

At the Tamanaca, we were advised to remain on the premises until our meetings were done. When it was time to leave, the cars would line up again for our conspicuous dash back to the airport. After clearing the special customs line, we'd head back to the U.S., or to Argentina or Brazil to discuss strategic ideas with other national oil companies like YPF and Petrobras.

After several discussions where we outlined how restructuring and privatizing PDVSA could boost its competitiveness against the Big Oils and secure lasting prosperity for Venezuelans, it was time for our final presentation—to convince them to choose

---

29. Ibid

Morgan Stanley to lead the restructuring and IPO of PDVSA.

Our presentation and Q&A session in Caracas in July of 1998 went smoothly, and I was confident we would secure the mandate. The proposed privatization of PDVSA would necessitate an overhaul of its accounting and reporting protocols, leading to much-needed transparency and promising transformative benefits for both the country and the company. Our proposal seemed impossible for the government to refuse, especially given the multi-generational economic and social benefits it offered.

Leaving tropical Caracas behind, we thought we could make PDVSA's value proposition very attractive to a wide range of investors and anticipated receiving the advisory mandate by that fall. However, things didn't go as expected. While CEO Luis Giusti was steering both PDVSA and Venezuela toward promising economic futures, a showdown with OPEC's kingpin, Saudi Arabia, lay ahead and would alter Venezuelan history and impact the global economy.

The crux of the issue was Giusti's belief that Venezuela, potentially the world's lowest-cost oil producer, should not adhere to its OPEC production quota of 2.8 MMBPD with Venezuela's output exceeding 3.4 MMBPD as 1998 began. This stance directly challenged OPEC's policy, which relies on each member country producing at agreed-upon levels to maintain market stability.

Giusti argued against the logic of OPEC's quota system, pointing out the paradox of selling higher cost oil (like that from the U.S. and North Sea) first, while lower cost, more economically viable barrels from OPEC countries were left untapped. He reasoned that low-cost producers shouldn't have to cut production and lose market share to non-OPEC competitors due to the specific needs and circumstances of some producers, especially poorer ones like Venezuela.

Consequently, Venezuela planned to ramp up its output,

doubling production to 6.4 MMBPD by 2006. This move would place Venezuela as OPEC's largest oil exporter to the U.S., a market position guarded fiercely by Saudi Arabia during the prior two decades. Unsurprisingly, this plan did not sit well with Saudi Arabia, which sought quota cooperation and was unlikely to tolerate loss of market share to Venezuela or any other country. The dilemma harked back to the mid-1980s when Saudi Arabia's attempt to support prices at the cost of market share had failed, slashing their oil revenues. Despite comments from the Saudis that they might raise production to drive down prices and punish the Venezuelans at the June 1997 OPEC meeting, the warnings went unheeded. At the November OPEC meeting, the war of words continued, leading to a deadlock. Unbridled production increases followed, and oil prices collapsed, falling from $20/bbl at the start of 1998 to $13/bbl by mid-year.

The decline in oil prices led to major financial strains in Venezuela since most government revenues came from petroleum. The 1998 presidential election campaign between the incumbent, Rafael Caldera, and the populist challenger, Hugo Chávez, was especially impacted. Ironically, Caldera had pardoned Chavez from prison in 1994, where he served time for the failed coups he led in February and November of 1992. Caldera did this to pacify the insurgent military force, but as a newly free man, Chavez was able to gather support to run for president. And that he did.

In a surprising turn of events, Hugo Chávez won the presidential election in December 1998 partially due to the significant fall in oil prices and the economic havoc it created for Venezuela. Our proposal to privatize PDVSA was rejected by the new government shortly thereafter. Chavez's governance strategy mirrored the tactics used by the neighboring Castro regime in Cuba from 1959 to 1961—implementing wealth-redistribution laws, con-fiscating large estates, nationalizing energy assets from companies like ExxonMobil and ConocoPhillips, dissolving the parliament, arresting opposition leaders, and manipulating elections.

The result was an economic disaster in Venezuela. Oil production plummeted from 3.2 to 0.5 MMBPD, the largest decline of any country in the world since 1998. This dramatic drop was fueled by mismanagement, corruption, economic sanctions, and flawed policies such as currency and price controls, which accelerated the country's sharp economic downturn.

The crisis deepened when Chavez ally Nicholas Maduro was elected president in 2013, leading to further deterioration in living standards, widespread poverty, and the migration of over 8 million people—almost 30% of Venezuela's population.[30] Today, hyperinflation persists, essential goods and services remain scarce, and a small group of political and business elites have consolidated power and resources. A staggering $150 billion in external debt remains in default.

In hindsight, critics have questioned Caldera's earlier decision to pardon Chávez and his cronies. As the policies of Chávez and later Maduro took effect, criticism of Caldera intensified, with many attributing the hardships of the past 25 years to his pardon.

The Heritage Foundation reports that the regime not only bankrupted PDVSA but also engaged in illicit trafficking. Despite U.S. sanctions, Venezuela has found support from Iran, Russia, and China, helping it to sidestep these restrictions. Whether it becomes a full-fledged strategic satellite of these countries and spreads their authoritarian ideologies across the continent remains to be seen. While neighboring Latin American countries have seen per capita GDPs double, Venezuela has witnessed a stark decline, severely affecting most of its population over recent decades.

Despite these grim conditions, the situation may worsen. The July 2024 presidential election, claimed to have been won by Maduro, was labeled a "serious breach of electoral principles" and one that "cannot be considered democratic" by the Carter Center. The U.S. recognized opposition candidate, Edmundo

---

30. The U.S. did not recognize Maduro as the legitimate winner of the 2013, 2018 or 2024 presidential elections in Venezuela.

González Urrutia, as the legitimate winner, indicating that the election process was deeply flawed and not reflective of the will of the voters.

Reflecting on what might have been, I can't help but ponder the potential trajectory for PDVSA and Venezuela. The country had the opportunity to mirror Norway's success, benefiting not only its current citizens but also future generations. It still does.

6

The Golden Age of Refining

The refining and marketing (R&M) sector of the energy industry may be the least understood part of the petroleum value chain. So, for those who know which fundamental factors drive performance in R&M stocks, it can also be one of the best areas to invest your money.

Honestly, I was a slow learner when it came to R&M investments. In my career on the investment side, I found it tough to make sense of the research that investment analysts put out there. I spent years trying to understand the basics and what really drives the value of companies in the R&M sector.

I was always struck by the sheer amount of "Street" research reports filled with data on how much refineries were producing, industry profit margins, and so on, updated almost every day. Even now, this kind of information is everywhere. But the analysis seemed to be mostly retrospective and offered little in the way of predicting future investment value in the bigger picture.

When I reached out to sell-side analysts in North America our discussions primarily centered on supply, demand, utilization, inventories, and margins specific to the region. And the case was the same in my interactions with analysts from Europe and Asia. They all appeared to be experts in the latest trends within their respective local and regional markets, maybe because they had free access to the information on government energy websites. The discussions, however, tended to focus narrowly on short-term details rather than on the potentially more impactful medium-term outlooks, which was surprising in an industry known for its deep cyclical nature and long cycles.

After years of stagnation and no significant progress, my faith in "Street" research for this sector dwindled. I reached out to three of the world's largest refiners at the time—BP, Exxon, and Shell—and requested meetings with their R&M groups to gain a better understanding of the drivers of performance. Through these discussions, I learned that most sell-side analysts were missing the mark—not because they lacked effort or intelligence, but because their methods of assessing market fundamentals were flawed. At least according to the world's largest players.

So, starting in the 1990s, armed with an understanding of the approaches of these major players, I set out to build the most value-added commodity and equity research framework in R&M on Wall Street. The market frameworks of the major refiners formed the foundation of my approach, but I supplemented it with elements that I thought were economically important.

Because the models they used were complex, I had to simplify them to be able to convey their insights to commodity and equity market investors. And by doing so, I would be able to clearly present my analysis on the future of refined product commodities and the implications for R&M stocks. I was confident that this approach would lead to some of the best calls ever seen on Wall Street in the R&M sector.

My methodology rested on two key principles. First, assessing refining supply, demand, and inventory should be made on a global scale due to the interconnected nature of margins across different regions. For example, North American margins are not set solely by local factors, but also by dynamics in the Atlantic Basin— including Europe and Latin America— and beyond. This interconnectedness implies that any method focusing solely on the U.S. market is likely to miss the mark in predicting investment outcomes. The same holds true today.

The rationale behind this global link in margins lies in the similarity of manufacturing costs across refineries with comparable setups, energy requirements, etc. and the relatively low costs of transportation and storage compared to manufacturing costs. For instance, let's say that gasoline prices on the U.S. East Coast are $2.00 per gallon. If a major unexpected refinery disruption occurs, like with Superstorm Sandy, the market may need to source more expensive supplies, potentially from Europe, where production costs might be $2.40 per gallon. After considering another $0.10 per gallon for transportation costs, gasoline would be resupplied to the East Coast at about $2.50 per gallon, assuming all else remains equal. Until cheaper local supply can be restored, it remains profitable for gasoline to be shipped from Europe to the U.S. East Coast. See the connection there?

And it's not just short-term connections that affect margin; medium-term linkages exist as well. Imagine ExxonMobil's Baton Rouge refinery has a technological or process edge, that helps to reduce costs. In a commodity-driven industry where companies mainly compete on lower costs due to limited product differentiation, ExxonMobil would naturally want to extend this cost-saving advantage to its other refineries, like those in Antwerp or Singapore, so they could benefit as well.

However, these advantages are usually only temporary because competitors eventually catch up. While patents are protected, the transfer of knowledge and expertise means that unique advantages don't last forever. "Human capital goes up and down the elevator every day," as the saying goes. In environments where manufacturing costs are similar and transportation costs are relatively low, refined products tend to move toward the most profitable markets around the world.

This global connection is underscored by the fact that more than 70% of the refined products consumed worldwide are shipped by sea. This results in a strong correlation—almost 90%—between the profit margins of refineries in North America, Europe, and Asia. So, any analysis that only looks at the U.S. market, ignoring the global context of supply and demand, is unlikely to yield accurate forecasts or insights.

The second tenet of our methodology focused on the global supply of "light products" such as gasoline, diesel, and jet fuel—the main drivers of global demand and the ones that generate most of the profits in the refining sector.

By analyzing how the supply of light products matched up against demand, we could estimate how much of the refining capacity was being used, or the utilization rates.[31] We thought these rates would be a good indicator of the profit margins refineries could expect in their key areas of profitability. Since these margins directly affect the profits and stock prices of R&M companies, our strategy was designed to predict how well R&M stocks would do, assuming the valuations were justified, or priced reasonably in the market.

Unlike traditional Wall Street research, which often only looked at the growth and utilization rates of distillation capacity, our approach looked at the output from both distillation and conversion units.

Distillation is the basic process in refining where crude oil is heated and separated into different components, like gasoline and diesel which are high value products, but also into fuel oil which is a low value product that sells below crude oil. Distillation capacity is widespread and has been in surplus, with profits cycling around zero for decades.

---

31. Utilization rates refer to the percentage of a refinery's total production capacity that is used. It is calculated by dividing the actual amount of crude oil processed by the refinery by its maximum possible processing capacity, then multiplying by 100 to get a percentage. High utilization rates indicate that a refinery is operating near its full capacity, while low utilization rates suggest underutilization of the facility's production potential.

Conversion processes, on the other hand, are more advanced techniques that further transform the basic components from distillation into higher-value products, like high-octane gasoline, jet fuel, and liquid petroleum gases like propane and butane. We placed higher importance on these units because they gave us a better picture of a refinery's ability to meet demand for the most profitable products. This nuanced approach helped us better understand and forecast the dynamics of the global refining market, beyond what traditional analyses based on distillation capacity alone could reveal.

To develop our global outlook, my research team and I evaluated every refinery project planned or under construction worldwide, updating our analysis twice a year and looking four years ahead. Initially, we also gathered historical data to test our hypothesis and create a multi-year framework. This effort required significant contributions from key associates over the years: Paul Coppola, David Donnelly, Sioban Hickie, Sean Maher, Chris O'Neill and Chai Zhao.

Our comprehensive methodology was unique, as far as we knew. This might have been due to our position as the top energy research team on Wall Street which our firm ensured was well resourced but also because of insights from Morgan Stanley's commodity group, which was the largest on Wall Street with revenue near $1.5 billion annually according to the Wall Street Journal. Our research budget and the synergies with our street-leading commodities group surely put us in a position to succeed in relation to Wall Street peers.

We regularly monitored 300-400 refinery projects worldwide and relied on engineering and construction consulting firms for up-to-date data on these refining and petrochemical projects and new ones too. While we purchased raw data from these firms, our value was in how we processed it, applying engineering yield factors to predict growth in light products capacity on local, regional, and global scales.

Our forecasts for global supply growth of light products were then compared to our demand predictions to gauge future utilization rates. Since our model showed a strong correlation between utilization rates and refining margins in the specific way that we calculated them, we knew we had an approach that was big and proprietary—one that would make a lot of money for investors.

While other analysts often echoed industry statistics from government sources, we dedicated our efforts to forecasting light product utilization rates several years into the future, which we thought were key to predicting refining margins, earnings and stock price performance. We were just waiting for the right moment and an impactful report title to make our analysis public and, hopefully, make our R&M predictions famous.

However, global commodity markets frequently experience prolonged oversupply periods, as seen in the late 1990s to early 2000s and in more recent periods too. During the first five years of applying our methodology starting in the late 1990s, our analysis indicated that supply growth would outpace demand, leading to lower utilization rates and margins. This resulted in weaker earnings and stock performance in the R&M sector, which confirmed our thesis. R&M stocks remained among the worst performers in the S&P 500 index.

So, we played the waiting game. Being patient was hard, but I remembered the lesson from Tony Gray about the importance of doing my homework, waiting until I had great ideas, and then making a move in the market. Our strategy fit that bill, but patience is always easier said than done for investors. Even though we were confident in our model—a tool we believed our competitors lacked—we needed to be closer to the moment when the "Street" would be caught off guard by rising utilization rates, margins, and earnings estimates. Such a scenario would likely lead to an unexpectedly strong performance of refining stocks, especially since we were starting from record low valuations.

We couldn't wait to challenge the prevailing Wall Street view that the bear market was long-term and that cyclical upturns would be both modest and short-lived. While we kept our powder dry, we believed we were close to the bottom of the cycle and that the negative sentiment on R&M stocks was overdone. While markets tend to be efficient most of the time, they aren't perfect. And we were ready to pounce as soon as our model gave the go signal.

It would quickly become clear whether our sell-side competi-tors had done the same level of in-depth, global analysis as we had. If they had, they would likely be issuing a similar recommendation to buy refinery stocks across all unregulated markets worldwide, just as we planned to do. If not, they'd be caught off guard by our strategy, and probably defend the opposing (and, we thought, incorrect view) to their demise. Or at least that's how it had played out during the Era of the Super-Major. It would be a win-win for us, as we patiently waited for the perfect buying opportunity. We were lying in wait, anticipating our moment.

In the meantime, we identified another market inefficiency and capitalized on it with several seasonal trading recommendations that rewarded investors. We called this strategy "Straw Hats in Winter," drawing on the analogy that it's wise to buy straw hats during the winter when demand is low—few are gardening, boating, or golfing in the cold. Then, sell those hats in spring or summer when outdoor activities pick up, and everyone's looking for sun protection.

Our analogy highlighted a simple but effective way to think about seasonal cycles and market timing in refining:

"During January to May in U.S. refined products markets, demand exceeds supply, inventories decline, margins rise, and the 'Street' typically raises earnings estimates. While analysts convey their excitement through upgrades and refining stocks like Valero, Sunoco, etc. typically rise, the forward curve for refined products in June overestimated eventual, annual margins

80% of the time. Our call was usually to sell R&M stocks in the May-June period even when the stocks were surging.

"Indeed, strong profits in Q2 and Q3 were often extrapolated into Q4 and Q1, which is a period in which supply exceeds demand, inventories build, margins decline, and the sell-side consensus often lowers earnings estimates. Downgrades of investment ratings of independent refining companies often follow, leading to unfavorable performance in R&M equities late in the year.

"Every year, our seasonal call hinges on our outlook for supply, demand and inventories which drives our views on margins for refined products in the U.S. If we conclude that inventories will be lower/higher than that which is discounted by the forward curve in the futures market for refined products, then we surmise that gross margins and earnings estimates will be higher/lower than expected as well.

"While downward revisions to financial projections, in any sector are not positive, we become interested in R&M stocks at that point. At issue is that if the sell-side consensus did not behave in this way almost every year, the positive seasonal trade, which has worked in 15 of 18 years, would not have been possible."[32]

While our seasonal trading strategy proved to be a reliable way to make money almost every year leading up to 2003, placing mid-year sell recommendations on R&M stocks carried its own risks. The main concern was the possibility that the favorable seasonal trends might give way to broader, positive changes in the industry cycle. If that happened, the financial outlook for R&M companies and their stock prices could keep climbing for several years. However, because we thought we knew exactly how supply and demand were likely to change on a global basis over the next four years, we also thought we knew when the seasonal trade would transition into a cyclical one. Such a shift would mark the start of a significant positive

---

32. "Straw Hats in Winter" Meet the "Golden Age of Refining," Douglas Terreson, January 6, 2003.

investment phase for both U.S. and international R&M stocks. We were determined to lead the way on Wall Street, making the call to buy every R&M stock and waving the flag for this major investment opportunity.

In January of 2003, we thought our moment had arrived. Like with our "Era of the Super-Major" call, we laid out our prediction in a bold new report that we hoped would grab attention and make waves on Wall Street. We titled it "The Golden Age of Refining."

Here's how we laid it out: We started by acknowledging the obvious. The R&M sector had been underperforming, ranking poorly among the S&P 500's 80 or so sectors due to poor capital management and excessive investment, which led to an oversupply of refined products. Refining margins were painfully low, around $3/bbl, underscoring the sector's struggles. Additionally, the fact that these companies had consistently failed to earn their cost of capital over the past decade only contributed to Wall Street's negative view of the sector.

Despite this, I thought that a new, positive outlook on the R&M sector was warranted. Our stance went against the tide, but I viewed the negative consensus outlook to be stale and herd mentality at its finest. I doubted the "Street" had done their homework in refining like we had and were instead just coasting along with the historical negative viewpoint —more comfortable for them, but a perfect setup for a major market surprise if we were right. After all, the common wisdom on Wall Street says that it's better to fail conventionally with everyone else than to take divergent non-consensus views and fail unconventionally. By now, you can likely see that I never played by that rulebook. I believed that all bad things had to eventually come to an end, and that the refining sector's time had finally come. Plus, the consensus was almost always wrong at market extremes.

Our view was that growth in global light products demand would rise at three times the rate of supply in the coming years. This imbalance, we believed, would increase utilization rates from 89% to 97% and cause refining margins to surge. Given the high operating leverage in refining, the increase in financial projections would stun Wall Street and R&M stocks would skyrocket if we were correct. The Wall Street Journal quoted me saying: "Buy them all; it won't matter which ones you own."

We thought we had what legendary investor Michael Steinhardt described as the key ingredients for market success: to know something others don't know, to think ahead of the curve, and to anticipate when something is going to happen.

We were sure of our stance but were not surprised that most investors doubted our optimistic forecast. Their skepticism was understandable; very few had ever seen a profit from investment in R&M stocks, except during our seasonal "Straw Hats in Winter" trades. The market's history of disappointments in refining had taught investors to be wary. Many analysts before me had fallen on their swords. However, that I was the top-rated Big Oil analyst on Wall Street lent significant credibility to our predictions and investors paid heed. Still, we found that investors remained leery overall.

My Wall Street competitors seemed mostly amused by my call with most doubling down on their pessimism to differentiate their views further. One competitor even put a $0 price target on Tesoro's stock, which traded near $8 per share at the time. This was the first and only time I can recall an analyst putting a $0 price target on a stock, much less an industry leader like Tesoro.

The oil companies were not overly supportive either. Bruce Smith, CEO of Tesoro told the Wall Street Journal: "This may not be the Golden Age but it's certainly not the dark ages, which is where we were."

Further, Petroleum Intelligence Weekly quoted industry R&M leaders saying that "the industry has worried for years that capacity is running out, but it has always solved the problem through continuous capacity creep." Another leader chimed in, "I have every confidence that with the incentives that the market is providing today, refiners will get very clever in finding new ways to meet further growth in demand."

While we considered those factors in our model, most observers doubted that industry recovery was ahead. However, as I marketed the call to investors and provided the specific plant-by-plant outlook that supported my outlook for supply, it was clear that clients had not seen R&M research that was this detailed before, especially on a global scale. Word began to spread in the investment community and demand for my time began to rise as traction increased with institutional investors, hedge funds, and sovereign wealth funds—my main clientele. This was a promising sign; I believed we were onto something big, and the lack of major pushback from investors suggested I might have the treasure all to myself.

Sure enough, R&M margins began to rise during the first half of 2003. After increasing our financial projections, we indicated that "while our annual earnings estimates for the 'pure play' refiners are no longer 75% above consensus, as they were in December of 2002, they remain well above consensus projections. Additionally, the bias for revision to our earnings estimates is to the upside."

It's unusual and risky to make predictions that are far beyond what most Wall Street experts agree on; in this case 75% above the consensus when estimates that are 10-15% above peers are significant outliers. Such bold forecasts can cause people to question the credibility of the call and dismiss it as unfounded. We knew this though and wanted investors to call us and ask more about our approach, believing that they would come away as convinced as we were about the positive outlook.

So, I doubled down. In an interview with the Oxford Energy Review in Oxford, England, I pressed the call by saying that

"2003 will be a good year in global refining but that 2004-06 will be the best three years of the past three decades, with 2006 the best year of all." This was a bold statement, especially three years out in such a challenging, deep cyclical industry. I was confident my call would prove correct though. And it did. The recovery in refining margins gained steam, increasing from $3/bbl in 2002 to $4.50/bbl in 2003. Consensus earnings estimates jumped by 600%, starting from a low base. R&M stocks surged by 80% in 2003, but we thought that the best was yet to come.

In January of 2004, we stated that because "growth in demand will exceed that of supply by a 2:1 ratio in 2004 and 2005, inventories will remain low and margins will rise significantly, surprising the consensus of Wall Street analysts.[33] The Wall Street analyst consensus appears to disagree with our viewpoint with earnings for R&M companies projected to decline modestly in 2004. The Wall Street consensus appears to utilize margins of $4.00-4.15/bbl in making earnings estimates for the companies, which is well below Morgan Stanley's weekly refined products model of $5.80/bbl. We have increased our projections for margins in R&M in North America, Europe, and Asia by 20-25% today."

In the stock market, shifting expectations are everything. Refining margins that are 50% above what most analysts predict are substantial outliers, and if correct, this would lead to significant gains in earnings estimates and, in turn, stock prices.

Our forecasts were on point: refining margins hit $6.50/bbl in 2004, and profits for R&M companies tripled. R&M stocks soared, increasing by 300% over the first two years of my prediction, 2003-2004.

Given this remarkable performance, many constituents suggested that I take a victory lap for this career-defining success and downgrade the R&M stocks. I remember a meeting with the legendary Barton Biggs at Traxis, who initially thanked me for my persistence in getting his fund involved in what was one

---

33. "The Golden Age of Refining," Douglas Terreson January 16, 2004

of Wall Street's most contrarian bets at the time. He went on to say that while he thought I knew more about the refiners than anyone on Wall Street, he cautioned me that "only egotists and fools try to pick tops and bottoms," and that an individual is only as beloved as their most recent performance.

While I always valued the wisdom from Barton, I really believed in my call and expected more from it. A lot more. Besides, the Wall Street consensus continued to oppose my view instead of doing the work to look into my research methodology that would surely change their minds. If they had, they would reach the same conclusions that I did, and it would be a sign that future positive surprises would be less likely and that we should call off the dogs. I wasn't being a maverick just to be one; I thought that I had insights that my Wall Street competitors didn't, and it was premature to change course.

Because they were overlooking what could be the biggest investment opportunity in the energy sector since the Era of the Super-Major five years before, my competitors were feeling the heat. A common tactic on Wall Street to gain an edge—and slow down someone else's momentum—is to try and poach their team members. Right on cue, my top associate, Sean Maher, got an offer from the Head of Energy Research at UBS to switch firms and start covering R&M stocks there, a move that could have significantly advanced his career by giving him his own research coverage and at a well-known firm.

As the job offer discussions advanced, UBS wanted Sean to bring my refining model with him. This was problematic for a couple of reasons. First, taking the model to UBS could have been seen as stealing intellectual property, potentially leading to legal action and bad press for UBS. Second, given my well-known stance on the R&M sector, if a competitor suddenly started publishing my model and claiming it as their own, investors would surely notice, especially given my high profile.

Sean, being a person of high integrity, ended talks with UBS that same day. The market had already spoken, and the results validated our hard work. I promoted Sean to lead analyst on four smaller R&M stocks, and he eventually took over the Integrated Gas and Midstream franchise. I remember telling him, "Sean, you've worked harder and longer for me than anyone. You've done great work and you know the program—it's time for you to have your own coverage. Go get them, and congrats on your franchise!" Sean has since had a strong career and is the Chief Economist at Phillps66 today.

As we headed into 2005, we continued to recommend the purchase of every R&M stock in every major market—North America, Europe, Asia, and others—to further distinguish our call from our peers.

In early 2005, we indicated that "based on our proprietary, global refinery-by-refinery analysis, growth in consumption (4.5 MMBPD) will outpace that of capacity (1.3 MMBPD) by a 3:1 margin during the 2005-2007 period, underscoring our Golden Age of Refining investment thesis. If so, the consensus of Wall Street analysts which project profits in R&M to decline by 35% in 2005, hold a viewpoint which we feel will prove wholly misplaced.

"Besides our own analysis in North America, our views draw from analysis in Europe and Latin America by Irene Himona and Christian Audi. Important inputs are also received from Russia (Craig Kennedy), China/Taiwan (Howard Wong), South Korea (Kenneth Whee), Australia (Stuart Baker), Japan (Lalita Gupta) and India (Vinay Jaising) as well, rounding out our global approach.

"With Morgan Stanley's global research capabilities, and the reality that the time involved to permit, schedule and construct new refining capacity approximates three years, all global projects should have already been included in our projections through 2006, and possibly 2007.

"While our projections for demand growth have increased modestly in recent months, our estimates for capacity growth have not changed since May, which was the last time that we provided our outlook for global refining capacity. An updated report is planned later in the year, which will be the next time that global survey data becomes available. Our outlook for 2007 will be expanded upon at that time."[34]

Indeed, refining margins climbed to record levels, reaching $10.50/bbl in 2005 and $12.00/bbl in 2006. While starting from a low base line, profits for major R&M companies like Valero, Sunoco, and Premcor skyrocketed by 50 times during my "Golden Age of Refining" call. While most of the gains were driven by strong performance in their main businesses, companies also smartly used the extra money to expand through acquiring other companies. Industry leader Valero grew from five refineries to 17 by 2008. Companies were investing in things that would make them more profitable and increase their value, which is exactly what they were supposed to do.

Normally, when companies experience a period of high profits and reinvest in growing their business during a cyclical upturn, it ends up being a bad move for investors. But this time was different. Even as spending relative to depreciation increased, I backed the strategy of growing through acquisitions at that point in the cycle, as entities were creating real economic value under normalized[35] conditions for refining margins.

The consistently high refining margins indicated a need for more investment. And with some companies looking to sell their plants for less than what it would cost to build new ones, buying these refineries made a lot of financial sense. Entities that purchased plants below these "replacement costs" enhanced their returns on investment, which in turn increased their stock values. While some deals were more successful than others, nearly all of them benefited shareholders, especially in the early to middle stages of this boom.

---

34. "The Golden Age of Refining" Circa 2006, Douglas Terreson, January 18, 2006

35. "Normalized" refining margins refer to the margin level required for marginal players to achieve returns that approximate the cost of raising funds through debt or equity. These levels are often approximated by the rolling 5 or 10-year average refining margin on the US Gulf Coast. Normalized margins provide a basis for comparison that mitigates the impact of short-term volatility and reflects more stable economic conditions and cost dynamics within the industry.

Because of my credibility in the R&M sector, Morgan Stanley, with me as the lead analyst, spearheaded the stock offerings for major players like Valero, Sunoco, TOSCO, and Premcor. I really enjoyed working closely with CEOs like Valero's Bill Greehey, Sunoco's Jack Drosdick, Marathon's Gary Heminger, and TOSCO and Premcor's Tom O'Malley. We spent quality time with their teams in the offices, on golf courses, and in the field.

Although I was highly supportive of the companies and their management teams to the point where some questioned my objectivity, they justified it by making decisions that aligned with shareholder interests. The assets acquired with the capital we raised during my "Golden Age of Refining" period still form the core holdings of today's largest U.S. R&M firms.

Institutional Investor magazine indicated that year: "'Morgan Stanley's Doug Terreson has distinguished himself by developing a long-term thesis and sticking to it,' says one money manager. The analyst's ongoing 'Golden Age of Refining' call—beginning in 2002, Terreson predicted that refining margins in 2004–2006 would be the strongest in a generation—has been 'deadly accurate and exceptionally well timed,' says another. WealthVest said 'Terreson was dead right. It was maybe the best sell-side research call I can remember. Paradigm shifts like an industry going from a dog to a secular winner start in deep pessimism making a big call like that a career risk.'"

During 2006, the stocks rose further. By mid-year, the average performance of stocks in the R&M sector had increased by 1,700%. In contrast, the S&P 500 index had a return of 55% over the same period. Of course, some stocks did better than others with Tesoro rising by 2,000% during my "Golden Age of Refining." "Otherworldly" may seem like an exaggeration, but it best describes market performance in R&M during our call.

However, the call was aging, and most Wall Street analysts had capitulated and now agreed with our view. This kind of shift is a key signal in investing—the more popular a position becomes, the less likely it is to be profitable.

In our mid-2006 update, we suggested that the refining sector's high profits and cash flow were fueling more investment, with supply of light products likely to exceed demand during 2007-2009. Refining margins and profits had likely peaked, and we decided it was the right moment to step back.

"Easy Money Made" was the title of my downgrade report in summer 2006. Downgrades typically don't sit well with investors, especially coming from someone considered the leading voice or "axe" in the sector, but most large institutional investors were prepared for this one. Though the stocks took a significant hit for almost a week following my downgrade, those who had followed my advice from the start recognized they had made one of the best investment decisions of their careers. They were grateful and a lot of goodwill was created with our investor base. The corporate sector was thankful as well, although with the R&M management teams showing strong commitment to creating value and aligning with shareholder interests, they deserved much of the credit.

Overall, R&M stocks went from being "un-investable" to being the market darlings of S&P 500 by the end of the phase. We had made what was arguably the call of the decade in the energy sector—perhaps even in the entire market—and had won a major upset victory, defying the Wall Street consensus every step of the way. It underscored Warren Buffet's quip that "the stock market is designed to transfer money from the active to the patient."

While my "Golden Age of Refining" title resurfaces on Wall Street every few years and to varying degrees of success, it is unlikely that any four-year call in *any* S&P sub-sector of meaningful market capitalization will ever deliver a return of 1,700% over four years. One of the main reasons being that I just laid out in this chapter how to accurately forecast the global refining cycle several years in advance and the fact that information is more widely dispersed now. Anything is possible though.

The remarkable performance we saw could never have

happened if the years leading up to our call hadn't been marked by poor financial results in global refining. This poor performance made peer sell-side analysts confident that the negative trend would continue. While they stuck to their pessimistic views, their positions crumbled when earnings estimates, valuations, and share prices surged unexpectedly.

Like the Super-Major phase that preceded it, the "Golden Age of Refining" had a transformative effect on the industry because "once assets changed hands, they would probably never be available again," reshaping the competitive hierarchy and distinguishing the winners from the losers. The phrase "Golden Age of Refining" became industry nomenclature and remains a significant part of its history today. For investors, management teams, and myself, it was an exhilarating time.

The call to sell R&M stocks in mid-2006 proved prescient. Although I didn't predict the Global Financial Crisis in 2008 that affected all industry sectors, my research had already pointed to the end of the R&M cycle and to overvalued refining stocks. Following my downgrade, R&M stocks plummeted by 75% in the subsequent year. In both the Super-Major and Golden Age phases, our analysis foresaw disruptive changes that would reshape the industry for years to come. Our predictions proved true, and we were glad to have our name on it.

The success of our predictions clearly indicated that we were looking at different investment factors than our competitors on Wall Street. While I didn't read competitor research, I suspected that they were too focused on the short-term, high frequency margin data rather than the medium to longer-term fundamentals of the global R&M sector. For this reason, they missed the forest for the trees. Otherwise, they would have shared our forward-looking view and made investment calls that were similarly profitable to ours. The Wall Street Journal would have quoted some other analyst saying: "Buy them all. It won't matter which ones you own."

To me, medium-term competitive dynamics and broader strategic shifts in the industry were the most intriguing and profitable aspects to analyze. However, it seemed research competition was limited in this segment of the market. This is especially true today where sell-side analysts are often charged with covering more than 50 stocks, compared to the maximum of 12 that I handled in my career. This workload leaves them little time to dig into the energy commodities that are often key to predicting stock price movements, which was a specialty area for me and my team. At times, it felt like we were competing against ourselves in this highly complex but profitable niche of the market.

After the Golden Age of Refining ended in 2007, the industry didn't perform as well in the following decade, with R&M lagging behind the S&P 500. This was in line with our predictions that supply growth would outstrip demand by 15% and utilization rates would level off around 90%. We didn't expect major changes in margins, and that turned out to be the case. Although there were highly profitable periods due to fluctuations in crude oil prices, weather events, and regulatory changes, the overall investment landscape within R&M was lackluster and more attractive opportunities could be found elsewhere in the S&P 500.

Years later, after I had joined the team at Evercore ISI, it looked like global refining was set to experience another period of positive surprise. In early 2018, we tuned up our R&M machine and published a new report titled: "It's Not Your Father's Golden Age but We'll Take It."

While the publication of our report may have been early since most of the major catalysts that we envisioned were unlikely before 2020, we wanted to garner investor mindshare early, and to enable them to reacquaint themselves with the R&M sector and its constituents since the sector had not held the spotlight for a while.

If investors agreed with my positive views, they would have enough time to build large positions in R&M stocks, which was my goal for my investor clients. In addition, because Evercore ISI was not overly positive on S&P 500 during 2018-2019, significant underperformance in R&M versus the overall market seemed unlikely. Indeed, R&M stocks matched S&P 500 during the period, so the opportunity cost of being early was minimal.

There were three key points to our view. First, "Evercore ISI's assessment of every refining project that is planned or under construction worldwide, of which there are 300 projects, indicates global growth in demand (4.1 MMBPD) will exceed that of capacity (3.4 MMBPD) in 2018-2020. Gross margins and feedstock spreads will exceed expectations during 2018-2020, in our view."

Second, "the International Maritime Organization (IMO) requires an 85% reduction in sulfur in marine fuels by 2020. Of the non-compliant fuel pool of 4.0 MMBPD: scrubbers (0.4), LNG (0.1), new diesel supply (0.5), desulfurization (0.5), higher conversion (0.3) and distillation utilization (0.8), blending (0.9) and non-compliance (0.5 MMBPD) will balance the market. Because most are high-cost options, prices for low sulfur crude oils (inputs) and refined products (outputs) are set to increase significantly in relation to high-sulfur varieties during 2018-2020. Consensus will be surprised by the strength in distillates: diesel and jet fuel prices, in our view."

Thirdly, the sell-side consensus was much less constructive on R&M, suggesting that earnings estimates and share prices could rise significantly if we were right. We indicated that "if margins in the forward curve come to fruition, consensus estimates in R&M must rise by 40%. R&M earnings stand to rise significantly and when applying historical valuation multiples on leading valuation measures in R&M (P/E, P/B and P/CF), we remain buyers. Refiners are Pledgers too with return of capital near $40 billion during 2018-2020 which compares to R&M equity value of $125 billion."

With this new refining call, we felt that we were back in business after a decade in the proverbial wilderness. While access to information was much greater than during the "Golden Age of Refining" and the Street was never likely to miss the estimates for R&M companies by a factor of five to 10 times again, enough positive catalysts were ahead for R&M stocks to perform well, in our view. We told investors that while R&M stocks were unlikely to rise by 1,700% ever again over a four-year period, 200-300% moves were probable. This was still an assertive, bold call.

Like the initial phase of my "Golden Age of Refining" call, the early signals from refined products markets were mixed. Bulls and bears both claimed victory although neither were fully correct because the stocks were mostly unchanged in 2018 and then again in 2019. Heading into 2020 though, we felt that the time had arrived and that the major catalysts that we had been waiting for would materialize. Significant surprises were probable in the R&M divisions of Big Oil and R&M companies and fireworks were ahead for their equities in the stock market.

It turned out that we were right but for the wrong reason, and in the wrong direction too. The tragedy of the COVID-19 pandemic led to record declines in demand for refined products as global economic growth and mobility cratered. Supply growth exceeded that of demand by almost 10 MMBPD leading to the highest level of refined products inventory on record by the end of 2020. Prices for West Texas Intermediate (WTI) crude oil fell to a record of negative $37/bbl for a brief period signaling significant market distress. The S&P R&M index declined by 65% during the first quarter of 2020, reflecting this ultra-negative outcome.

Refining margins declined below cash production costs leading to temporary reductions in output for lower cost players and complete plant shutdowns for those of the higher-cost variety. This started the market rebalancing process though with over 4 MMBPD of refining capacity eventually closing permanently. With demand recovering as global economies reopened, markets rebalanced, and our fundamental call was in play again but not before 2021.

Indeed, refining margins increased from $5/bbl in 2020 to

$9/bbl in 2021 to record levels of $27/bbl in 2022 and 2023.

While gasoline prices were strong, diesel prices rose by 70% more than gasoline.

This market outcome validated the two primary tenets of our call. First, that global balances for refined products would tighten. And second, low-sulfur diesel prices would surge because of the International Maritime Organization (IMO) 2020 fuels transition.

Modifications in Russian crude oil and refined products supply surely played a role post the invasion in February 2022, as did the European embargo of Russian refined products in February 2023, which I did not predict.

Profits at the "Big 3" U.S. R&M companies, Marathon Petroleum, Phillips66, and Valero, rose to record levels and their stocks doubled by 2024. While refining fundamentals were lackluster during the ten-year period between the original "Golden Age of Refining" and "Your Father's Golden Age," R&M management teams led by Mike Hennigan at Marathon Petroleum, Greg Garland and Mark Lashier at Phillips66, Greg Goff at Tesoro, and Joe Gorder at Valero positioned their companies to prosper along the way. They fully recognized the transition in the industry from growth to maturity and managed their companies in a disciplined way while retaining upside to positive cyclical and regulatory events.

Their value propositions balance capital investment and share-holder distributions which almost always leads to superior share-holder outcomes in deep-cyclical commodity industries. Because R&M companies under their leadership were the best capital managers in S&P Energy since the Great Recession, they outperformed Big Oil, E&P, and Oil Field Service peers by a whopping 200 percentage points in the equity market since that time.

While their energy peers later adopted the same value-based model that had allowed the "Big 3" to prosper, R&M entities remain among the best companies and most reliable investments in S&P Energy today.

Like the Era of the Super-Major, the Golden Age of Refining spread substantial prosperity among corporates and investor stake-holders alike and was another dreamlike experience for me. We designed an approach that connected refined products economics to share price performance irrespective of whether our methodology was sanctioned by oil companies or Wall Street competitors. This approach served as our guiding star in uncharted waters, and we held an unwavering commitment to it. Because we were confident in our approach, we challenged the status quo in the face of widespread skepticism. Substantial prosperity followed and being at the heart of the action was truly rewarding.

7

Crude Oil and the Chaos of 2008

The year 2008 started like many others. Our energy team was performing well and life in Houston was good. While the city is the fourth largest in the U.S. and has the normal amount of hustle and bustle, I had purchased the house of former U.S. Olympic track and field superstar Carl Lewis several years earlier and had the privacy and emotional space that I needed. Our home sat on two wooded acres, complete with a pool, playground, batting cage, and ample space for my son and his friends to practice their pitching wedges right in our backyard.

Life in Houston for us was quintessentially suburban—quite a change from my New York days. My wife and I engaged in local charities, my daughters threw themselves into soccer and dance, and my son thrived in youth basketball and baseball. Though my contributions to soccer and dance were limited to the cheering section, my experience in various baseball and basketball leagues lent me enough "expertise" to coach youth sports. Even in my mid to late forties, I found myself always looking for a league to play in or coach.

I coached an 11 and 12-year-old basketball team in the Inner-City Youth League of Houston's rough Third Ward, with our games at Jack Yates High School. In a stark contrast, I also coached my son Todd's basketball teams from kindergarten through second grade at the Post Oak YMCA, made up of his classmates at River Oaks Baptist School. To me, teaching life lessons, developing skills, and encouraging team play was top priority. But we also won championships in both leagues, which was fun and gave the kids—and their parents—a sense of pride.

My inner-city teams competed in the 1 Corinthian 13 League, started by my friends Prince and Sheila Cousinard. Besides their own four kids, they often provided a home for five to six additional kids facing family instability due to domestic violence, substance abuse, mental health issues, or family breakdowns. Many of my players came from the Cuney Homes, a hotbed of violent crime in Houston. Some were essentially homeless and tracking them down for practice and games became a routine challenge. I did everything I could to keep the team together and be a positive force in their lives.

Over the six years I coached inner-city basketball, we rarely saw many parents at the games, a notable difference from the other local teams I coached. My assistants—Sean Maher and my son Todd—and I would be out for about four hours, several times a week with our kids. My wife was totally on board with it, always backing us up. After every game, the kids insisted on eating Cici's Pizza. They preferred it over the closer and arguably tastier Pizza Hut, which I found out later was because they could load up on the all-you-can-eat buffet, and the manager would also let them take extra pizza home with them (which we were happy to pay extra for, of course).

Meanwhile, coaching baseball at Post Oak Little League in Houston's Memorial neighborhood brought its own set of joys. My team went undefeated and clinched the championship in the Minors Division in 2007. We eagerly anticipated moving up to the next age group, the Pee-Wees, in 2008. The league's annual draft in January, followed by an 18-game regular season running from February through April, tested our endurance and teamwork. My son Todd was drafted by the Horned Frogs, a team I was asked to coach before the draft by Tommy Fatjo and

John Shepard, who had deep knowledge of the league's dynamics from the previous season. Despite the Frogs' rough season, the year before, when they won only three out of 17 games, we were excited about the potential of the upcoming season and the opportunity to work alongside coaches like Tommy and John.

Coaching youth sports, whether it was with my children or those of others, provided a sense of purpose and fulfillment, and I also enjoyed the daily interaction with players, parents, and other coaches and especially the much-needed break from the Wall Street scene. The joy of play, learning, and teamwork was gratifying and provided a different type of satisfaction compared to work achievements.

While family life in Houston was thriving, ominous developments were unfolding in the investment world that would soon culminate in one of the most turbulent years in the global economy over the last century.

The year started with the major market indices near record highs and further gains expected through 2009. Investors were optimistic about the global economy and corporate earnings, with U.S. consumer confidence and employment in positive territory. However, there was about to be a major shift.

Threats were emerging from the housing bubble that had started in the early 2000s driven by easy access to credit, soaring home prices, and speculative investments in real estate. By 2008, the subprime mortgage sector, which comprised loans to borrowers with poor credit histories, started to collapse. As home values fell, these borrowers increasingly defaulted on their mortgages.

Financial institutions had bundled many of these subprime mortgages into complex financial products like mortgage-backed securities (MBS) and collateralized debt obligations (CDOs). Despite the risks, these financial products were widely held on the balance sheets of investment banks and insurance companies. While losses were expected, they were initially considered manageable.

The positive outlook was reflected in the share prices of leading investment banks like Bear Stearns, Lehman Brothers, Goldman Sachs, J.P. Morgan, Merrill Lynch, and Morgan Stanley, which were near all-time highs at the start of 2008. In other words, the market seemed to think there was no reason for concern, though some investors believed that a crisis was looming.

In the energy sector, I had just declared the end of the Golden Age of Refining, and downgraded R&M stocks several months earlier. Although refining margins were expected to remain strong, the "Street" had become hyper-bullish on R&M shares, making their equity valuations less appealing after significant gains.

Despite this, my outlook on the energy sector as a whole remained positive. I maintained overweight ratings on the Big Oils and E&P companies, both of which were larger market sectors than R&M.[36] My perspective was bolstered by my view that the prices of crude oil, natural gas, and refined products would rise, which would enhance profitability and drive share prices higher in the energy sector from 2008-2009.

Like many other sector-specific analysts, I was an expert in my area of research but still needed insight from the army of strategists, economists, and analysts at Morgan Stanley on potential areas of concern outside of energy. In turn, with petroleum considered the lifeblood of the global economy, the firm was reliant on my views on oil prices—as were investors, corporates, and governments around the world.

In my energy team, the structure was clear: while all members had input into the oil price forecast, only one person—typically the head of the energy group, which was me—was responsible for maintaining the models and representing the team's view publicly.

---

36. "Overweight" refers to an expectation that a sector or stock will exceed the average return of other sectors or stocks. It urges investors to allocate a larger portion of their portfolios to the area compared to its weight in a benchmark index. It implies a positive outlook and confidence in future performance.

This structure was the same for our Natural Gas and Drilling Rig Count forecasts, managed by the E&P and Oil Field Service analysts, respectively. These designated team leaders served as our public voice on these matters, and I deferred to their expertise in public discussions. Having one consistent and reliable voice proved more effective, and every team member agreed to this framework before joining Morgan Stanley. Analysts were expected not to encroach on each other's areas of expertise.

We wanted to prevent mixed messages and counterproductive competition within our team, which could lead to intense conflicts typical of Wall Street. We had observed situations where, when oil or natural gas prices rose and media attention increased, individual team members would seek their 10 minutes of fame at the expense of the team. We had also witnessed what would happen to the newfound "expert" when prices fell and the spot-light dimmed—these same individuals often retreated to their primary areas of expertise and went radio silent on prices, leaving the official spokesperson to sort it out with the sales team and clients on their own. Our goal was to avoid these scenarios and the resulting internal strife that is caused.

Although I was often told that forecasting oil prices accurately was impossible, I disagreed. My model explained nearly 80% of oil price fluctuations during the past decade or so. We demonstrated in refining that investors could accurately predict commodity prices if they understood the right variables to consider. For oil, recognizing the fundamental economic drivers as well as geopolitical influences, particularly policies in the Middle East, was crucial.

In my view, several factors influenced oil prices. On the demand side, we knew that economic growth leads to increased industrial, transportation, and construction activities, all of which require oil. This, in turn, leads to higher household incomes which then leads to increased demand for goods and services that rely on oil such as for transportation and heating and cooling. Conversely, during economic downturns, demand for oil typically decreases as both businesses and consumers reduce their energy consumption. The relationship between global GDP growth and oil demand is positive for these reasons. However, oil demand is also affected by technological advancements, governmental policies, and shifts in consumer behavior, which can alter oil intensity over time.[37] These factors are vital components of any forecasting methodology.

On the supply side, the economics of investing in oil production and the budgetary needs of OPEC countries set a baseline for equilibrium oil prices. Although the oil market usually operates under fully competitive conditions, OPEC's influence introduces an oligopolistic element. Geopolitical events such as political unrest, conflicts, and tensions in oil-producing regions also play a critical role in affecting supply too.

Overall, the price of oil is subject to a dynamic mix of economic, political, and social factors that can cause rapid fluctuations. My goal was to integrate these factors into a well-defined and accurate forecasting model that could be conveyed clearly to investors.

Our outlook for global demand, supply, and inventories relied on baseline data from the IEA, OPEC and the EIA. We also used information from other sources around the world that we deemed to be reliable and valuable. Annual meetings with industry leaders from Saudi Arabia as well as periodic discussions with counterparts in Brazil, China, India, Kuwait, Norway, Russia, the UAE, Venezuela, and other key nations, gave us a significant competitive edge.

We observed that the dynamics of demand and supply, which affect inventories, are closely linked to oil prices. This is because inventories serve as a short-term marginal supply source since demand is inelastic in the near-term, meaning price changes have little immediate impact on quantity demanded. As a result, inventories reflect market pressures. When inventories are low, prices tend to rise as buyers compete for limited supplies.

Conversely, when inventories are high, prices often fall as sellers look to unload excess barrels.

---

37. Oil intensity refers to the amount of oil required to produce a unit of economic output, typically measured as barrels of oil per unit of GDP or per capita energy consumption.

Because the model explained most of the variation in oil prices over prior decades, I knew that we had something great over the years. In fact, this was the most predictive commodity price forecast model that I ever encountered during my tenure on Wall Street. The public accuracy and reliability of our model opened doors to high-level discussions with many investors, corporates, and government agencies around the world.

Counterintuitively, because my methodology was proprietary, we published the relationship between oil prices and inventories each month to reduce the likelihood that it would be "borrowed" by Wall Street competitors. Plus, being transparent enabled me and my clients to see my potential biases and to open the door for debate when needed. While I didn't read competitor research, and others may have had more predictive models for crude oil prices, they were never brought to my attention by my loyal investor and corporate base. This is not to say they didn't exist.

As 2008 approached, our team held a positive outlook on all three energy commodities and energy stocks too. We projected strong global economic conditions would render an increase in oil demand of 3.5 MMBPD over 2008 and 2009, a healthy gain. Although oil supply was expected to increase by an even larger amount of 4 MMBPD and overall inventories would likely grow, the key to our positive price forecast was the expected decrease in oil inventories adjusted for demand.[38] This particular measure, which we believed was often overlooked by others, was a critical driver of oil prices in our model and was the factor that set our forecast apart from the consensus over the years.

Due to modest declines in days-of-inventory, our analysis pointed to a modest rise in oil prices. Brent crude averaged $61/bbl through Q3 2007, and in our October 7, 2007 report, we forecasted a move to around $65 in 2008. The estimate reflected our nuanced view of supply-demand dynamics and a slight

---

38. Inventories adjusted for demand can be calculated by total inventories divided by demand in barrels per day.

decline in adjusted inventories—an outlook nearly identical to OPEC's.

However, the market had other ideas. As the group met on October 16, 2007, oil prices were surging unexpectedly, surpassing both my and OPEC's projections and approaching $85/bbl. This rapid and unanticipated price escalation compelled the organization to state:

"We strongly believe that fundamentals are not supporting current high prices and that the market is very well supplied. There has been no interruption in crude supplies and OECD commercial inventory levels remain above five-year levels. Forward cover, which stands at 53.5 days, is at a comfortable level.[39]

"The rising oil prices which we are currently witnessing are, however, largely being driven by market speculators. Persistent refinery bottlenecks and seasonal maintenance work, ongoing geopolitical problems in the Middle East and fluctuations in the U.S. dollar, also continue to play a role in pushing oil prices higher. Additional political tensions, seen during recent days, are also pressurizing oil prices upwards.

"OPEC continues to strive for a balanced market and a fair price that is favorable for both consumers and producers. As part of its mission to keep the market well supplied, and as agreed in September, the Organization will raise output by 500,000 b/d from 1 November 2007."[40]

While higher oil production and inventories usually lead to lower prices, oil continued to increase and to exceed both mine and OPEC's expectations. Brent crude oil rose to $90/bbl as 2008 commenced and to $95/bbl by the end of February 2008. By March of 2008, prices remained in an upward trend, surging

---

39. Days forward cover refers to the number of days that existing oil inventories can meet demand without additional supply. It is current oil inventory levels divided by the daily demand rate. It helps assess the adequacy of oil reserves in relation to consumption.

40. Press Statement by OPEC Secretary General, HE Abdalla Salem El-Badri, October 16, 2007

to record levels of $110/bbl. My "face was getting ripped off" according to a prominent hedge fund client at a luncheon I hosted in mid-town Manhattan.

However, as the subprime mortgage crisis deepened, the value of credit assets plummeted triggering negative economic impacts. Rumors spread in the market about liquidity issues at Bear Stearns and concerns about its solvency. These rumors caused a severe loss of confidence among investors and trading partners, leading to a rush to withdraw funds and sever ties with the firm, effectively causing a run on the bank. The situation worsened when the company's stock price collapsed, exacerbating the liquidity crisis.

To prevent other failures that could ripple through the financial system, the U.S. Federal Reserve stepped in. This emergency intervention facilitated the acquisition of Bear Stearns by JPMorgan Chase at a drastically reduced price of $2 per share, a sharp decline from its $75 per share value in January. However, the market was unnerved, and concerns about the stability of other financial institutions and the overall financial system rose leading to widespread uncertainty about the potential for a broader economic fallout.

Following the collapse of Bear Stearns on March 14, 2008, as economic turmoil escalated, an updated outlook for the oil market was warranted, and I published mine. On top of the financial crisis, oil prices were rising rapidly leading to a full-blown media frenzy. Constituents both inside and outside Morgan Stanley looked to me for an updated view given rising economic chaos.

I was widely expected to shift my stance and align with the bullish consensus. Instead, I indicated that market fundamentals had deteriorated during the previous six months and that increased caution was warranted regarding oil prices. Meaning, rather than turn positive, I doubled down, and became more negative. I indicated that gains in oil supply would now exceed that of demand by almost 2 MMBPD, which would lead to a staggering increase in global inventories from 45 to 55 days of demand—a new record. While I believed and defended my new oil price forecast of $95/bbl for 2008, I noted that even if I was wrong and oil prices continued to rise, it was unlikely that energy stocks would see substantial gains, as the market would view any such increases as unsustainable.

My negative stance did not sit well with oil bulls, both within and outside of Morgan Stanley, and criticism of my position intensified. Within Morgan Stanley, strategists, economists, and even sector analysts—who typically did not focus on commodity prices—began offering their insights. It seemed like everyone had become an oil price forecaster overnight with or without actual economic models or experience.

My position was also in stark contrast to the prevailing Wall Street consensus, which seemed to be raising forecasts daily to align with rising market prices. Indeed, key competitor Goldman Sach's stated: "We believe the current energy crisis may be coming to a head, as a lack of adequate supply growth is becoming apparent. The possibility of $150-$200/bbl seems increasingly likely over the next six to 24 months, though predicting the ultimate peak in oil prices as well as the remaining duration of the upcycle remains a major uncertainty." Other competitors indicated that oil could rise to $200 or even $300/bbl which underscored the tenor at the time.

While I realized that the complexities of the oil market sometimes surpassed my ability to fully grasp them, I believed my methodologies were among the best on Wall Street. Even though pressure was mounting for me to capitulate to the overwhelmingly bullish consensus, I stood my ground. I had been here before—I was no stranger to challenging the status quo—and my predictions had proven correct again and again. The only question was how long I could survive on Wall Street with such a seemingly detached and erroneous forecast. The intense scrutiny and the daily barrage of criticism was wearing me down. However, I felt that a few more shoes had to drop, specifically three more shoes had to drop, before I admitted defeat.

The first involved a decline in oil demand caused by high oil prices, which our data suggested was already underway. The second involved a temporary condition in refined products markets that was propping up oil markets but expected to abate around mid-year. The third involved the exit of speculators from the oil market once prices began to fall, leading to a rapid unwinding of positions.

Starting with the first item, we believed that our models for price elasticity of demand were the best on Wall Street and that they enabled us to see when and by how much high oil prices were affecting oil demand.[41] This information is important to energy investors because when consumption falls, OPEC is usually unable and sometimes unwilling to reduce supply quickly enough to prevent inventories from building and prices from declining. Energy equities no longer rise as oil prices increase towards unsustainable levels with share prices declining thereafter.

Our methodology gathered end-user prices for gasoline and diesel monthly from 57 countries, accounting for 96% of global oil demand over the prior decade. The data set therefore contained around 30,000 price points which when compared to oil demand in these same countries were expected to indicate pressure points in the market. And, voila! The resulting scatter plot showed the oil price levels at which oil demand was weakening by country, region and globally. We were confident that no other Wall Street firm had this data, which showed that demand destruction was underway and poised to accelerate if oil prices rose further. If so, the IEA, OPEC and EIA which provided the baseline forecasts for global oil demand for Wall Street analysts, would be making negative revisions to their outlooks in coming months, supporting my position.

---

41. Price elasticity is calculated as the percentage change in quantity demanded divided by the percentage change in price. A higher elasticity indicates that consumers are more sensitive to price changes, while a lower elasticity suggests they are less responsive.

Indeed, economic impacts almost always occurred when global consumer spending on crude oil and natural gas reached 8-9% of GDP; and with oil prices near $115/bbl, petroleum costs per unit of GDP were near the threshold of previous petroleum induced economic shocks. While we noted that the effect of the global wealth transfer and trends in petroleum intensity had to be considered too, our work suggested that demand destruction would be a significant, negative catalyst in the oil market in coming months.

The second shoe involved anticipated weakness in refined products markets, which had strengthened to record levels and pulled crude oil prices higher. The driver of the strength was surging demand from non-OECD countries, notably China, which was ramping up for the 2008 Olympics, and supply constraints related to new environmental regulations in the OECD.

We reasoned that "because almost every barrel of crude that was sold globally was purchased by a refinery, that demand and prices for oil were influenced by refining economics." This perspective—that the value of crude oil would fix at a level that connected to refining margins and not just near-term inventories or medium-term economic factors like reinvestment economics and OPEC's budgetary needs—was met with raised eyebrows from many investors. The idea that crude oil had limited intrinsic value without the refining process, given limited substitution options, challenged conventional wisdom and was a difficult concept for many to grasp.

However, the margin of diesel over crude oil rose from $15 to $43/bbl in the first half of 2008, leading refiners to bid up the price of crude oil to capture high spreads. Additionally, record spreads between low and high sulfur fuels incentivized processing of low-sulfur crude oils which increased in price in relation to heavier, higher sulfur varieties. While the market was optimistic, weakness in demand and gains in capacity were set to lower utilization and margins, relieving pressure in refined products markets. We anticipated this outcome would unfold within a few quarters.

The final catalyst involved the unwinding of massive speculative positions in crude oil and refined product markets. Like other commodity markets, oil is driven by the physical market dynamics of supply and demand, but speculators play a role too. Although the impact of speculation was difficult to quantify, it appeared to be significant in the first half of 2008.

I expected that once the oil market recalibrated to fundamental equilibrium price levels—as it always did—that prices would plummet, vindicating my predictions. However, because I didn't know how long this would take, I didn't engender much confidence with investor clients.

To truly grasp the magnitude of what was unfolding, we need to step back and examine the historical context that led us to this point. The story of commodity regulation in the U.S. is one of good intentions gradually eroded by the relentless tide of financial innovation. It all began with the Commodity Exchange Act of 1936, a well-meaning piece of legislation designed to keep markets liquid without inviting excessive speculation. The Act struck a delicate balance, allowing legitimate hedging while placing limits on speculative positions. It was responsible legislation, aimed at preventing the kind of price bubbles that could wreak havoc on the American economy.

But as the years rolled by, the regulatory landscape began to shift, subtly at first, then more dramatically. The creation of the Commodity Futures Trading Commission (CFTC) in 1974 was meant to be a step forward in market oversight. However, as financial futures gained popularity in the 1980s, the CFTC's attention drifted away from traditional commodities. This shift would prove to be a crucial turning point, setting the stage for what was to come.

The real game-changer came in 1991. The CFTC, in a decision that would have far-reaching consequences, granted commercial exemptions from position limits to swap dealers.[42] On the surface, it seemed innocuous enough—these dealers

---

42. A swap is a financial derivative contract in which two parties agree to exchange cash flows or other financial instruments over a specified period. Common types include interest rate swaps, currency swaps, and commodity swaps, used to manage exposure to fluctuations in interest rates, exchange rates, or commodity prices.

were just hedging their over-the-counter swaps transactions, right? But this seemingly small change opened Pandora's box of speculative opportunity. Suddenly, Wall Street banks had a loophole big enough to drive a truck through. Speculators could now bypass position limits by engaging with these banks, effectively undermining the very purpose of the original 1936 Act.

This loophole, born from decades of legislative tinkering and market evolution, set the stage for a perfect storm of speculation. The once-staid world of commodities had morphed into a high-stakes casino, with oil as the marquee game. The regulatory frameworks, originally designed to prevent excessive speculation, had gradually been hollowed out from within. Financial innovators seized upon these gaps, creating sophisticated instruments that allowed speculation to balloon beyond what the original legislators could have imagined.

By the late 2000s, with returns on U.S. equities near zero over the previous decade, investors sought higher returns in "alternative" assets. Given that crude oil prices had quadrupled compared to the S&P 500 with only a 0.25 correlation in the 10 years leading up to 2008,[43] major commodity swap dealers like Goldman Sachs, Morgan Stanley, J.P. Morgan, and Barclays Bank began promoting commodity futures as an asset class offering "equity-like returns" that increased diversification, hedged against inflation, allowed bets against the dollar, and reduced overall portfolio risk. Supported by these claims, mainstream financial consultants advised large institutions to adopt a "long only," buy and hold strategy for commodities futures, similar to those for stocks and bonds.[44]

---

43. A correlation of 0.25 indicates a weak positive relationship between crude oil prices and the S&P 500. For investors, low correlation can be attractive because it implies that crude oil and the S&P 500 can provide diversification benefits. By investing in assets with low correlation, investors can potentially reduce the overall risk of their portfolio while still maintaining the potential for returns from different sources.

44. Long only is an investment strategy whereby securities are bought with the expectation that prices will increase over time. Unlike short-selling, which involves betting on the decline in the price of a security, long-only investors hold their positions for the potential of price appreciation and profit from rising market values.

This led to the rise of "Index Speculators," a new class of investors who allocated capital across the 25 key commodities futures included in major indices like the S&P, the Goldman Sachs Commodity Index, and the Dow Jones AIG Commodity Index. As capital flowed into these commodities, prices and speculation surged dramatically. Indeed, the open interest in these 25 largest and most important commodities, with oil representing a third of the total, rocketed from $13 billion to $300 billion between 2003-2008—a 25-fold increase. This compared to a total market value of commodities near $2.0 trillion at the time.

The unprecedented nature of this surge was alarming. While commodities are usually correlated due to energy input costs and other factors, one would expect to see prices of some commodities going up and prices of others going down if pure economic factors were at work. This broad rise in all 25 commodities during this period suggested a simultaneous demand shock. While possible, such an event had never happened before in history. Humes' contention that reason is the slave of passion seemed to be operative, as economic realities were cast aside in favor of speculative fervor.

While comparing incremental purchases in the physical commodity markets to incremental purchases in the commodities futures markets is not exactly an apples-to-apples comparison, it helps in understanding this phenomenon. Index Speculators increased their demand for petroleum nearly as much as China, which accounted for a third of the global oil demand growth during the period. Moreover, they bought more futures contracts than both physical hedgers and traditional speculators combined. This herd mentality and fear of missing out is vividly described by Charles MacKay in his book, "Extraordinary Popular Delusions and the Madness of Crowds:"

> "Men, it has been said, think in herds: it will be seen that they go mad in herds, while they only recover their senses slowly, and one by one."

Such a mania appeared to be present in oil markets in 2008.

Making matters worse, Index Speculators were overwhelmingly "long-only" and not particularly price-sensitive, since being fully allocated to the commodity asset was their main goal.

Indeed, the positive price trend that emerges from excessive speculation attracts further attention and capital from other speculators, contributing to the expansion of the bubble. As new speculators jump on the bandwagon, it exacerbates the vicious cycle of rapidly escalating prices and increased market volatility. This scenario was playing out in the oil market, where a classic speculative price bubble was forming. Financial players were driving up demand artificially, focusing on acquiring exposure to oil with little regard for supply, demand, and other fundamental factors that traditionally influence prices. It was like an avalanche gaining momentum, growing more powerful and destructive. The result was significant price distortion, underlining the principle that money moves markets and prices.

The primary beneficiaries appeared to be the largest dealers of commodity swaps—Goldman Sachs, Morgan Stanley, J.P. Morgan, and Barclays Bank—who reportedly controlled 70% of the commodity index swap positions at the time, and by mid-2008 were the largest holders of NYMEX WTI crude oil futures contracts.[45] Just as with their positions in MBS and CDS, high prices benefited them as long as they remained high, but not so much if prices were set to collapse, as I envisioned for the oil market. If so, the Wall Street adage that "it's okay to be late, just don't be last" would apply to the income statements and balance sheets of these companies.

Further complicating matters, the surge in commodity speculation led to upward prices in other areas, particularly for food, creating significant hardship in less developed countries. Since energy can constitute up to 30% of crop production costs, rising energy prices typically lead to higher food prices.

---

45. "The Accidental Hunt Brothers," Michael Masters, July 31, 2008

This effect was evident in the U.S. Producer Price Index or PPI, where food and energy make up a third of the index. The double-digit rise in the U.S. PPI during the first half of 2008 did not bode well for the U.S. or the global economy, illustrating a key difference between speculative bubbles in capital markets versus commodities markets. That being that when internet or tractor stocks double or triple in value, the livelihood of the average citizen is not affected. The same is not true when commodity prices such as energy and food skyrocket, as the average citizen's livelihood is directly affected, particularly in poorer, developing countries.

So, I planned to stay the course, betting that high oil prices would cause oil demand to crater, and with supply rising, oil prices would decline. If oil prices fell precipitously, which was my call, the will of speculators would be broken and sales at any price would follow as their losses mounted.

What happened next is probably best described by a New York media outlet in an article from September 2008:

"Douglas Terreson, the Morgan Stanley analyst who said that independent refining and marketing companies were undervalued, was the bank's chief oil analyst. The award-winning, nationally recognized Terreson had fielded questions in relation to oil prices and futures since the mid-1990s. On March 14 of this year, he said that oil would settle at around $95/bbl for the remainder of 2008. Moreover, Terreson also concluded that oil would retreat to around $83/bbl for 2009.

"This would be Terreson's last forecast for Morgan Stanley. Two short months later, Dow Jones Newswires reported that Terreson had been ousted in a round of layoffs. Two weeks after that, Morgan Stanley said that oil could reach $150 a barrel.

"This speculation set off a round of speculative fervor never before seen in the market. Goldman Sachs immediately followed suit by forecasting oil to roar beyond $150, saying it could hit $200 a barrel in the near future. Oil prices were off to the races, with the investment banks in full lobbying mode while pointing the finger at China and India.

"In retrospect, the turning point appears to be Morgan's $150 forecast. It fueled the apprehension of the media and Wall Street alike. Americans were quick to do the math and knew that the spike would mean $5 per gallon at the pump. Maybe more. Suddenly everyone recalled the 1970s, and new terms such as 'stay-cation' were on everyone's lips.

"So, where did this $150 number come from? Morgan Stanley no longer has a spokesperson for oil. Nor are they willing to comment on the decision to forecast crude oil futures at $150/bbl by someone who 'doesn't deal in oil.' For more than a decade this had been the exclusive domain of Terreson. Yet a month after the report that Terreson had been laid off, Morgan Stanley issued a statement claiming that Terreson voluntarily left his position at Morgan for the promise of higher pay from a hedge fund.

"Not so, according to a Morgan Stanley employee familiar with the circumstances surrounding Terreson's departure, who asked not to be identified in this story. Taken aback by the confusion surrounding Terreson's reason for leaving, he says, 'I knew they had a rightsizing, but he said he was retiring. He was getting ready to head off into the sunset.' And, just like that, Terreson was gone.

"Terreson, once an integral part of the Houston community and a star in the financial sector, seemingly disappeared from the city altogether. His home phone has been disconnected. His former co-workers were unsure of his whereabouts. And almost no one from the firm at which he spent years as a superstar in his field wants to discuss why."[46]

---

46. "How Wall Street is Screwing America," Jerod Morey, The Long Island Press, September 2008.

The oil price forecast was officially removed from my portfolio and reassigned in May 2008. My last day at Morgan Stanley was July 8, 2008, which ironically was three days before the all-time peak in oil prices at $147/barrel on July 11, 2008.

While some believed that I had missed something and that my model had finally met its match, I knew my approach was sound and that the market would come my way. The experience taught me to trust my instincts and the value of rigorous analysis and to be willing to stand apart from the crowd, even when it's uncomfortable. True conviction, I learned, comes not from following the herd but from having the courage to follow the evidence, wherever it may lead.

I left Morgan Stanley with a sense of mutual appreciation and on good terms, ready for the next chapter. With my head held high, still hopeful about my future, I packed up my family for our move to Alabama. And—as if right on cue—oil prices started to decline, plummeting to $37/bbl by Christmas. Overall, oil prices averaged $98/bbl—within 3% of my projection of $95/bbl—for 2008. In the end, I almost hit the bullseye—and bullseyes rarely happen in my line of work. But you can't deny it...numbers don't lie on Wall Street.

8

The Pledge

In Fairhope, my days were simple yet fulfilling. I shuffled between my golf course and beach houses in Point Clear and Ono Island. Besides coaching my daughters in girls' softball and my son in baseball, I planned on playing in the local men's basketball and softball leagues. We joined the Fairhope Methodist Church and settled into the community. This life of leisure looked promising, but I expected another professional endeavor.

I stayed intellectually engaged by managing my family office and serving on a couple of boards. Leaving the relentless pace of Wall Street behind was incredibly freeing—I enjoyed the extra personal space and time to explore a life less dictated by my work schedule. For years, my intense focus on the energy sector had kept me from noticing the broader world around me.

Living in a small resort town near where I grew up was perfect for raising a family. It was filled with friendly faces and daily activities. While some recognized me from my energy commentary in prominent publications or TV spots, most people were unaware of my past, which suited me fine. While professional visibility was important for a high-profile analyst career, I valued my privacy and anonymity. In the grand scheme, I felt what I did was relatively unimportant, especially given the global hardships I'd seen firsthand and my experiences coaching in less privileged areas.

As spring 2009 rolled in, I was deep into coaching Little League baseball and both of my daughters' softball teams and gearing up for Fairhope's men's basketball league. My days were spent mostly at the ballpark surrounded by 6 to 10-year-old kids. This lively and fun atmosphere was a refreshing change from the past two decades of my fast-paced life.

In baseball, I noticed that the younger the players, the more intense the games—and the parental involvement. Despite some parents voicing concerns about fairness, our coaching decisions were always backed by performance data and supported with mid-season tryouts for key positions, which I shared with parents when any concerns came up.

Ensuring that each child was treated fairly and learned the basics of the game and sportsmanship was important to me. I wanted all my players to look forward to returning to the ballpark each season. Most kids were thrilled to be drafted to our team because of the positive atmosphere and our reputation for being championship contenders almost every year.

Girls' softball had a different vibe altogether. Unlike the boys, most girls weren't dreaming of the big leagues but were there to have fun. For them, it was more about the candy and cheers during the games, the snow cones afterwards, and hanging out with their new friends. They went through countless buckets of Double Bubble each season—no other brand would do. I found myself regularly in Aisle 7 at the Fairhope Wal-Mart, stocking up on those large buckets every other week. Our season always ended with a pool party, which was a big hit.

Like most kids and their parents, our team preferred winning over losing. As coaches, we focused on teaching the basics, promoting sportsmanship, and using data to evaluate players, develop strategies, and hone skills, just like my coaching days with the Frogs in the Post Oak Little League in Houston.

The use of data surprised some of my fellow coaches, who

came from a variety of backgrounds like plumbing, butchery, landscaping, dentistry, and law. They often thought that analyzing data would be too time-consuming and questioned its value. However, it really involved just basic math and algebra and was certainly easier than the complex models I was used to building on Wall Street. Plus, it satisfied my weekly craving for crunching numbers.

My daughter Catherine's team, the Cherry Bombs, won the league championship with only two or three rough innings throughout the entire season of 12 games. Meanwhile, Virginia, who was consistently my lead-off hitter, maintained a .700 batting average and was part of teams that nearly snagged the championship several times. Her future as an Alabama State Champion in cross country gave her an edge on the basepaths, making her tough to tag out. Virginia's strategy was to hit toward third base every time she was up to bat, leveraging her speed to first base to her advantage.

In the younger divisions of girls' softball, "coach pitch" is the norm, meaning coaches pitch to their own players. Our data showed that the winning teams typically scored around seven runs, and scoring above that significantly increased the chances of winning. Thus, a strong offense was crucial. However, if a coach couldn't pitch well—failing to deliver pitches the kids could hit or adjust for each player's strengths—the team's offensive performance usually suffered. This often led to a slide to the bottom of the standings.

Unfortunately, these coaches often let their egos get in the way and were reluctant to step aside for better pitchers to take the mound, which caused frustration among both players and parents as the season progressed and the losses mounted. Essentially, whether a team became accustomed to winning or losing often boiled down to talent, the quality of coaching and the willingness of coaches to put their players' needs first.

In boys' baseball, success was often related to these same factors, team dynamics, and whether favoritism, commonly known as "Daddy Ball" was prevalent. Consequently, within the first few weeks of a 20-team league, it was usually possible to identify and eliminate teams with unfavorable characteristics, narrowing down the likely contenders to five or six teams. Remarkably, these teams were often in the running for the championship by season's end. Once we identified the best competition, we monitored these teams to gain strategic insights for future matchups, especially as the season-ending tournament approached.

You may be surprised to hear this, but I found striking similarities between managing an 8-year-old girls' softball team and selecting the best energy stocks for investors. Initially, the process involved setting a baseline of empirically proven factors that correlate with successful performance. The next step was to monitor whether there was effective execution in those critical areas known to drive success. If execution fell short, or if complacency, conflict avoidance, favoritism, or other negative influences interfered with making tough decisions, it led us to seriously question the potential for success. Of course, leadership, communication, teamwork, skill development, and positive reinforcement were key ingredients for success too.

I played basketball weekly at the Methodist Church and was excited to be the sixth pick in the city basketball league draft. I was looking forward to a relatively solid level of competition. Just a few days before our official first game, we were in the middle of a half-court five-on-five game, and I was in the corner of the gym about to head down the baseline on a right-to-left crossover. As I headed to the hoop, a loud crack echoed through the gym. Everyone looked around, stunned, trying to pinpoint where the noise came from. Since I was the only one sitting on the floor, it didn't take long before it dawned on me that something was wrong—I suspected it was my Achilles tendon.

About an hour later, Dan Matthews, an orthopedic surgeon who had played basketball at the Citadel and whom I had looked forward to facing on the court, confirmed my fears. He told me that after surgery, I'd be in a boot for several months. While the news was a blow, it also felt like a sign that my plans for leisure and early retirement at 47 might need a rethink. Either way, it seemed my basketball days were now behind me.

Not long after, David Ginther, a former client from Waddell and Reed in Kansas City, reached out to see if I would be open to returning to the sell-side. He mentioned that the market missed my voice and hinted that he knew of an opportunity that may interest me. I told him that the only offer I would even consider entertaining would be from International Strategy and Investments. As luck would have it, that's exactly who it was.

ISI was an iconic Wall Street firm led by the legendary Ed Hyman, the top Wall Street economist for 40 years according to the Institutional Investor poll. Ed's consistent ranking as the #1 economist out of 25 to 30 global competitors yearly is an unparalleled career achievement.

While ISI was doing well in 2010, Ed saw the bigger picture. He knew that if ISI expanded its best-in-class macro analysis to include specialized fundamental research in sectors like energy, healthcare, and technology, its revenue base would broaden, and its macro product would be stronger due to inputs from industry specialists, potentially making ISI an attractive acquisition target for a larger investment bank.

Part of this expansion involved putting together an all-star team of analysts by cherry-picking the top players on Wall Street. I was the third hire and tasked with building the top energy research franchise, leveraging my previous experience at Morgan Stanley.

Choosing ISI was straightforward for me. First, working closely with Ed promised valuable insights into global economic trends, which would significantly improve my commodity forecasts and stock picking and enhance my ability to be the top Big Oil analyst on Wall Street again.

Second, because Ed was arguably the most renowned analyst

in the history of Wall Street, I would have a front row seat to the best way of producing and marketing research to the largest investors in the world. This proved to be a game-changer for me. I quickly retired the conventional and uninspired "Soviet style" template that was prevalent on Wall Street and adopted Ed's user-friendly format with PowerPoint charts and graphs, concise commentary, and clear investment opinions. I incorporated video presentations and made my research more accessible which immediately led to a significant increase in traction with investors and leaders in industry and government too.

Third, ISI was highly efficient and entrepreneurial with minimal bureaucracy. Because most analysts built their franchises from the ground up and were leaders in their categories, no one had a deeper understanding of the competitive dynamics in their market or had more at stake in case of competitive errors. Most analysts were experienced senior types who felt a research director would not add value, and so almost everyone was happy that we didn't have one. Plus, the firm made clear their expectations for performance through an annual or semiannual meeting that covered outcomes, goals, compensation, and plans for improvement. Our team comprised driven, self-sufficient individuals who thrived on autonomy and wanted to be rewarded for excellence.

Most of my colleagues at ISI also had interesting lives outside of work which made them enjoyable to be around. There were former Davis Cup tennis players, numerous low-handicap golfers, and college athletes from several other sports too.

Ed and Vinayak Singh assembled a team that felt like the perfect fit for me, offering both fairness and a pure, competitive meritocracy that I believed was ideal for Wall Street. Their commitment to doing "first-class business in a first-class way," a mantra that resonated with me from my early days at Morgan Stanley, was equally appealing. I looked forward to teaming up with them and hoped to build the top energy team on Wall Street all over again.

Importantly, ISI also let me work from Fairhope—an

unusual arrangement since almost every Wall Street analyst was required to be in New York City circa 2009. My argument was that our investor clients wouldn't care where I lived if I was adding value to their investment process. Not to mention that having a two-minute commute across the golf course every day to a smaller office free of distraction would allow me to be much more productive. Both turned out to be the case as I consistently placed at the top of the investor polls while at ISI. No doubt my outstanding quality of life was a factor in this success and probably added years to my career.

My first day at the firm in June of 2009 was a microcosm of what lay ahead. After Ed introduced me during the morning meeting, he indicated that he, Vinayak, and I would join several clients for dinner. We were instructed to meet by the giant aquarium in ISI's offices after the market closed around 4 p.m. I looked forward to dinner and didn't ask questions. We met up, went downstairs, and climbed into a black car that took us from Midtown to the 23rd Street heliport along the East River waterfront. From there, we boarded a helicopter to East Hampton where we took another black car to the Maidstone restaurant for dinner.

Our dinner guests were an impressive group of luminary investors—Marty Cohen, Dan Loeb, George Soros, Marty Zweig, and Dwight Anderson—most of whom I knew during my time at Morgan Stanley. These guys were in their prime at that time and the dinner conversation flowed around geopolitics, economics, and specific investment insights, each one bringing a deeply informed perspective.

George Soros shared insights from his recent book, discussing his reflexivity theory against the backdrop of the efficient market hypothesis. He credited this concept with helping him foresee and navigate the 2008 financial crash during which time his Quantum fund rose 10% while the average hedge fund declined 19%. While some parts were abstract and I didn't understand them all, his main point was that positive feedback processes, by reinforcing themselves, can drive systems away from equilibrium, sparking movements in the opposite direction and potentially leading to market bubbles. George believed that his concept of reflexivity offered a better framework for explaining and predicting events, arguing it should be taken seriously as an addition to our understanding of reality. Given his exceptional performance during the crisis, his insights commanded everyone's full attention.

After dinner we flew back to Manhattan. I have to say, the helicopter flight with Ed and Vinayak was a major upgrade from those of my days as an oil field engineer in the stormy Gulf of Mexico a few decades earlier. I was excited to be at the firm.[47]

When I settled into my new role at Evercore ISI in the early 2010s, the energy market was looking optimistic. During the Era of the Super-Major between 1998-2008, the return on equity for S&P Energy soared from 20% to 200% of the S&P 500's return on equity,[48] reaching levels not seen since the early 1980s. Energy profits made up an impressive 25% of S&P 500, making it the third-largest sector in the market by 2008. Investors responded by raising S&P Energy's share of S&P 500 from 4% to 14% by the end of the period. Energy not only

---

47. ISI was successful with its strategy and was purchased by Evercore in 2014 for $440 million in stock. Evercore equity quadrupled since the acquisition. Today, Evercore ISI consistently ranks as a leading research firm on Wall Street. An impressive distinction is that it often has the highest number of analysts ranked #1, 2 or 3 in the II poll, despite having significantly fewer total analysts than larger firms such as JP Morgan and Merrill Lynch. Their research quality is outstanding and used by leading investors around the world.

48. Return on Equity (ROE) measures the profitability of a company in relation to its shareholders' equity. It is calculated by dividing a company's net income by its shareholders' equity. ROE indicates how effectively a company utilizes its equity capital to generate profits and is used by investors to evaluate a company's financial performance and management efficiency. The rise in the energy sector's ROE from 20% to 200% of the S&P 500's ROE indicates an unusual and substantial improvement.

outperformed all other S&P 500 groups during the Super-Major phase but did so by a significant margin, doubling the performance of the next closest sector.

The future looked bright for energy stocks, assuming companies remained committed to the value-centric approach that had driven their success. And early indications were positive that shareholder alignment would remain robust. Companies were selective with investment because entities were striving for higher returns on capital and improved company valuations. With balanced increases in oil supply and demand, crude oil prices were healthy too. This was the model for success for an increasingly mature, highly cyclical industry, and prosperity prevailed across the sector.

The understanding between investors and energy company management teams was clear: investor support would continue as long as the companies adhered to the value-based approach and their results remained competitive with other sectors of S&P 500. Positive performance on capital allocation, cost reduction and portfolio management were key factors and expected to lead to strong results on full cycle metrics such as returns on capital employed and economic value added (i.e., ROCE and EVA). These were the standard benchmarks for evaluating companies in other cyclical industries, and they played a significant role in determining market valuation. Performance on these metrics was important as investors were always looking for the highest potential for value creation, regardless of the market sector.

At the same time, any departure from the successful approach of the prior decade would prompt investors to divest energy stocks, a quid pro quo that was made clear to energy management teams. Although investors were optimistic that emphasis on value creation would continue, my interactions with some of the world's largest institutional, sovereign wealth, and hedge fund investors revealed they were on watch for deviations in strategy. This was their job.

While it started slowly, cracks in the façade began to appear in 2010 and 2011. Capital investment began to climb both in absolute terms and relative to shareholder distributions, signaling the first deviations from the value-based model. The trends were also unfavorable when compared to other sectors of S&P 500.

In North America, the escalation became stark: investment surged from $120 billion in 2009 to an astonishing $270 billion by 2014. U.S. E&P companies led the way, with spending jumping from $100 billion to $237 billion, accounting for 90% of the overall rise. This spending spree focused on developing shale resources, which saw oil production leap from 1.0 to 4.0 MMBPD by 2014, with an additional 1.0 MMBPD expected in 2015. Some Wall Street analysts even began to suggest that there was a "call on U.S. shale," as if Saudi Arabia would sit by idly and cede control of the global oil market to debt-heavy, high-cost marginal U.S. E&P players.

U.S. E&P companies could not spend money fast enough, turning to Wall Street to raise more capital whenever funds ran low, only to spend it again. From 2010 to 2014, they spent 130% of their cash flow and planned to continue overspending to expand shale production.

Overseas spending ramped up as well, from $300 billion in 2009 to $480 billion by 2014. Brazil, Canada, Iraq, Kazakhstan, Russia, and Saudi Arabia led the way in oil supply investments, while spending on natural gas, especially LNG, was notably high in Australia, Papua New Guinea, and Qatar. Because everyone seemed to be increasing spending at once, many investment projects were plagued by delays and cost overruns. According to the IHS Herold Global Projects Database, large oil and gas projects, as well as those in infrastructure and mining, were typically 80% over budget and delayed by an average of 20 months! The result was financial performance that fell short of expectations.

Increased spending is not inherently problematic as resource companies need to replace and expand production to justify their existence. However, if such growth comes at the expense of economic value, resulting in a lower market valuation, it is counterproductive. It was crucial for energy sector management teams to accurately assess whether potential investments would deliver value. If not, reallocating capital to reduce debt, buy back equity, or even consider the sale of the company could be better for shareholders.

As spending ramped up, the assumption was that reinvestment opportunities were plentiful and that returns would be high. However, this assumption was questionable because new investments in U.S. were focused on shale oil and gas which had very different characteristics than conventional wells and minimal performance history.

For companies that forged ahead and spent to grow production even at the expense of returns and value creation; valuation and share prices would eventually falter, and it was only a matter of time. While more growth may seem more appealing than less growth in all industries, the Wall Street Journal quoted me saying, "the market is indifferent as to whether companies are larger or smaller but instead that they become more valuable." This was the hardest learned lesson for energy investors and corporates over the past three decades.

Companies tried to ease investor worries by offering optimistic projections based on selective financial metrics like EBITDA (earnings before interest, taxes, depreciation, and amortization)[49] but without showing the connection to overall financial results. While EBITDA measures a company's profitability in its core operations it does so without considering the impact of financing decisions, accounting practices, or tax jurisdictions. Since it only offers a partial view of financial performance, it was akin to taking your temperature with a thermometer that only went to 50° F.

And Wall Street E&P analysts embraced the practice. Despite ROCE being a reliable indicator of a company's performance and valuation across all major market sectors, analysts focusing on E&P argued that ROCE and EVA weren't applicable due to various timing and other factors. While some points were

---

49. Internal Rate of Return is used to evaluate the profitability of an investment. It represents the annualized rate of earnings on an investment over its holding period, considering the timing and magnitude of cash flows.

credible, legendary investors like Warren Buffett generally scoffed at such viewpoints saying: "people who use EBITDA are either trying to con you or they're conning themselves. Use of EBITDA has cost a lot of investors a lot of money." Buffet's former partner Charlie Munger put it more bluntly: "Every time you see the word EBITDA, you should substitute the word bullshit earnings."

Wall Street E&P analysts urged investors to buy companies that were rapidly increasing production, suggesting that substantial outspending of cash flow in early-stage assets was normal and would eventually lead to positive outcomes for shareholders. This advice persisted even though the geological potential, technological learning curve, and overall returns from U.S. shale operations were unknown at the time.

While these companies were boosting their production levels, they were simultaneously eroding value with each dollar invested. In other words, they were compounding value destruction because the more they invested, the more their returns, market valuation, and share prices were likely to fall. To improve transparency and show that capital was being invested effectively, we recommended that E&P companies report the performance of their shale businesses separately from their traditional oil and gas activities. That not one company took me up on my suggestion was a major red flag.

While this "dash for growth," as some called it, was like that which led to massive value destruction prior to the Era of the Super-Major when S&P Energy declined from 28% to 4% of S&P 500 during 1980-1998, Wall Street E&P analysts cheered the new models promoted by management teams. They also supported management incentive pay packages that rewarded production growth without regard for value creation. The phrases ROCE or CROCI, our preferred metrics, quietly disappeared from corporate financial commentary, and investor concerns rose across the sector.[50]

---

50. CROCI or Cash Return on Capital Invested measures the cash earnings generated by a company as a percentage of the capital invested in its operations. It divides gross cash flow by the total capital invested. CROCI illustrates the efficiency in generating cash returns from investments and is useful in comparing

The industry had essentially returned to its old ways, moving away from the value-based approach that had brought prosperity during the Super-Major phase. As the pursuit of growth, even at the expense of value, regained its foothold, my research methodology and my insights increasingly fell out of favor. Some began referring to me as an "artifact," "fossil," and even a "dinosaur," —respectfully, if such a thing were possible.

Honestly, I didn't understand the business model or the slangy, code-like discussions between E&P analysts and E&P management teams at the time. I admit that "I didn't get it" and incoming calls from investors that were still involved in the sector declined significantly.

The divide between my approach and the prevailing one among Wall Street E&P analysts was reaching a critical point, with one of us on the verge of being disrupted and made obsolete in the market. With U.S. E&P companies showing a ROCE of just 7%, even as oil prices soared above $100/bbl in 2014, it was clear that value destruction was pervasive and that a day of reckoning was ahead. At least it was to me. Investor sentiment reflected my concerns with energy short interest reaching a record level—two standard deviations above the norm. In practical terms, this indicated that investor negativity toward energy stocks had only been matched or exceeded 5% of the time over the previous decade.

The "buyer beware" principle was alive and well, and so "Caveat Emptor" became the title of my investment theme for energy stocks. I believed the oil and gas industry was rapidly moving in the wrong direction and that significant change was needed.

By mid-2014, with U.S. shale output growth in overdrive, troubling signs began to threaten the stability of the global

---

performance of companies within the same industry. It is closely related to ROCE which also measures a company's efficiency in using capital to generate returns.

energy sector. Because healthy economic growth is essential for healthy oil demand and prices, steady gains in GDP are important for energy companies. However, economic concerns were mounting, with the IMF describing the global recovery as "modest, laborious, and fragile." This assessment was consistent with Ed Hyman's outlook, which I echoed in my June 2014 commodity and energy strategy report to investors.

If economic growth and oil demand weakened, OPEC would need to reduce supply to balance the market as they had done in previous years. However, based on my conversations with industry contacts in Saudi Arabia, this was increasingly unlikely, implying that a price war may be ahead. This would be disastrous for many U.S. shale players given their high debt levels.

Initially, the Saudis were content for U.S. E&P companies to spend at high levels to grow production while oil prices were low earlier in the decade since geological "sweet spots" were confined to only 20 U.S. counties and U.S. E&Ps were rapidly depleting their best prospects. However, as oil prices climbed above $100/bbl, there was growing discontent in the Kingdom over higher-than-expected expansion in the U.S. and the resulting loss of revenue and market share.

In September 2014, my concerns were confirmed when Dr. Ibrahim Al-Muhanna, whom I met in Saudi Arabia Oil Minister Ali Al-Naimi's office in Riyadh a decade earlier, made discreet but concerning comments on the topic. While it barely made the news wires, he said "Saudi Arabia is unwilling to make cuts without a contribution from others. It has to be collective action."

This was problematic to me because I thought "others" meant non-OPEC players such as Russia and Mexico, and that output cuts from those countries were highly unlikely.

Dr. Al-Muhanna was regarded as "the power behind the power" as the trusted communications advisor to four Saudi oil ministers starting in the late 1980s. While most energy investors had not heard of him, I always regarded his commentary as "market signaling" during my career. It colored my views on the oil market and my price forecasts. He was a secret weapon of sorts for me and my oil price forecast on Wall Street over the years.

As oil prices hovered around $100/bbl in fall 2014 and the market remained optimistic, I anticipated that lower demand and higher supply were on a collision course in the oil market. In October, I was set to travel to the Kingdom of Saudi Arabia, Qatar, and the UAE with 10 of my top institutional investor clients, hoping to unravel the complexities before other investors in global equity and commodity markets.

Our first meeting was in Abu Dhabi, United Arab Emirates, a major hub for the oil and gas industry. Here, we attended the Abu Dhabi International Petroleum Exhibition & Conference (ADIPEC), one of the energy sector's largest and most prominent events. ADIPEC attendees include government officials, CEOs, policymakers, energy specialists, and innovators, making it the Middle Eastern counterpart to CERAWeek held in the U.S.

In Qatar, we met with executives at ConocoPhillips and Qatar Energy at the Qatargas 3 facility, their world-class LNG complex near Doha. The rapid modernization that has unfolded in Qatar since my initial visit in 1998 always stuns me.

Next, we visited the King Abdullah Petroleum Studies and Research Center (KAPSARC) in Saudi Arabia, where my long-time friend Adam Sieminski, a senior advisor to the board of trustees, hosted us. We also spent time with my late friend Ford Fraker, the former U.S. Ambassador to Saudi Arabia. Following discussions with Aramco's management in Dhahran, we toured the Manifa Field, an engineering marvel. Our visit to the Middle East was well-timed, just about a month before OPEC's next meeting on November 27.

We concluded that oil market policy was indeed shifting in the Kingdom. Based on Dr. Al-Muhanna's recent book there were three major changes underway. First, "some in the Ministry, thought that Saudi Arabia's policy was protecting the interest of some high-cost producers such as U.S. shale oil, Russia, Canada and Brazil" and that "Saudi Arabia had lost control of the oil market."

Second, because "oil demand in Saudi Arabia was rising at twice the global rate, higher production was needed to sustain exports because demand-side adjustments were likely to be difficult." Both factors portended higher sustained output from Saudi Arabia.

Finally, Minister Al-Naimi believed that "expensive oil, such as shale, could not survive low oil prices. If prices went to $80/bbl, not only would investments stop but production of expensive oil would decline and the fall in production would be deeper if prices fell to $50 or $60/bbl." His position was supported by an IEA report in October of 2014 that indicated that oil prices below $80/bbl would threaten a whopping 2.6 MMBPD of global oil production.

These points were made crystal clear on our visits to the Middle East. After returning to the U.S., James West, perennially the top Oilfield Services analyst on Wall Street, and I published a research report detailing our meetings in the Middle East. In early November, we hosted a conference call with investors to share our insights. The consensus widely believed the comments of OPEC Secretary General el-Badri who indicated that Saudi Arabia would announce output reductions of 0.5-0.8 MMBPD at their upcoming November meeting. This led to widespread expectations of a cut in production and higher oil prices.

We disagreed. In our published report and on our conference call with investors we indicated that "because Saudi Arabia's financial position is very strong today, and maybe because their security system is stronger as well especially in relation to the pre-Arab Spring condition, it seems like they are less motivated to support prices at higher levels.

" When considering that a production response from OPEC later this month would effectively transfer production from poor producing countries in OPEC to rich producing countries such as the U.S., which would not sit well with the local population, nor would it be in Saudi Arabia's best longer-term interest, we doubt that OPEC will lower output on November 27.

"So, while the combined market imbalance is not onerous by historical standards that is in relation to 1986 and 1998, it is meaningful enough such that a broad set of contributions from interested parties will likely be needed to restore market balances and for prices to be sustained at higher levels over the intermediate term. That is, OPEC leaders appear content to let the market sort it out and while lower prices will elicit changes to demand and supply, it will not happen overnight but instead over a few quarters."

If this were the case, oil prices would decline, and we advised investors to reduce positions in energy stocks. Our call was significantly opposed to consensus, which broadly accepted the public statements from the head of OPEC. Our position turned out to be correct though as OPEC agreed to roll-over quotas in November 2014. Dubbed the "Thanksgiving Day Massacre," the oil market was stunned, and prices collapsed and fell much lower than we thought.

In Saudi Arabia Oil Minister Ali Al-Naimi's book, he summarized the situation of growing supplies from high-cost sources and weaker than expected demand: "I don't think it's fair for us to defend prices just for the sake of defending prices. It will come at the expense of market share. If we want to cut back, then it has to be collaborating with other non-OPEC producers who need to come to the table."

This meant supply reductions would be required from Russia, Mexico, Kazakhstan, and other non-OPEC players who did not normally participate in efforts to balance the market. In that case, a new supply management consortium would be needed, and its construction was likely to be time-consuming.

Indeed, the process stretched out as oil prices remained low throughout 2015, hitting an unusually low point of $30/bbl in February 2016. Prices eventually recovered later that year after OPEC and non-OPEC countries agreed to cut supply. While our caution toward crude oil and energy stocks was warranted, our outlook wasn't bearish enough; energy stocks fell by 35% by the end of 2015, significantly underperforming the S&P 500.

While there were many confident views about the resilience of U.S. shale and its economic viability at lower crude oil prices, the market would deliver the ultimate verdict. It reminded me of the debate between Saudi Arabia and Venezuela in 1998 as to who had the lowest break-even price on oil production. The fact that the largest E&P companies faced a collective cash flow shortfall of $35 billion even with oil prices near $100/bbl indicated a brutal reality check was ahead for many E&P boards and management teams and their sell-side cheerleaders.[51] This turned out to be an understatement as 450 U.S. E&P and Oil Service companies eventually declared bankruptcy.

In 2016, with oil prices around $50/bbl, we calculated that E&P spending needed to drop by 40%, or an astounding $100 billion, to achieve cash flow neutrality.[52] Despite their reluctance, collapsing cash flows and the drying up of debt and equity markets forced companies to cut back on investments. The rig count dropped below the level necessary to replace production in key shale regions like the Bakken, Permian, and Eagle Ford and the rout was on.

Not only did output growth stop, but production fell by around 1.0 MMBPD during 2016-2017, with other non-OPEC countries also seeing production declines due to lower oil prices impacting cash flow for investments.

---

51. Cash flow shortfall of $100 billion indicates the external cash needs from equity or debt financing for the industry at oil prices of $50/bbl.

52. Cash flow neutrality refers to the point that a company's cash inflows from operations (such as revenue from oil sales) equal its cash outflows (such as operating expenses and capital expenditures). With oil prices of only $50/bbl, cash outflows were significantly higher than inflows, necessitating a reduction in spending or new sources of debt or equity.

Ultimately, expectations for non-OPEC supply growth declined by almost 3.0 MMBPD between 2014-2016 supporting the IEA's original assessment. With the ROCE for U.S. E&P standing at just 3% in 2016, using normalized oil prices of $75/bbl, the debate over whether heavy shale investments would reward shareholders was settled.

Rapid increases in investment had obscured significant financial and strategic misjudgments, leading to vast value destruction. Investors continued to divest the sector, forcing widespread reevaluation among U.S. E&P boards and management teams.

As the #1 ranked analyst in the II poll, my research reached most major energy investors, management teams, and boards worldwide. My stance was well known—if not, it could easily be discovered through my widely disseminated research reports and video content. "Everyone knows Doug," as the CEO of one of the Super-Majors responded when asked the question at a meeting.

With the industry in a difficult position, I hoped to use my platform to lead another major movement that would boost industry prosperity and, admittedly, maintain my relevance in the market. I thought that if my thesis was well-reasoned and included a credible path to value creation, that widespread adoption would lead to positive change in the industry—returning to a more prominent place among the 10 other sectors of S&P 500.

Because many of the questionable practices that the E&Ps were employing were also in place at Big Oil and Oil Service companies, we expanded our message to include the whole energy sector. We wanted every large U.S. Energy company under our revival tent and focused our message on the 30 largest U.S. energy entities contained in S&P Energy. Because there would be a trickle-down effect on smaller companies if we were successful, widespread industry change was expected.

Like my "Era of the Super-Major" and "Golden Age of Refining" theses, we were starting from an unenviable position. S&P Energy had declined from 14% to 6% of S&P 500 during 2008-2016 because Big Oil, E&P, and Oil Service companies used shareholder capital in unproductive ways. There was simply too much capital chasing too few advantaged investment opportunities and the situation was exacerbated by U.S. energy companies backed by private equity which increased from 40 in 2006 to 120 by 2016.[53] One U.S. E&P CEO jokingly remarked to me that all one needed to be an energy private equity firm was "a phone, a dog, and a pick-up truck." And that was the way it seemed. Because many private players followed the same destructive investment practices of the public entities, the market was crowded with undisciplined players, making prolonged hardship likely.

International markets were becoming more difficult too. Companies like Sinopec, PetroChina, Statoil/Equinor, and Petrobras rose in prominence and captured investment opportunities once dominated by the Super-Majors. Their market capitalizations were nearing those of BP, Shell, and Chevron by 2016. This was well before the privatization of Aramco in 2019—a milestone for which Evercore served as an advisor—and yielded market capitalization greater than all five Super-Majors combined.

Amidst challenging structural conditions, poor capital management, governance issues and low oil prices, the energy sector faced dire straits. Our proposed remedy was contained in our new report: "The Pledge for Greater Capital Discipline and Enhanced Corporate Governance," a.k.a. "The Pledge," in 2016.[54]

The solution we proposed for every company in S&P Energy was laid out in three specific criteria outlined in the

---

53. Cambridge Associates
54. Taking the Pledge, Douglas Terreson, October 18, 2016

Pledge. Once a company met all three conditions, we dubbed them Pledgers. Their stocks would be added to our list of buy-rated stocks at Evercore ISI and were expected to post superior performance in the stock market. There would be no exceptions for any company to the three criteria.

The first criterion required companies to reprioritize investment toward growth in returns and away from growth in output.[55] Companies would acknowledge the imbalance between capital formation and competitively advantaged investment opportunities with disciplined capital spending even if oil prices rose. That is, entities were to keep investment flat even if oil prices increased above normalized price levels of $75/bbl, with surplus capital returned to shareholders.

The level of capital investment was no longer to be dependent upon the level of cash flow and borrowing capacity but instead on the number of projects that would create economic value at normalized oil and gas prices. While the Pledge did not require companies to reduce spending, it did require them to show how higher spending would lead to increased returns and distributions to shareholders over an investable timeframe.[56] [57]

Secondly, companies were to eschew partial profitability measures such as EBITDA, EBITDAX (EBITDA before exploration expenses) and other flavors of the month, both at the business unit and corporate levels. This was because of the financial ruin that their emphasis had created, and the disconnect with the economic interests of shareholders. The adage that "companies can grow EBITDA and destroy economic value with one hand-tied behind their backs" was prominent in U.S. Energy.

We recommended a return to financial measures like ROCE and EVA because they provide a complete financial picture and

---

55. Returns in this case meant Return on Capital Employed or ROCE. Output means production of oil and gas.

56. Hess, under CEO John Hess, had high spending but provided investors a clear path to value creation on its investments.

57. Shareholder distributions typically refer to dividends, special dividends, and share repurchases.

connect to a company's true value in the market. Phrases like "return on capital" and "return of capital," which had mostly vanished from investor materials across the energy sector, stood to make a comeback under the Pledge, driving the kind of success the energy sector saw during the Super-Major era from 1998 to 2008.

Third, the value-based metrics that we espoused were to be tied to CEO compensation to better align management's incentives with the economic interests of shareholders. With the Environmental, Social, and Governance (ESG) movement picking up steam, addressing executive pay relative to performance was crucial to avoid becoming targets for activist investors, especially with poor share price performance in energy. Companies were smart to come on board with this initiative, as activists ramped up activity just a short time later.[58]

"The Pledge for Greater Capital Discipline and Enhanced Corporate Governance" was a call to action for every company in S&P Energy, including giants like ExxonMobil and Chevron, E&P firms such as EOG and Occidental, and service providers like Schlumberger and Halliburton. We aimed for a near-complete reversal in strategy from a growth oriented to a value-based model. By implementing new capital management policies, adopting new performance metrics, and aligning CEO pay with shareholder value, we believed prosperity would return, and the industry would regain its competitive edge against other sectors of S&P 500.

We stated: "Because every Big Oil and E&P company indicates that value creation is occurring, identification of the drivers, including production growth (or declines), margin gains etc. all the way to how higher ROCE and free cash flow will materialize and be returned to shareholders would lead to increased investor interest. Companies would get credit for the

---

58. Activist investors purchase shares or options in a company with the goal of influencing its management and strategic direction, often pushing for changes to increase shareholder value, such as cost-cutting measures, restructuring, or changes in corporate governance.

value creation that they indicate is occurring through higher valuation and stronger performance in the equity market. By contrast, Big Oil, E&P and Service companies that do not commit to plans for higher returns and shareholder distributions are deemed to not have the assets, strategies, and management teams to do so. They will remain unsponsored in the equity market, in our view."

While our "Caveat Emptor" theme to avoid energy stocks unless they conformed to our Pledger value-based model was brusque in the eyes of some, I had a duty to my investor clients, and it wasn't to be a cheerleader for destructive behavior. Companies were being impaired, and we were certain that conditions would worsen. Energy share prices were going to decline further absent change in our view.

I reiterated my published research position every month and reinforced it through monthly videos and quarterly investor conference calls. Despite the onset of "Pledger fatigue" among some investors and corporations, I maintained that without adopting a new direction, companies were on a path to failure, and it was only a matter of time.

While I had positive personal and professional relationships with most CEOs in the industry, I knew that some of these relationships were unlikely to endure considering my uncompromising stance. Suggesting that the value propositions and business models of nearly every company in the sector were obsolete was bound to be met with pushback from CEOs, especially since their strategies were approved by their boards of directors and presented to investors as the best use of shareholder capital.

As the S&P Energy sector's share of the S&P 500 dwindled from 14% in 2008 to 6% by 2016, I projected a further decline to around 2% by 2020 if substantial changes were not made. S&P Energy was about to have its grave danced on, so to speak, which was not in my or my industry's best interest. No disrespect to the late, great, and always interesting Sam Zell the original "grave dancer."

Because many CEOs, especially of small companies knew

that they would never be able to satisfy the criteria of the Pledge, they probably also knew that it was always a trap for them and a game they could not win. The end game for them was to be acquired by an entity that also prioritized partial profitability measures like EBITDA, hoping that mergers which emphasized such measures would elicit a favorable market response. This assumption was flawed because changes in EVA explained most of the MVA post mergers and combinations of this type were routinely punished in the equity market. This was a greater fool's game at its best although it did enable some management teams to cash out of increasingly obsolescent business models before performance deteriorated further.

My partner at Evercore ISI, James West, kept me abreast of CEO thoughts in the Oil Service sector. In short, management teams were not enthusiastic about my "do or die" mandate for the industry. One CEO wished us good luck before informing us that we were kicked off the beer and barbecue circuit in Texas! This was unfortunate because James and I both like Texas and the beer and barbecue circuit (and golf too), but we were convinced that our tough love approach was in the best interest of both investors and the industry at large.

Overall, the response from industry was "thanks, but no thanks." The message from most of the companies was that once oil prices and cash flow improved and their financial health was restored, they would resume aggressive spending and focus on boosting production. They believed investors preferred seeing growth in production over higher return on investment, and thus planned to return to the prior path. However, this approach was likely to fail for two critical reasons.

First, the relationship between returns and company valuation is strongly connected, with an 80% correlation in the U.S. and 70% internationally across all 85 industry subsectors of the entire stock market. It was unrealistic to think that investors expect value creation from the other 81 sectors of the market when determining their investments' worth but would not expect the same from the four sectors within energy—namely, Big Oils, E&P, Oil Services, and R&M.

Second, the "Red Queen" effect was in full force in U.S. E&P and was set to pressure financial outcomes further. My Red Queen analogy came from "Through the Looking-Glass and What Alice Found There" by Lewis Carroll. In the book, the Red Queen tells Alice, "It takes all the running you can do, to keep in the same place. If you want to get somewhere else, you must run at least twice as fast."

The analogy with U.S. shale was that "E&P proclamations for outsized returns and production growth drove capital inflows into U.S. shale. However, few shale players earn ROCE above capital costs after more than a decade of heavy investment. E&P total shareholder return (TSR)[59] was near zero along the way."

We went on to say: "Importantly, as the production base grows, higher spending is needed for stable output with maintenance spending to exceed 80% of the total by 2021. While consensus envisions lower E&P ROCE, declining prospect quality and lower productivity will pressure returns beyond that point. ROCE in U.S. shale has likely peaked in this scenario." U.S. E&P valuations were set to collapse, in our opinion.

And this outcome unfolded: "Deteriorating investment economics and declining capital available for growth did indeed portend peak returns (ROCE) and production growth in U.S. shale. While U.S. E&P valuations collapsed, falling from 22 to 12X (P/E), further declines are likely. U.S. shale entities must reduce spending further to stop the decline in returns, valuation, and share prices, in our view."

Further, we stated that "an important outcome of our Pledger movement is that the historical investment model which assumed that higher oil prices would always lead to higher share prices in energy is disrupted. Higher oil prices, cash flow and production growth will likely remain negative for shareholders as

---

59. TSR stands for Total Shareholder Return. It measures the total return received by a shareholder through both capital appreciation (changes in stock price) and dividends over a period. It provides a comprehensive view of the overall performance of an investment.

increased investment renders diminished returns. Consolidation is the natural path forward for E&P companies either at current share prices or lower share prices in the future." A new strategic phase stood to shrink the number of players and enhance the quality of investment portfolios and investment economics, especially for first movers.[60]

While the response and feedback from most companies was not encouraging, that wasn't the case with the investment community. Investors in North America and Europe—which are the two largest markets for energy equities—overwhelmingly embraced my Pledger call. They agreed that the competitive structure was unfavorable and that consolidation or widespread changes in corporate behavior were requisite for energy to be investable again.

Investors pledged to continue to avoid energy stocks unless there was change and specifically until value propositions became competitive with those from other sectors in the S&P 500. Their position was underscored by institutional holdings in energy, which had declined to decadal lows, and by short interest which remained abnormally high. The latter effectively represented bets against CEOs in energy, which were highly profitable during the period.

The call for change from activists in the energy sector was getting louder too. Well-known activist investors like Carl Icahn, Elliott Management, and Engine No. 1 were reaching out to me, and I suspect my Wall Street peers, more and more about what they considered to be flawed policy on energy capital management and corporate governance. To back up their criticism, they pointed to the collapse in ROCE from 35% near the end of the Super-Major Era in 2008 to 0% in 2014, even though oil prices were similar between the two periods. Their positions would become validated in the court of public opinion, something energy companies would later learn.

---

60. "The Red Queen," Douglas Terreson, February 2, 2019

Even though the idea behind the Pledger initiative was appealing in theory, and investors appreciated my enthusiasm, determination, and confidence, they were skeptical about the likelihood of actual change occurring within the energy industry. In the meantime, they looked for better investment opportunities in other sectors. Even so, I refused to give up because I knew I was on the right track having formed and led a similar movement in energy a decade or so earlier.

If energy companies reformed their capital management policies with a longer-term perspective as the Pledge prescribed, I knew that positive results would be demonstrated in the stock market. Such a shift could potentially trigger a domino effect in corporate behavior like it did during the Era of the Super-Major. Because industry conditions looked likely to remain challenging in 2017, the time was right for new strategies that would serve shareholders. While I was optimistic, crucial tests that would determine the fate of the Pledge were on the horizon.

As 2017 began, I was fortunate to have prototypes for the Pledger model in the largest U.S. R&M companies and a few first movers in Big Oil and E&P too with which to start to validate my thesis in the market. In the R&M sector, fundamental conditions were healthy during 2010 to 2016 and capital was managed effectively which had led to positive performance in R&M stocks.

Phillips66 and Valero CEOs Greg Garland and Joe Gorder correctly anticipated the environment and institutionalized emphasis on selective investment, cost reduction, divestiture of non-strategic assets as key strategies. Shareholder alignment was demonstrated through balance between spending and shareholder distributions, with financial performance measured by value-based metrics such as ROCE, which connected to CEO pay packages.

Because their capital management frameworks were like successful ones in other cyclical sectors, these companies were more likely to have positive comparative performance and to be included in investor portfolios, than that of energy peers. And share price performance was indeed superior.

R&M peer Marathon Petroleum employed Pledger principles too under the leadership of CEOs Gary Heminger and Mike Hennigan. Because the three leading U.S. R&M companies had fulfilled the criteria of our Pledger framework, we recognized them as such in 2017.

In E&P, ConocoPhillips was the frontrunner. CEO Ryan Lance led a return enhancement program called "Value Proposition for a Disciplined, Returns-Focused E&P," aligning seamlessly with the Pledger theme. In prior years, the company reduced capital expenditure by 60% and divested non-core assets worth more than $15 billion to weather the storm. By 2017, they intensified their efforts with a multi-year plan featuring flat spending, divestitures of $5-8 billion, debt reduction of 25%, and a commitment to return 20-30% of cash flow through a $3 billion share repurchase program. ROCE was utilized as a management pay incentive too.

Despite initial skepticism from Wall Street analysts, with ConocoPhillips being the least recommended stock in either the Integrated Oil or E&P sector during its return enhancement phase, we considered the plan to be astute and never doubted CEO Lance's ability to execute it within the specified timeframe. At one point, I was the only prominent Wall Street analyst backing CEO Lance and his stock.

And ConocoPhillips was successful. As financial performance improved, the company eventually repurchased $25 billion of its debt and equity, which was a whopping one-third of its capital employed. ConocoPhillips' equity outperformed every peer in both the Integrated Oil and E&P categories in 2017-2018, providing needed momentum for my Pledger movement.

In Big Oils, BP under CEOs Bob Dudley and then Bernard Looney performed commendably. BP cut operating costs by $7 billion and reduced capital expenditure from $25 billion to $16 billion in previous years. Their 2017 initiative included divestiture of $5 billion in non-strategic assets and maintaining investment at 2016 levels until 2021. The company called it their new "value-based, disciplined investment plan" and introduced a ROCE target of 10% by 2021, with oil prices at $55/bbl.

CEO Dudley promised that the transformation would focus on simplicity, efficiency, and modernization: "We are benchmarking not only against our peers, but also other extractive or capitally intensive industries. This is an area where I know we have a lot still to learn, including how to be more efficient in running our operations, in managing our investments, as well as benchmarking ourselves against 'best-in-class,' and not only energy businesses."

BP clearly embraced the Pledger model, and it was music to my ears.

Chevron also prioritized value creation with its new plans. The company reduced operating costs from $30 to $25 billion and cut spending from $35 to $18 billion over the prior three years. In 2017, Chevron aimed for an additional $5 billion in expense reduction with investment to remain in the $18-20 billion range through 2020. The company refocused operations on the Permian Basin, Deepwater regions, Kazakhstan, and Nigeria, and expected to double its ROCE from 7% in 2016 to 14% by 2020, at oil prices of $60/bbl. The company also used ROCE in its executive pay programs. Performance in Chevron equity was strong with CEOs John Watson and Mike Wirth placing the entity on the path to success for shareholders.

Shell aligned with the value-based model too, achieving a 25% reduction in costs and a 35% decrease in capital investment in the years leading up to 2017. Their new 2017-2020 plan included another 10% reduction in costs, flat capital spending and divestiture of $15 billion in non-strategic assets. Shell also set a ROCE target of 10% with oil prices of $60/bbl. Surplus capital was expected to be significant and used to fund a $25 billion share repurchase program. CEO Ben Van Buerden employed an assertive plan for stakeholders.

Total announced an astute plan for stronger shareholder returns too. They raised their annual cost reduction target from $3 to $4 billion and lowered capital expenditures from $18-

19 billion to a new range of $15-17 billion for 2017-2020. The company increased its divestiture target to $10 billion and targeted ROE of 10% at oil prices of $60/bbl. Importantly, Total also planned to allocate surplus cash flow towards debt reduction and share repurchases, rather than higher spending—a key tenet of the Pledge.

Conspicuously absent from the list of companies adopting the value-based model was industry kingpin ExxonMobil. Investors were optimistic about the company's future though as management met with investors at its annual analyst day in New York City in March 2017. Darren Woods had recently become CEO of ExxonMobil, succeeding Rex Tillerson, who left to serve as secretary of state in the Trump Administration. I had known Darren for years and held him in high regard for his experience and capability.

Our concern for the company was that while corporate ROCE had declined from 34% to 4% since 2008—some of which was related to lower oil and gas prices—returns would be lackluster on new investments too. ExxonMobil's main projects included Kearl Oil Sands in Canada, Kashagan in Kazakhstan, XTO in U.S. Shale, and LNG in Australia and Papua New Guinea. With its balance sheet holding its highest debt to capital ratio in 20 years, investors anticipated a new direction.

The response from the company was more of the same though with key points on financial flexibility, disciplined investment, dividend growth and modest gains in spending very similar to the message from years past. While few investors envisioned major changes from the company since Woods had only been CEO for two months, investors were disappointed, nevertheless.

Overall, the combination of low oil and gas prices and unusually high debt levels required an operational, financial, and strategic pivot across the industry leading up to 2017. Crucially, the programs announced that year restrained spending, prioritized value-based metrics and channeled surplus cash flow to new share repurchase programs instead of higher spending—

core tenets of the Pledge. This marked a significant turning point for the sector particularly because the commitments were set to be maintained through 2020.

The stark reality, however, was that we had only eight companies out of 30 in S&P Energy which met the key criteria that we felt were needed for performance to improve and for share prices to recover. While somewhat promising, only around 25% of companies in S&P Energy had become Pledgers and held value propositions that were competitive with that which investors could get in other industry sectors.

This was not satisfactory, and S&P Energy was likely to extend market underperformance until adoption of the value-based model became widespread. Corporates that refused to take the Pledge were at a stalemate with investors, and equity market performance was set to remain poor. The road ahead looked long and arduous for me and my call. I hoped that investors would not tune me out and that I survived.

However, a remarkable thing started to happen in the stock market. Pledgers made up 80% of the top 10 performing stocks out of 30 in S&P Energy in 2017. This outcome was important because our central premise was that companies that adopted the Pledger model would generate higher returns and valuation and investors would reward them with superior performance in the stock market. If so, other companies would be encouraged to embrace the new model as happened during the Super-Major phase, especially since executive pay was primarily denominated in the shares of their companies.

Naysayers suggested that this unusual market outcome was coincidental, due to random movements in various stocks or not reflective of any underlying theme. In other words, I got lucky. My view from hundreds of meetings with the largest energy investors in the world was different. It was that investors were embracing my Pledger thesis, and that Pledger equities were becoming the preferred vehicle in long-only investment portfolios, whereas non-Pledger equities were often targeted for short selling in hedge fund portfolios. Investors were also clear that they planned to avoid investment in companies which clung to the unsuccessful model of their predecessors since performance was unlikely to improve without new strategies.

And it wasn't just anecdotal; my quantitative findings supported my views and refuted the naysayers too. That energy dispersion of stock market returns was low and intra-sector equity correlations were high, and the highest in S&P 500, suggested that variation of returns was explained by structural, systemic factors rather than idiosyncratic ones.[61] This means that a significant thematic play was being discounted by investors in the energy sector. We were sure that this was true and that the theme was the Pledge.

Indeed, the Pledger narrative increasingly dominated conversations in my meetings with investors and corporates as 2018 commenced. I thought that superior share price performance was a positive feedback loop for companies that chose the new, more optimal path for stakeholders. This trend suggested that Pledger stocks would outperform in the equity market for the foreseeable future. The anticipated corporate domino effect, a shift I had been hoping to see, finally seemed plausible.

With our thesis gaining a toehold with investors and corporates in 2017, my confidence grew. As 2018 began, an important test loomed in March when ExxonMobil and Chevron would hold their annual analyst day meetings. Investors would be gauging commitment to the value-based model from these standard bearer entities. With S&P Energy lagging behind the S&P 500 in seven of the eight previous years, investors anticipated new direction.

But it didn't happen.

---

61. Dispersion refers to the degree of variability or spread in the returns of individual stocks within a particular sector or market index. Low dispersion means that individual stock returns within the sector are closely clustered around the average return, indicating similar performance among stocks. Intra-sector equity correlations measure the degree to which individual stock prices within the same sector move in relation to each other. High intra-sector correlations indicate that stocks within the sector tend to move together, reflecting common sector-wide influences or market conditions.

ExxonMobil repudiated the Pledger thesis by announcing an increase in capital spending from $23 billion in 2017 to a whopping $35 billion per year during 2019-2024, justified by an "advantaged" investment opportunity set. The massive rise in spending was expected to lead to an increase in upstream volume of 25% by 2025. While guidance was provided for some financial measures, there were no targets for ROCE or EVA, nor were they emphasized at the meeting.

Investors were outraged that ExxonMobil appeared to be aligning with the production-compounder wing of the Wall Street analyst community and that priority for value creation and stronger share price performance was not higher.

I gave Chairman Woods the opportunity to neutralize these concerns in the public Q&A: "When considering the execution risk that plagued the Super-Majors during the past decade, are there changes to the capital budgeting process or project selection or is it really just an improvement in portfolio quality that gives you confidence that you're going to be able to deliver the new plan? And second, are changes to incentive compensation needed to drive these gains or do you think that management is already aligned with shareholders enough to accomplish your objective?"

Chairman Woods highlighted the robust capital management process inside the company and emphasized that competitive advantage was required for investments to proceed. Because the company had industry leading technology and was able to leverage advantages throughout the organization, they expected to be successful.

While management pay and performance was an unusual and awkward topic to bring up at an analyst day meeting for any company, investors felt strongly that shareholder alignment was poor at ExxonMobil and its Super-Major peers. Activists felt the same way and most companies seemed to underestimate the threat at the time.

Chairman Woods indicated that "our compensation system is very well aligned with the shares in the market. When our shares don't perform, our pay goes down. I mean, that is a one-for-one correlation. So, I would tell you that the incentives are there. I don't think that's the root of the issue."

Although ExxonMobil's management compensation was primarily in company shares, the value of these pay awards depended on their performance relative to other Super-Majors. The problem was that the other Super-Majors consistently posted negative EVA and underperformed S&P 500. This meant that management could receive substantial compensation as long as their value destruction was less severe than that of their peers, an outcome that investors found unacceptable. While ExxonMobil was not the only Super-Major that earned less than its cost of capital in the prior three years, it was the only one that investors thought resisted change, and increased alignment with shareholders. My sidebar conversation with Chairman Woods revealed that, al-though we found some agreement on aspects of my proposed framework, there was a significant lack of alignment overall—a disappointment both for me and for the growing groups of investors who were pushing for reform.

The next day Chevron met with the analyst community in Midtown Manhattan at the St. Regis hotel. Fortunately, their plan reflected close alignment with my value-based model. The company indicated plans to reduce spending and for it to remain low through 2020 and provided specific cost reduction and di-vestiture goals. Clear targets for cash flow and returns on capital were also provided which enabled investors to close the loop on the likely level of valuation and Chevron's share price. Chevron demonstrated complete alignment with our Pledger doctrine which was positive progress and an exhale moment for me.

My question to Chevron Chairman and CEO Mike Wirth went to the core of Chevron's commitment to the Pledge: "Mike, today's spending guidance indicates that Chevron's spending per distributions is going to decline by more than any of your Super-Major peers through 2020, which is important because this usually leads to higher returns and valuation. And so, while this is a really positive framework for investors, the risks have historically been, one, management's ability to stay committed when the oil and gas price rises and, two, to manage the transition internally. So, my question is, what are you doing to mitigate these risks? And why are you confident that Chevron's going to be able to manage its pledge successfully over the next several years for shareholders?"

Mike responded: "I've grown up in businesses where returns were always the focus. You always believe that the market tomorrow was going to be tougher than the market you face today, and self-help is the one thing you can control and the one thing you can focus on to get better. Growth in volume is not necessarily the objective. You can grow a lot of empty barrels that don't bring any value, so you really must think about growth in earnings and growth in returns. And if you have that mindset, you begin to set up your definition of success along those lines. You set up the metrics by which people are evaluated and compensated along those lines, and you drive that down through the organization so that everybody understands their piece. And so, I think really the challenge is for us not to be seduced by the price cycle. Prices will be higher, and prices will be lower in the future, and we can't build our business around a view on price. We need to build our business around a view on efficiency and competitiveness. How do we benchmark every single area that we operate versus the best operators, be that downstream or upstream? And how do you win in any environment? That's what I fundamentally believe is the right way for us to run our business. It's the way we're organizing ourselves and measuring ourselves."

This was exactly what the investment community wanted to hear. Investors bet that Chevron performance would be superior to that of ExxonMobil given substantial differences in capital management strategy. And that is exactly what happened. ExxonMobil not only fell behind Chevron but also trailed every other Super-Major peer for the third consecutive year in 2018. It was evident that investors were distinguishing between the two models, with the Pledge holding the winning hand.

In the E&P sector, Occidental joined ConocoPhillips in embracing the value-based model in 2018. However, throughout the E&P sector overall, phrases like "return on capital" or "return of capital" were still largely missing from annual reports and analyst presentations.

Instead, most E&P company value propositions emphasized increased spending and production growth. While industry consolidation had the potential to reset the structural and investment landscape and reframe the ongoing debate, this seemed improbable without another drop in oil prices. The pace of change in the E&P and Oil Service sectors was glacial and resistance remained firm.

The problem behind the problem was that corporate governance, specifically the financial incentives that were driving management behavior, were outdated and grossly misaligned with shareholders. Until it changed, results were unlikely to improve, leading investors to continue to avoid the sector and for short sellers to press their bets.

Our report titled "Energy's Corporate Governance and Share-holder Alignment Problem" was unambiguous and sought to expose shareholder misalignment, which was a needed last resort that we hoped would get the sector back on track.[62] We began by detailing the compensation structure for CEOs in the energy sector which was: 10% salary, 20% annual bonus, and 70% long-term pay.

While salary was fixed, annual bonuses were set by performance against preset goals and paid out in cash after one year. For Big Oil CEOs, annual pay incentives used worthwhile financial metrics like earnings, cash flow, and return on capital. For E&P CEOs, emphasis was on production growth and operational efficiency. Because the ratio of pay incentives for resource growth to value creation was a staggering 10:1 in 2016, shareholder outcomes were almost certain to be poor with E&P CEO pay incentives negatively correlated with TSR. This meant that E&P companies were investing shareholder capital in ways

---

62. "Energy's Corporate Governance & Shareholder Alignment Problem," Douglas Terreson, June 11, 2018

that were averse to shareholder interests.

Long-term pay structures, which were the largest part of pay packages, also presented problems. In this area, Big Oil CEO pay was mostly determined by ROCE and TSR relative to Big Oil peers. In E&P, TSR relative to E&P peers set 80% of compensation. Because few companies emphasized measures that connected to intrinsic value in the market, it was not surprising that valuation in the stock market was collapsing. This also explained why the energy sector was the worst-performing sector in the S&P 500 over 1, 3, 5, and 10 years.

Another important distinction was that energy and utility companies utilized TSR relative to peers more than the other nine groups of the S&P 500. The problem was that when the industry was in value-destruction mode, as it had been during the previous decade, CEO pay could remain high as long as management teams destroyed less value than their peers. This was obviously not the path to prosperity for shareholders in any industry and undermined shareholder alignment.

The effect that energy boards had by allowing CEOs to make target pay with median TSR, but against the worst performing sector in S&P 500, was that Big Oil and E&P ROCE was only 4% with TSR of -50% during the previous five years. By contrast, S&P 500 ROCE was at 11% with TSR at 40% during the same period. Because energy returns and valuation became the lowest of the 20 cyclical investment options in S&P 500, investors avoided the sector and institutional holdings of energy shares declined to 10-year lows.

Effectively, many energy CEOs were more incented to "follow the herd" or "closet index" than to grow value on an absolute basis. Because many investors were cognizant of this issue, they would remain aligned with our "Caveat Emptor." Avoid investment view on energy stocks, until it changed.

Continuing poor performance was not in anyone's interest and better practices were needed. The solution was for boards to provide annual pay incentives for CEOs that were positively correlated to shareholder returns. In longer-term pay plans, boards in other cyclical sectors like Industrials, Materials, and Technology required S&P 500 as a key peer comparator, setting a higher bar for performance which rewarded their shareholders with superior returns, valuation, and positive market outcomes. Investors preferred CEO performance to be benchmarked against S&P 500 too, like that of their investment management performance fees.

Slowly but surely, investor pressure began to shift practice in the energy sector. From 2016 to 2019, the ratio of E&P CEO incentives tied to production growth versus value creation dropped from a staggering 10:1 to a balanced 1:1. By the early 2020s, the S&P 500—once rarely used—had become the most common comparator for energy CEO pay, much to our delight.

As positive governance changes became widespread, the bar for performance rose across the energy sector. Some investors concluded that they could probably forego the 90% of sell-side research covering operational and financial factors and still get the energy stocks right if they understood the 10% on corporate governance, CEO pay incentives and alignment with shareholders. I concurred, especially for investors with medium to longer-term time horizons.

While it was remarkable that the Pledge delivered 80% of the top 10 performers in the equity market in S&P Energy in 2017, this highly abnormal outcome unfolded again in 2018. While I was confident that the result was not a coincidence, recurrence in 2018 ended the debate on the merits of the Pledge and its effects in the stock market.

Heading into 2019, I was confident that a "Three-Peat" was ahead, and that Pledger performance would remain superior. In our January report of the same title, we indicated that "the Pledge would remain the predominant investment theme in Energy." We stated: "It will be increasingly important for investors to further differentiate between entities with focused strategies for higher returns (Pledgers) and avoid those that cling to the failed growth at the expense of returns strategies of their predecessors (non-Pledgers). The former strategy was the path to prosperity for energy investors in 2017-2018. These companies provide credible pathways for value creation and return of capital to shareholders as is the case for successful companies in other sectors of S&P 500. Their equities are being sponsored by investors in the equity market.

"For companies that resist adoption of value-based strategies and CEO pay incentives, or to recapture lost value through consolidation, their equities will remain decoupled from crude oil prices, in our view. The reason: while higher oil prices will be positive for cash flow, production growth, and CEO pay, until CEOs are no longer incented to spend as returns diminish, higher oil prices will be negative for shareholders. Investors will continue to avoid these equities due to clear misalignment with shareholders.[63]

"The buy-side is enforcing the Pledge in that a strong positive relationship (80%) has materialized between E&P, ROCE, and valuation (EV/IC)[64] in the equity market. The trend will persist and companies that demonstrate Pledge-like behavior and post higher ROCE, will receive higher valuation and superior performance in the equity market, in our view. Their equities will remain the top 'long-only' investment opportunities in energy."

I pressed my bet because rising investor support for my movement gave me confidence that full industry adoption was ahead. For the first time, there seemed to be light at the end of the tunnel. While less than 30% of the companies in the S&P Energy index pledged allegiance to the model and broader commitment was needed, Pledger market performance was unequivocally superior. It seemed to only be a matter of time

---

63. "Three Peat," Douglas Terreson, January 22, 2019

64. Enterprise Value / Invested Capital is used to assess the efficiency of capital deployment by a company. It compares the enterprise value (market value of equity plus net debt) to the total invested capital, which includes both equity and debt. This ratio helps evaluate how effectively a company utilizes its invested capital to generate returns for shareholders.

before the rest of the energy sector adopted the model. The momentum was in our favor.

In March of 2019, the final major test of investor preference would unfold and in a high-profile way. The market would clarify whether Pledger outperformance was random, as the naysayers still hoped, or instead reflective of an underlying theme, namely adherence to our value-based model.

That month, Chevron approached Anadarko Petroleum with an offer to acquire Anadarko for around $64 per share in a 75/25 stock-cash bid. Occidental responded with an offer near $72 per share in a 60/40 stock-cash split. Because Chevron counteroffered, Occidental increased its bid to $76-per-share, payable 50/50 in cash and in Occidental stock. Because a higher bid from Chevron was value destructive based on our calculations—and oppositional to Chevron CEO Mike Wirth's pledge to conform to the value-based model—Chevron abandoned its pursuit.

Wirth stated: "Winning in any environment doesn't mean winning at any cost. Cost and capital discipline always matter, and we will not dilute our returns or erode value for our shareholders for the sake of doing a deal." This was Pledger doctrine at its finest. Occidental won the Anadarko acquisition sweepstakes.

While the transaction was accretive to EBITDA and would secure Occidental's dividend payments to shareholders, it was massively dilutive to ROCE. The market was about to demonstrate which financial measure had the greatest effect on share prices, with our bet squarely on ROCE, EVA, and MVA. The battle lines were drawn.

Because Evercore was the advisor to Anadarko on the transaction, I was restricted from verbal or written communication until the purchase closed a few quarters down the road. However, I estimated that Occidental's ROCE, valuation, and share price would decline by a third due to the transaction. They clearly overpaid for Anadarko and the winner's curse stood to be alive and well for Occidental. If so, it could potentially be one of the most questionable uses of shareholder capital in the energy sector in recent decades.

Investors sided with me, and Occidental equity collapsed from $70 to $45 per share between March when the transaction was announced to August when it closed. Occidental's underperformance, especially when compared to S&P E&P, the broader energy sector, and the overall market, was remarkable.

Because Occidental betrayed their prior pledge to the value-based model with the dilutive acquisition of Anadarko Petroleum, we downgraded the stock when my published research restriction was lifted on August 12, 2019.

The next day, activist Carl Icahn released an open letter to Occidental stockholders. The first part was taken verbatim from my report the previous day and contained my primary points:

"Then yesterday, a highly regarded Wall Street analyst published a report that we believe further confirms our views and further supports our thesis that the status quo at OXY is not working for stockholders. The analyst made the following observations:

- "The Company's 'Pledge' for greater capital discipline and enhanced corporate governance proved fleeting with ROCE [Return on Capital Employed] *to decline significantly* due to the Anadarko transaction."
- "The purchase of Anadarko makes Occidental larger but significantly less valuable."
- "…while the company indicates that it is 'focused on returns,' *the Anadarko transaction appears 30% dilutive to ROCE*. Because returns are well associated with valuation in the equity market in energy…Occidental's equity declined by 30% since the transaction was announced. *It is the worst performer of U.S. large-capitalization E&P companies in 2019.*"
- "Occidental's capital management choice is problematic because of *significant value destruction*, but also because it contrasts with management's stated emphasis to be 'focused on returns.' *The move also violates the company's 'Pledge' for greater capital discipline and enhanced corporate governance.*

"OXY has repeatedly pledged to act prudently and has repeatedly pledged to exercise capital discipline. But, how quickly OXY's pledges were abandoned when CEO Vicki Hollub and the Board, in my opinion, believed their company could become an acquisition target, and therefore quickly pivoted to purchase Anadarko at almost any cost, which they believed, would serve as a de facto poison pill against an acquiror."[65]

While I have not always agreed with Carl over the years (or with many other investors, activist or otherwise, and vice versa), I agreed with the main content of his letter. Primarily because I wrote it the day before.

Regardless, we were emboldened by the market response which completely aligned with our Pledger doctrine. While Occidental stock fell further and declined to less than $10 per share during the COVID year of 2020, the shares have still not recovered to the level before the Anadarko transaction and have been among the worst performers in the E&P group since the transaction in 2019.

During the rest of 2019, my Pledger movement continued to gain support. By the end of the year, the Pledge had again delivered 80% of the top 10 performers in the equity market in S&P Energy—a highly improbable stock-picking outcome in any sector, and in any market anywhere in the world. This outcome could only have happened had the buy-side embraced the Pledge enabling it to become the predominant investment narrative in the global energy sector during 2015-2019. Our call was that a "Four-Peat" was ahead in 2020.[66]

With superior market performance for Big Oil, E&P, and Oil Service companies that embraced the new model (which was really an old model with a new name) the number of holdout non-Pledger companies diminished by 2020. The tide had clearly turned with a key barometer of capital discipline and shareholder alignment—capital expenditures per unit of shareholder distributions, falling from an astonishing 8:1 at the

---

[65]. This last paragraph in quotes was not in my research report and instead was from Icahn's letter directly.

[66]. "Four-Peat," Douglas Terreson, January 21, 2020

beginning of the decade to 2:1 for 2020-2021E.[67] It bordered on career suicide for CEOs to fight the movement at that point given the positive response in the market to companies that conformed. The implication was that the whole industry was indeed adopting the Pledge and that positive performance was ahead.

Concise plans for disciplined capital management and how spending would be balanced with shareholder distributions started to reappear in investor materials with phrases such as return on capital and return of capital becoming prominent again as well. Corporate commentary on production growth, EBITDA, EBIT-DAX, etc. became replaced with more useful commentary on regular and variable dividend yields, and ROCE. To my delight, energy CEOs even started using free cash flow yield to compare the outlook of their company to those of peers to highlight the superiority of their value proposition in the market.

The industry had come full circle and superior market performance by the Pledgers silenced any doubt about the merit of the Pledge. Maybe I wasn't a "fossil" or a "dinosaur" after all.

With this positive new direction, a more constructive investment outlook was warranted, and it was time to retract my negative "Caveat Emptor" investment call and turn positive on energy stocks. Our timing appeared exceptional because sellers of financial ESG products had convinced many investors that non-financial factors (chosen by their firms and conveyed through their financial products), would increasingly set share prices, disrupting centuries old relationships between returns and valuation in markets.

Consequently, money poured into renewable energy investments like wind and solar power, and away from traditional energy sources like oil and gas. This shift was driven

---

67. E is estimated.

by expectations of high investment returns in non-traditional energy sources and that the financial viability of fossil fuel business models would be greatly diminished in the long term. This projection came from expectations of decreasing demand and new regulations supporting cleaner energy and suggested that traditional energy investments would not be profitable or sustainable in the future. In other words, the terminal value of energy assets, which estimate the future worth at the end of a forecast period, for fossil fuels was expected to approach zero, much sooner than previously anticipated. While the market share for fossil fuels had only slightly decreased during the previous decade, from 86% to 82% of the global energy mix, greater losses were expected and in rapid fashion.

As the ESG fund raising model gathered steam, price to earnings ratios approached 50 for Clean Energy ETFs, meaning investors were paying $50 for every $1 of earnings these companies made. This was unusually high compared to price to earnings ratios of eight in traditional energy and 20 in S&P 500 especially since most clean energy companies weren't creating any economic value.

Advocacy groups forced many pension funds and other institutions to divest positions in traditional energy and sentiment towards oil and gas investments plummeted. This created significant headwinds for investors in traditional energy leading to a surge in capital costs for new investments. The mania reminded me of the dot-com bubble of 2000—a time when tech stocks soared in value based on metrics like website visitors and click through rates instead of solid financial metrics like future profitability and return on investment. It also reminded me that while technology significantly outperformed energy and other "old economy" sectors during the earlier period, the craze marked the bottom for the energy sector and that it saw exceptional performance in the stock market over the next decade.

In the current landscape, I felt that peak negativity and peak uncertainty had arrived in energy, and it was time for me to call off the dogs and retire my negative "Caveat Emptor" investment call on Big Oil, E&P, and Oil Service stocks that we had pressed for several years. The light was turning from red to yellow to green, slowly but surely.

By summer of 2020, the drumbeat of activism was becoming even louder too which seemed likely to be the final catalyst that we needed for the entire energy industry to adopt the Pledge. Incoming calls from activists focused on companies that maintained and defended models that were proven to be value destructive.

In discussions with investors and corporates, I indicated that companies underestimated the threat from activists and that those who remained misaligned with shareholders would find themselves in the crosshairs. This was especially true given the contrast in equity market performance between companies that adopted our value-based model and those that stubbornly continued to invest for growth but without public goals for value creation.

My friend Dan Rice's sons, Toby and Derek, started the wave as they were frustrated with results at EQT, a large natural gas company. They sought to replace the entire board and management team. To the surprise of many, they won 80% of the votes for their 12 nominees to the EQT board. The margin of victory was stunning and rebuked the incumbent management team, which had significantly underperformed S&P E&P, S&P Energy, and S&P 500 over the previous three years. It underscored that contempt for shareholder misalignment and lack of management accountability was palpable across the energy sector.

In the Super-Major category, ExxonMobil remained the only holdout to the value-based model. The company maintained that their portfolio of investment opportunities was higher quality than peers, which justified heavy investment. Investors clearly disagreed though as ExxonMobil's stock had underperformed S&P Energy and S&P 500 in four of the past five years.

The facts of the matter were that ROCE declined from 27% during the last two years of CEO Lee Raymond's tenure in 2004-2005 to 2% during 2019-2020, even though oil prices were slightly higher in the more recent period. EVA collapsed as well, falling from over $20 billion to $13 billion during the same timeframe. Because Super-Major peers BP, Chevron, Shell, and Total were already compliant with the Pledger framework, Exx-onMobil underperformed every other Super-Major in the stock market by a whopping 25 percentage points since the Pledger phase began in 2017.

On December 7, 2020, armed with many of these basic points, Engine No. 1, led by Chris James, wrote an open letter to Exx-onMobil's board of directors. The firm proposed changes to strategy and four new board members to be voted on at the May 2021 shareholder meeting. The Wall Street Journal indicated that ExxonMobil was chosen because it had "drawn the ire of a number of large shareholders for its lackluster performance and refusal to engage."

Engine No. 1's key issues were several-fold. First, "ExxonMobil significantly underperformed and has failed to adjust its strategy to enhance long-term value. Second, a focus on chasing production growth over value has resulted in an undisciplined capital allocation strategy and has destroyed value even during periods of higher oil and gas prices. Third, a refusal to accept that fossil fuel demand may decline in decades to come has led to a failure to take even initial steps toward evolution, and to obfuscating rather than addressing long-term business risk. Finally, a lack of successful and transformative energy experience on the Board has left ExxonMobil unprepared and threatens continued long-term value destruction."

Following the release of the letter, the market was abuzz with debate, and I was inundated with calls from investors and corporates. While most believed that Engine No. 1 was unlikely to be successful since they held only $250 million in ExxonMobil equity which equated to 0.02% of the company's shares, I disagreed.

Companies underestimated how fatigued investors were by misguided capital management, unconnected pay and performance, and overall lack of accountability for poor results from management teams. While I agreed that ExxonMobil's portfolio was improving and probably even underestimated, I thought that they would face an uphill climb with their activist threat, and this proved to be true.

In response to Engine No. 1, the company announced a reduction in capital spending of $10 billion, a new target for production growth of zero—which compared to 25% previously for 2025—and new emissions intensity reduction targets. While most were core tenets of the Pledge, we doubted that these concessions would neutralize the threat. There was a lot of water under the bridge with institutional investors, and Engine No. 1 knew it because they were in communication with many of the larger ones every week.

A rule of thumb in proxy contests is that only 70% of shareholder votes are cast, which, in this case, meant that Engine No. 1 might only need around 35% of total votes to get to the winning majority of 51%. Because shareholdings at Black Rock, Vanguard, and State Street exceeded 20% of the total, garnering these votes and those at a few other large institutions would get them over the threshold.

Because many of the larger institutions were members of the Climate 100, and ESG momentum was strong and probably peaking at the time, Engine No. 1 expected their support. This was Engine No. 1's strategy, and because other large investors indicated to me that they would not support ExxonMobil mostly due to poor financial results and resistance to change, Engine No. 1 won the shareholder vote for three board seats.

Because ExxonMobil was the largest and most influential publicly traded oil company in the world in the prior century, this outcome was significant, placing every company in the industry on notice.

Regardless of whether our prediction that ExxonMobil would lose board seats to Engine No. 1 was accurate or not, the signs were clear. The Pledge had become the prevailing corporate strategy in the energy sector well before Engine No. 1's letter to ExxonMobil in late 2020. Successful activist campaigns at EQT, ExxonMobil, Marathon Petroleum, Occidental, and others indicated that the status quo threatened CEOs and boards, no matter how large the company.

In early November of 2020, my outstanding associate Chai Zhao and I prepared our lengthy 60-page upgrade note. It was longer than normal to leave no room for doubt about our new investment viewpoint. As analysts, we always try to identify major turning points in sectors. Little did we know we were about to make a call so precise and improbable that it would mark a defining moment in my 35-year career. The extraordinary timing of our upgrade would only become apparent in the weeks and months ahead and in ways we hardly could have predicted.

While the damage was extensive with S&P Energy falling from 14% of S&P 500 in 2008 to only 2.8% in late 2020, we thought the worst was over. Like the Golden Age of Refining, we thought the negative trade was crowded, failure was priced in, and all bad things had to come to an end.

Even though investing in energy stocks was widely perceived to be high-risk and low reward, we believed the opposite and that energy equities had not only stopped going down but were probably set to rise, especially with positive catalysts ahead. All the ingredients for another upset victory in the market were present just like in the Era of the Super-Major and the Golden Age of Refining, especially if the clean energy bubble popped which seemed likely due to misconceptions regarding economics, chemistry and physics.

Our positive upgrade report was released pre-market November 9, 2020, and was titled "Time to Lean In."[68] Our new call to buy energy stocks would surprise some investors because we had been negative for several years starting with our "Super-Major Revival" report in August of 2015. We conveyed confidence in our call by recommending that investors double or triple weight the energy sector, which is an unusually bold position for an analyst or strategist on Wall Street.[69]

---

68. "Time to Lean In," Douglas Terreson, November 9, 2020

69. Double-weighting and triple-weighting in a stock portfolio refer to strategies where an investor allocates two or three times the typical or benchmark weight to a specific sector. This approach reflects a strong conviction about the sector's future performance. For example, if the benchmark allocation for the technology sector is 10%, a double-weighted position would be 20%, and a triple-weighted position would be 30%. This strategy increases exposure to the targeted sector, amplifying potential gains if the sector performs well, but also increasing risk if the

Our primary points were as follows: "Because the Pledge has become the default corporate strategy for every energy company and consolidation is transferring spending and resources to fewer, more disciplined hands, an investable industry structure is emerging. Combined with stronger oil and gas prices and unusually attractive fundamental, quantitative, and technical factors, the outlook for energy stocks is positive.

"Fundamentally, energy ROCE will rise vs. S&P 500 in 2021-2022 and possibly in sustained fashion. Driving the gains are higher oil prices, substantial declines in operating and capital costs, and stronger capital discipline across the sector. Governance policy whereby CEO pay incentives elicit strategies which connect to economic value are materializing and will be supportive too."

Indeed, "Chevron and Phillips 66 were joined by Apache, ConocoPhillips, Hess, Noble and Pioneer as entities that use S&P 500 as a peer comparator for CEO pay. S&P 500 is clearly a higher bar for CEO pay than energy peers, which were the worst performing sector in S&P 500 over 1, 3, 5, 10 and 20 years. If S&P 500 becomes a significant part of the comparator peer group for CEO pay, then value propositions would become more competitive with S&P 500 on a sustained basis. Investment interest would return to the sector as well, in our opinion.

"Quantitative catalysts support our call as well. Energy places in only the 1st percentile[70] on our composite measure of financial expectations, valuation and technical factors going back to 2000. The implication is that energy has been this attractive only 1% of the time during the past 20 years.

"Technically, our 'Double Bottom for the Ages' call remains operative. Evercore ISI technical guru Rich Ross concurs especially with the recent breakouts in crude oil and various

---

sector underperforms.

70. The 1st percentile indicates the value below which 1% of the observations or data points fall in a dataset. It is often used in statistical analysis to understand the distribution and relative positioning of values within a dataset.

energy indices."

Rich remains the best technical analyst on Wall Street today and demonstrated as much with his correct, highly contrarian market call on S&P 500 in 2023-2024.

We also highlighted the inverse correlation between energy's placement in S&P 500 and 10-year forward returns.[71] We indicated that "if CEOs remain committed to the Pledger value-based model as they all indicated last week at our energy CEO conference, then returns and valuation should rise, and S&P Energy should approach 7% of S&P 500 around 2024."

We thought our note contained everything an investor needed to confidently purchase energy stocks. As the equities rose, we envisioned our report earning a place of honor on the walls and bookshelves of investor offices, a trophy-like outcome for those that followed our recommendation. Energy was expected to be the best performing group in S&P 500, as it was during the Era of the Super-Major.

Energy stocks surged 14% on the day of our upgrade, one of the greatest single-day gains in four decades.[72] While the magnitude of the move was surreal, we indicated the gains would continue if companies stuck with the value-based model. They did, and S&P Energy tripled, becoming the best-performing sector in the S&P 500 by a wide margin. Moreover, the sector went on to post its strongest three-year performance relative to S&P 500 in half a century.

Notably, our upgrade coincided with the exact day S&P Energy reached its lowest price level relative to the S&P 500

---

71. The inverse correlation between energy's placement in the S&P 500 and 10-year forward shareholder returns indicates a cyclical pattern where high returns attract more investment, leading to declines in returns toward the mean. Low shareholder returns often result in capital outflows and increases in returns to the mean.

72. A 14% single day gain in S&P Energy is extraordinary, occurring only 3 times in the last 40 years. However, factors such as the covering of substantial short positions in energy which we knew were near record levels before our upgrade, and a 1.3% gain in S&P 500 supported energy stocks that day too.

in my 35-year career—on both the buy and sell sides. Yes, you read that correctly. The odds of releasing a major upgrade report on the precise day of a sector's bottom are incredibly low, given the complexity, intricacies, and unpredictability of financial markets. While not quite winning-the-lottery rare, it's wildly improbable.

Remarkably, November 9, 2020, also marked the lowest point for energy stocks relative to the market since record keeping began in 1911, as confirmed by our colleagues at Crude Chronicles. In over a century, through wars, recessions, and oil shocks, energy had never traded lower versus the market. To call the bottom that precisely—on that very day—is the kind of things that doesn't just defy odds; it borders on the surreal. Frankly it still feels a little eerie.

While ExxonMobil performed poorly prior to adopting the Pledger model, performance surged in the aftermath. Its stock rose 300%, which compares to original Pledgers BP, Chevron, Shell, and Total at 200%. It was ExxonMobil's best two-year market performance in the equity market in over 50 years as investor confidence in corporate governance, capital management and shareholder alignment rose.

We remained confident that CEOs would stay committed to the Pledge for many of the same reasons they did during the Era of the Super-Major. Specifically, as management teams performed on the value-based model and their share prices rose, they would become empowered to stay the course.

We turned out to be right, and S&P Energy rose from 2.8% of S&P 500 at the bottom in November 2020 when we upgraded the energy group, to 5.6% at the writing of this book.

Mission accomplished.
Now for the caveats.

Like the Era of the Super-Major, our Pledger theme wasn't the sole catalyst for positive change during the period; other significant factors also played a role. It's important to recognize that reductions in operating costs were required at all energy companies, following the sharp decline in oil prices in 2014-2015, and the sustained market weaknesses in 2016-2017 and again in 2020. While companies can only save their way to prosperity for so long, enhanced cost efficiency was undeniably beneficial.

Second, I do not downplay that the companies might have eventually developed and implemented our capital management model on their own. Although the momentum was clearly headed in the wrong direction when we started our Pledger crusade, it could have eventually shifted, especially if CEO pay incentives were properly aligned with shareholders. When early adopters of the Pledge received a positive response in the market, they were empowered to extend their plans to the medium-term. This was a turning point and other companies had to follow. As I said before, "the Pledge was an old model but with a new name."

I also credit the buy-side for effecting the changes prescribed in the Pledge, just as they did during the Super-Major period before it. Investors pressed companies to embrace strategies that were successful in energy and in other cyclical sectors too. That Pledgers were 80% of the top 10 energy stocks in 2017, 2018, and 2019 underscores that the buy-side embraced the Pledge and that adherents to the value-based model were being purchased for portfolios while holdouts were not.

Strategies that emphasize selective investment, balancing spending, and distributions—key principles of the Pledge—are set to continue driving prosperity in the energy sector, much like during the Era of the Super-Major. Catalysts for change often come from unexpected places. Ultimately, it makes no real difference where an idea comes from, but whether it gains traction to eventually have an impact.

Although the gains from the Pledge have not yet reached the heights of the Era of the Super-Major—when S&P Energy's share of the S&P 500 climbed from 4% to 14%—or matched the Golden Age of Refining—which saw a 1,700% increase in R&M stocks—energy shares have tripled off the bottom and the best may be yet to come for energy investors.

9

Can't Deny It

Every angler has that one story—the perfect catch, the battle for "the big one" that got away, that unforgettable day on the water. Tales usually told around a campfire or at the local bait and tackle shop. For me, it's all about a deep-sea fishing tournament that could make even the most seasoned fishermen sit up and listen. And this memoir would not be complete without it. Here's my story.

The Gulf Coast hosts a series of bluewater fishing tournaments, known collectively as the Gulf Coast Triple Crown Championship. This prestigious circuit includes three fiercely competitive events: the Orange Beach Billfish Classic in Orange Beach, Alabama, the Mississippi Gulf Coast Billfish Classic in Biloxi, Mississippi, and the Emerald Coast Blue Marlin Classic at Sandestin, Florida, which lead up to the Blue Marlin Grand Championship, also in Orange Beach. The latter is broadcast live on television and streamed online, earning its title as the "Greatest Show in Sportfishing."

Held in June and July, these tournaments normally draw 80 to 90 boats, from sleek 40-footers to stunning 100-foot yachts. These boats, worth up to a cool $10 million and often crewed by five or more, come from Florida, Texas and even the Caribbean. With around $2 million in prize money at stake in each event, competition is fierce. The real stars are in the Blue Marlin category, with the heaviest catch taking home the big trophy, though there's also cash on the line for the largest Yellowfin tuna, Mahi, and Wahoo.

The "bluewater" in the Gulf Coast Triple Crown Championship isn't just a name—it's a nod to the striking blue depths at the edge of the continental shelf. That's where the tournament's prize fish—Blue Marlin, Yellowfin tuna, Mahi, and Wahoo—like to hang out. As NASA oceanographer Gene Carl Feldman explains, the ocean's blue color isn't about the water being blue; it's actually clear. "A glass of water will, of course, appear clear as visible light passes through it with little to no obstruction. But if a body of water is deep enough that light isn't reflected off the bottom, it appears blue." So, when we talk about bluewater fishing, we're really talking about fishing in the deep, open ocean where the water is so deep and clear that it takes on that beautiful blue hue.

On Ono Island, my backyard was a mere 29 miles from the edge of the continental shelf in the Gulf of Mexico—perfect for serious bluewater fishing. Our boat, a 48-foot Viking we called *Can't Deny It*, had twin Mann 1,110 horsepower engines that could propel her over 40 miles per hour, although our cruising speed stayed in the low thirties.

Can't Deny It was equipped with all the comforts of home: three staterooms, two bathrooms, and a kitchen—we even had a washer and dryer on board. When we weren't fishing, we could grill and watch TV on the back deck. With a 1,000-gallon diesel tank plus an extra 250-gallon bladder, we could easily cruise 150 miles out into the Gulf and spend two to three days living the dream, surrounded by nothing but water and sky.

While *Can't Deny It* may seem luxurious and well-equipped, it actually stood on the modest side compared to our competitors. Most boats in the tournaments were larger and faster, with more advanced electronics and comfort technologies. The typical boat measured around 60 feet and cruised at speeds of 40-45 knots. Many were outfitted with state-of-the-art omnidirectional sonar, which scans the water beneath and around the boat and gives detailed graphics of both bait and predator fish nearby. Captains could quickly assess whether prize fish might be close by, and if not, they would move to more promising fishing spots to optimize their time on the water.

These advanced sonar systems come with a hefty price tag, around $250,000, but despite not having this cutting-edge technology on our boat, we never felt it was necessary for winning.

Sea Keepers were another technology added to many competitive fishing boats. These devices, basically sophisticated computer-controlled gyroscopes installed below decks, work by generating torque through a rapidly spinning flywheel. The force from this torque transfers to the hull, smoothing out the boat's ride by counteracting wave action. Impressively, Sea Keepers can reduce a boat's roll—its side-to-side motion—by as much as 95%, which is a real game changer in terms of comfort as it helped mitigate seasickness, fatigue, and anxiety on board. While we certainly preferred a smooth ride, we knew that rough water was just part of the game.

I purchased *Can't Deny It* in May 2018, just before the start of the 2018 bluewater season. Since she wasn't set up for bill fishing, we hauled her out at Barber's Marina in Elberta, Alabama, to get started on the upgrades. Besides stocking her with essentials like cleaning supplies, linens, and bedding—as you would outfit an apartment—we also added a new stereo system, updated marine electronics, underwater lights, and a fighting chair on the back deck. Everything was installed just in time for the Mississippi Gulf Coast Billfish Classic in Biloxi, the first of three major tournaments, which kicks off in early June.

The tournament in Biloxi, like the others on the bluewater circuit, is a well-orchestrated carnival of sorts and a whole lot of fun. Boats start arriving on Tuesday to participate in a golf tournament. The registration fee, usually around $5,000, secures a preferred spot at the dock. Wednesday afternoon features the captain's meeting, attended by the captain, the first mate, and other crew members, to go over rules and regulations. This is fol-lowed by a kick-off party complete with great food, sponsor gifts for the teams, and usually live music. Final wagers are placed at this party and continue into the next morning, with categories ranging from $500 to $10,000 for each of the four fish types. Betting across the board on every money category for each fish typically costs around $80,000. The larger money categories, attracting fewer players, offer better odds of winning, but tend to be dominated by the larger, faster boats with advanced technology and professional crews. A portion of the money raised at these tournaments goes to charities.

Most tournaments kick off on Thursday morning. The boats gather about a mile off the beach for a noon shotgun start. Once the starting gun fires, it's a mad dash to the spots captains believe hold the most promise, with fishing permitted anywhere in the Gulf of Mexico.

My captain, Bo Keough, had been with me for many years, previously on my boat *Reel Happy*, a 41-foot Albemarle. The crew was led by my son Todd, who managed the team on each outing, and included four of his high school friends: Will Beard, Richie Prince, Pete VanLingen, and Mac Waller. Depending on the tournament, others like Harry Ladas, Thomas Leland, and Will Parker would rotate in. All the boys were teenagers and had fished together for years on my boats. Captain Bo and I found that a crew of five was our sweet spot. We were there to have a good time but make no mistake—we were there to compete and believed we could go toe-to-toe with the best.

I knew each of the boys well, having coached some in Little League and joined others on hunting and fishing trips, along with attending numerous social functions with their families. They were also among the hundred or so interns who had worked on my summer research projects over the past decade. These projects held commercial value for me and bolstered their college applications and resumes, with me as their reference. It was a win-win.

Preparation for our tournaments was extensive and began as soon as the previous one ended. This meant ongoing repairs and maintenance for engines, generators, air-conditioning, and electronics. We meticulously checked and updated every piece of tackle and gear. *Can't Deny It* had a knack for attracting marlin, and we wanted her to be streamlined, quiet, and effective in the heat of competition.

Our approach was thoroughly detailed. We always started with brand new line on all our reels, making sure every reel was serviced to perfection, and double-checked that the drags were set just right. The knots and swivels had to be faultless, and the hooks razor-sharp. We couldn't risk missing out on the winner's circle due to faulty equipment, lack of preparation, or subpar gear. Even the onboard cameras needed to be in top working order to document everything. Managing the slew of state and federal fishing and vessel licenses was also part of the drill—it was a lot to keep track of.

Our typical offshore setup had Captain Bo and me at the helm while our crew manned the back deck, also known as the cockpit. The boys treated this space like their "office" and were incredibly proficient in all things marine-related, even though they were by far the youngest crew in every tournament. They were confident and skilled on the water, always eager to prove themselves against the top competitors on the circuit.

Bill fishing is often described as hours of boredom punctuated by moments of sheer pandemonium, making experience and well-established procedures important. When a Blue Marlin is on the line, the intensity on deck skyrockets, and it's crucial that everyone knows exactly what to do. Good communication between the captain, the mate, and the crew is essential. Team *Can't Deny It* thrived on this chemistry and always looked forward to competing fully prepared. In every sense, bill fishing is a team sport.

The Emerald Coast Billfish Classic, held the last week of June at Baytown Marina in Sandestin, Florida, was my favorite event in the Gulf Coast Triple Crown Championship. The marina is not only equipped with excellent docking facilities but is also surrounded by top-notch hotels, golf courses, shops, and restaurants, making it a perfect spot for team members' families to enjoy a week-long stay. The event attracts thousands of lively spectators each year.

Our boys covered most of the entry fee themselves, and I handled all other expenses. I believed that working to earn their share of the fee would be beneficial for them—it certainly was for me at their age. They also pooled money for the Calcutta, wanting to have a stake in the game themselves. We placed bets on *Can't Deny It* for tuna, Mahi, and Wahoo. When my son Todd asked about betting on Blue Marlin, I half-jokingly told him, "If we don't bet on Blue Marlin, we'll win." And I added that winning Blue Marlin would make us tournament champions and bring in plenty of money anyway. Fishermen are a superstitious bunch, after all. Only time would tell how our bets would play out.

Captain Bo Keough was something of a local fishing legend, and we were fortunate to have him at the helm. Bo was deeply woven into the fabric of the local captain community along the Alabama and Florida Gulf Coasts, with an uncanny knack for knowing where the fish were—and where they were likely to be next. I delved into data science and spent time with providers to discuss potential fishing hotspots.

We subscribed to services like Hilton's and Roff's, which provided daily satellite screenshots of the Gulf of Mexico. These were invaluable, offering detailed maps and imagery that showed us altimetry, chlorophyll levels, temperature, currents, watercolor, and eddies—key indicators of nutrients and bait presence. We analyzed this data to better understand temperature breaks, where opposing currents meet and often signal nearby rips.[73] If sea grass is stacked along these rips, fishing tends to be highly productive.

While many other teams had access to the same data, the

---

73. A "rip" in offshore bluewater fishing refers to a visible line in the ocean where different water masses meet, often resulting in changes in water color, temperature, or surface texture. These areas are known to attract baitfish and larger predatory fish, making them prime fishing spots. Fishermen look for rips as indicators of productive fishing areas due to the convergence of nutrient-rich waters.

way we manipulated and interpreted it often led us to different fishing grounds. Sound familiar? Turns out, fishing is a lot like investing on Wall Street.

At Emerald Coast, Bo and I were on the same page about where to fish, though he had the final say if we disagreed. We opted to head 130 miles south of Destin, as both veteran captain insights and my data analysis suggested it would be the best location. The area, known as Lloyd's Ridge, is remote, located due west of Tampa and not well-known. While considered a low-probability spot by some, we were undeterred. We thought we had done our homework and that we knew something that others didn't.

We left Destin with the rest of the fleet at noon on Thursday, reaching our chosen location by 4 p.m. Right away, it was clear we had made a great choice. The surface was bustling with flying fish, Bonito, Blackfin, and Skipjack tuna—favorites in the Blue Marlin diet. Our marine electronics showed that larger fish lurked below as well. The steady winds and rolling seas were ideal, much preferable to gusty winds and choppy waters based on my extensive bill fishing experience. From my days in commercial fishing, I could recognize a promising fishing spot, and this certainly looked like one.

We also found an impressive weed line in the vicinity, so we began trolling our favorite lure, a red and black Aloha Beauty, at 6 knots in about 3,000 feet of water. Weed lines, often seen as golden oases offshore, are typically made up of sargassum—a brown macroalgae filled with tiny air bladders that keep it afloat and give it a bright yellow-gold to dark amber-brown color. These mats of grass form a floating ecosystem that supports fish, crabs, worms, and shrimp, making them hotspots for attracting larger fish. With the combination of the current and the weed line, the area showed great potential.

We typically fished with seven baits in our spread, a technique known as the "Tonga Tactic" which is popular in the South Pacific. We rigged small lure heads with ballyhoo baits on the left, right, and center outriggers. These were complemented by teaser baits on the left and right, which we operated from the bridge, trailing about 30 yards behind the boat. We also ran flat lines 10-15 yards off our stern to stir up the water and draw fish closer.

Once we dropped our lines, the action was fast and furious. We landed a Blue and a White Marlin, along with several Wahoos, Mahi, and Yellowfin tunas. Unfortunately, our Blue Marlin was under the tournament minimum of 108 inches, so we released her—tournament rules impose hefty fines for keeping undersized fish, and most Blue Marlins caught are released as a conservation measure.

We fished until dark, then stored our gear. With the seas calming, we grilled hamburgers and fresh steaks from the Yellowfin tuna we'd caught earlier on the back deck. The mood was upbeat about the next day's prospects, especially since few boats were in our vicinity. We felt we had the perfect spot mostly to ourselves.

By Friday morning, the boys had our lines back in the water before sunrise. Despite choppy 3-4-foot seas, we were pumped about our piece of water. We fished there until 11 a.m., catching more fish but not the prize we were after. We then tried our luck to the west for a bit before returning to our original location, which still teemed with bait and had that promising, transitional look often favorable in bluewater fishing.

A few hours later, excitement peaked. At 3 p.m., with Captain Bo and I at the helm and the boys on deck, music blaring, I spotted a giant Blue Marlin surging up from the depths right into our spread. She hit the right flat teaser with her bill and dove back down. Bo and I shouted, "Blue Marlin!" alerting the crew. Seconds later, our 80-class Penn reel was screaming. The marlin had taken the Aloha Beauty on the port outrigger, and the battle was on.

Angler Will Beard hurried into the fighting chair as Mac Waller strapped him in and pivoted the chair toward the fish, careful not to touch the rod which would have disqualified our team. Captain Bo put *Can't Deny It* into reverse to back down on the marlin, flooding the cockpit with seawater up to the boys' knees. Seeing a few feet of seawater on my back deck 130 miles out in the Gulf of Mexico amid 4-foot seas always set me on edge, but Bo had done this many times and knew exactly what he was doing. Besides, Viking designs its sport fishing vessels to drain water quickly, which was definitely a good thing.

Todd, Richie, Pete, and I quickly reeled in our other baits and moved any unnecessary gear away from the cockpit while making sure our cameras were rolling. The game was on, and Team *Can't Deny It* sprang into action.

And the fight was nothing short of spectacular. Blue Marlin are powerful, aggressive fighters known for their hard runs and breathtaking aerial acrobatics. Given that females can weigh up to four times more than males, we knew we had hooked a big girl. She leapt several times, and from her jumps, we could tell she was definitely big enough to keep—if we could manage to bring her onboard. This is when strategy, tactics, and clearly defined roles really come into play.

The plan was for Will to maintain pressure on the fish and work with Captain Bo to bring her close to *Can't Deny It*. This could take anywhere from 30 minutes to 8-10 hours, depending on the fish's size, how it was hooked, our fighting tactics, and various other factors.

Once the marlin was near, Todd, our wireman, would grab the leader and guide the fish to the starboard gunnel, near the tuna door. Then, Pete and Richie, our bigger team members at around 6 feet and 200 pounds, would gaff the fish and haul her through the door.

"It's almost like ballet. It takes a lot of orchestration and choreography. Everyone has their job. It's a fascinating team sport to watch," is how Dr. Ellen Peel from the Billfish Foundation describes it.

I was always uneasy with Todd as our wireman, a critical job in the final stages of a marlin fight. When the fish gets close to the boat, the wireman wraps the wire leader around his hand to control the fish so another angler can either gaff the fish (if it is to be boated) or release the hook. In "The Big Rock: Inside the High-Stakes Hunt for the Elusive Million-Dollar Marlin," author Bethany Bradshear recounts a harrowing incident where a fish made a sudden, unpredictable move that pulled the wireman off the deck into 10,000 feet of water, never to be seen again. Although such outcomes are rare and specific techniques can minimize risks, the danger is always in the back of my mind.

Gaffing the fish is another intense moment in the chaotic, high-stress process of landing a huge marlin. A gaff is a stainless-steel pole with a large hook on the end, designed to secure a large fish and pull it aboard. Missing the gaff, or a "yip," often results in a lost fish, so the pressure was on Pete and Richie to perform flawlessly. Pete had missed a few big Yellowfin tunas earlier in the season, but we believed he was ready this time. He and Richie understood that they might only get one chance and needed to make it count.

Our marlin was large and strong, and the fight went on for hours before it began to tire and show signs of exhaustion. As it neared *Can't Deny It*, the tension mounted—there was so much that could go wrong during the wiring, gaffing, and hauling the fish through the tuna door to the back deck. As Todd brought the fish closer, we could see it was legal size, likely between 115-120 inches long and she looked heavy.

She made one last run, but the next time Todd brought her close, Pete and Richie set the hooks in her like pros. In seconds, the fish was on the back deck, and the celebration erupted. She measured 120 inches in length, and based on her girth, the formula for estimating marlin weight, suggested she was between 700-750 pounds. Considering a 600-pound marlin would win many tournaments, we were thrilled, believing we had a real shot at the crown. We secured everything and set course for Destin, Florida.

We docked at Baytowne Marina in Sandestin around 10 p.m. Friday night. Unfortunately, the weigh scales were closed, so we had to wait until Saturday afternoon to weigh our catch. This delay was problematic because the intense Florida sun would surely cause our fish to lose some water weight over the next day, possibly as much as 5%. To minimize the loss, we wrapped her in a comforter from the master stateroom and kept her wet, hoping to preserve her weight for the next 18 hours. Exhausted from the physical demands of being offshore in moderate seas for a few days, we slept soundly that night.

Saturday morning, we were up and counting down the hours until *Can't Deny It* could weigh its Blue Marlin. At Emerald Coast, the scales open at 4 p.m., and boats with fish to weigh must be inside Destin Pass by 6 p.m. Teams typically only bring their catch to the scales if they believe the fish is heavy enough to compete for prize money. These fish are kept on ice below decks until weighed, and after the weigh-in, they are donated to the local food bank.

Can't Deny It was first in line, thanks to Captain Bo having positioned us right next to the scale the night before. As our marlin was prepared for weighing, tension was high among the crew. We believed our catch was competitive, but the scuttlebutt from the fleet suggested that other boats had landed big fish as well. As our marlin was hoisted vertically, the scale's readout briefly went dark, then the display flickered to life, showing 699.2 pounds! We were overjoyed, feeling a surge of hope that we might just clinch the win, though the wait through the next several hours was agonizing.

That weekend, around 40 Blue Marlins were caught, but most didn't meet the size requirements for weighing and were released. However, three teams were rumored to have caught marlin sizable enough to compete: *Reel Fire* from Biloxi, Mississippi, *You Never Know* from Road Harbor, British Virgin Islands, and celebrity chef Emeril Lagasse's *Aldente* from Destin.

Watching these boats approach the scale and their catches being weighed was nerve-wracking. Their marlin weighed in at 665, 640, and 476 pounds, respectively. Despite the stiff competition and having the youngest team in the 91-boat, $2 million tournament, we were the Emerald Coast Billfish Classic Champions. It was a phenomenal achievement for Bo, me, and our young crew. The celebration that night was unforgettable, surrounded by family, friends, and competing teams. Our boys truly were the toast of the tournament.

On Sunday morning, the closing awards ceremony kicked off at 9 a.m. Captains and their crews, now cleaned up and dressed nicely, gathered as the breakfast buffet served up an excellent spread. The tournament director thanked the sponsors and participants, also highlighting the significant funds raised for charity, includ-ing The Sandestin Foundation for Kids, Florida Environmental Protection Clean Marina Program, and The Billfish Foundation.

As the soon-to-be-crowned champions, we were the last to be called to the stage. As our names were announced, the other teams gave us a standing ovation, and most seemed genuinely pleased for us. One captain joked that it was like an amateur winning the Masters, but we never saw ourselves as amateurs or underdogs. We knew what we were doing and proved it in this tournament and others too. Winning the tournament established us as a formidable presence in future competitions as well, solidifying our status among the elite in the fraternity of champions at the Emerald Coast—the most prestigious event on the Gulf Coast Bluewater circuit.

After that victory, our young men became local legends, thanks to the high-profile nature of the tournament and the popularity of saltwater fishing along the Gulf Coast. Media outlets like USA Today, Marlin Magazine, In the Bite, Coastal Angler, and various television and radio stations across the southeast covered our story. Our prize winnings of $131,040 were shared among the captain, crew, and the boat.

Bound forever by this incredible experience, our team continued to fish in future tournaments. The boys' newfound fame made them highly sought after by owners of some of the most sophisticated yachts on the Gulf Coast. Their notoriety secured them excellent summer jobs during college from the Gulf Coast to the Bahamas, all the way to Bermuda. All's well that ends well!

Fishing and Wall Street have more in common than you might think. Whether you're casting a line or crunching numbers, it's all about reading the environment and knowing when to make your move and when to sit tight. Anglers learn to read the waters and make calculated moves, just like analysts keep their eyes on the markets, searching for the best opportunities to buy or sell. Both require a blend of patience, skill, and intuition—all of which our boys had despite their youth. The thrill of landing a big marlin and the satisfaction of a successful investment thesis may come from different worlds, but the skills and mindset behind them are remarkably alike.

Looking back on that experience, one thing's for sure—there may not have been a more fittingly-named boat for our crew that summer. *Can't Deny It*, indeed.

10

What About the Future?

As I look back on my decades-long career on Wall Street, it's clear that understanding the past is key to forecasting what lies ahead. Warren Buffett famously said, "In the business world, the rearview mirror is always clearer than the windshield," reminding us that hindsight often provides the clarity we need to make better predictions about the future. With that in mind, it's time to shift gears from looking back to looking ahead. So, what is the optimal path forward for the industry, and what does the future hold for energy stocks? These are the questions that investors care about deeply. In this final chapter, I'll share my insights for the ever-evolving energy sector.

Having notified Evercore ISI of my decision to leave in March 2020, I officially departed in July 2021 to pursue other interests. I'm still actively involved in the industry and frequently invited to speak on various company, industry, and market-related topics. I relish these interactions and debates, particularly seeing the oil and gas industry, its companies and management teams achieve their potential and have it reflected in the stock market.

Leaving when I did felt like the right thing to do, as the industry was poised on the brink of a prosperous period. The Pledger initiative I had championed had taken root, and by mid-2021, every major oil, E&P, and Oil Service company had adopted the model, reaping benefits for their shareholders. As returns on capital, valuations, and share prices surged, investors applauded the commitment to value creation.

The energy sector's value proposition regained competitiveness with other major sectors of the S&P 500, fulfilling the original goals of the Pledger and Era of the Super-Major movements. Market performance was strong, with the S&P Energy index not only outperforming as the best group in the S&P 500 but also doubling the results of nearly every other market group since our sector upgrade in November 2020. Future gains seem likely, with boards and CEOs feeling empowered to maintain their course, especially given the strong investor support for these new capital management policies in the equity markets.

Another factor in my decision to move on was the broader changes occurring within Wall Street research and investment banking. The industry landscape is shifting, with firms increasingly competing more with financial capital rather than intellectual capital that characterized the earlier, more exciting phases of my career. These shifts suggested that it was the right time for a new chapter. This doesn't imply that investment banks won't remain strong investments. They continue to be adaptable, innovative, and adept at navigating market fluctuations to grow profitability as evidenced by the quadrupling of Evercore's stock price during the past decade. Nevertheless, the evolving nature of research held less appeal to me.

A key shift in sell-side research regards MiFID (Markets in Financial Instruments Directive), which introduced new regulations aimed at enhancing market efficiency and competitiveness. These regulations cover a broad spectrum of financial activities, including trading, reporting, and disclosure. Prior to MiFID, investment banks and other financial institutions commonly bundled the cost of research with other client services, such as trading commissions.

Under the new rules, financial institutions must unbundle the cost of research from other services and directly charge clients for it. With greater transparency around these payments, spending is becoming more deliberate, and clients are unlikely to engage with as many research and trading firms as before—likely resulting in a reduced volume of research received. This shift coincides with mounting pressure on investment management fees stemming from the rise of passive investing through index funds and ETFs, which also reduces the demand for traditional sell-side research.

Facing pressure from regulatory changes and fee compression from buy-side customers, sell-side firms have scrutinized and reduced their expenses, leading to less investment in research departments. This will surely dilute research efforts and diminish the depth of analysis for commodities with the number of stocks under coverage per analyst doubling and tripling at some firms in recent years. The long-term effects will depend on how the industry adapts to the changing regulatory landscape and how market participants adjust their research practices to meet evolving investor demands.

Regardless, the new model does not favor business models that once allowed analysts the time, focus, resources, and freedom to make substantial, multi-year strategic forecasts—like those seen in the Era of the Super-Major, the Golden Age of Refining, Crude Oil in 2008, or the Pledge. This could fundamentally alter the nature and scope of equity research in the future.

Artificial intelligence (AI) has the potential to disrupt the financial industry and the work of Wall Street research analysts. With advances in machine learning and natural language processing, AI systems are becoming increasingly adept at analyzing vast amounts of financial data and generating insights and predictions that were once the exclusive domain of human analysts. Whether the marginal cost of research content is headed to zero is hard to know but the trend is almost certain to be lower.

To be fair, AI is not a perfect substitute for human expertise. There remain many areas where analysts maintain an edge—such as interpreting complex information, understanding market context and nuance, and making judgment calls rooted in experience and intuition. Moreover, the role of research analysts extends beyond predictions and data analysis. It involves building relationships with investors and corporate clients, identifying market trends, and offering tailored insights that align with client needs. These are areas where the human element still matters—and where machines fall short.

At a minimum however, the increasing use of AI and other advanced technologies will reshape the role of Wall Street analysts. As research becomes more commoditized, analysts will need to adapt by working alongside AI, using its capabilities to enhance rather than replace their insights. AI is most likely to augment the work of analysts—creating new opportunities, but also new challenges. Balance between real wisdom and artifical intelligence seems to be the optimal model in this area.

Overall, these new models contrast with my macro-micro hybrid model which sought to provide accurate commodity forecasts on global crude oil and refined product markets while providing best in class research on the 10 to 12 companies that I covered. The approach worked well with key energy macro calls enabling our energy teams at Morgan Stanley and Evercore ISI to be among the most highly rated energy groups ever on Wall Street, according to the II poll. These were by far the most fun, value-added, money-making calls in the energy sector during the past three decades. They enabled me to be the #1 or #2 ranked analyst in the Integrated Oil Category a record 20 times and a member of the II All-America team 24 times. I am appreciative of this historic level of support from the investment community, especially over such a long period of time.

Going forward, because the Pledger framework has become the central feature of capital management policies of Big Oil, E&P, Oil Service and R&M companies around the world, and fundamental conditions will likely be attractive, the investment outlook for the industry seems positive. Valuation is favorable as well, with the energy sector trading below the midpoint of the range on key valuation measures in relation to the past decade.

The fundamental outlook is constructive because growth in oil demand will rise at a healthy rate in the coming years and supply looks like it may be challenged to keep pace. Healthy markets for crude oil and refined products are the probable outcome.

On the demand side, consumption of oil is a function of income, population, and price. Starting with income, the IMF expects nominal global GDP to rise by 5.0% annually from 2024-2028. This compares to 4.2% annually during the past five years, which included the significant economic decline during COVID. While the IMF provides credible analysis on each region and the world in total, growth in China represents a key downside concern.

Global economic growth drove gains in oil demand of 1.6% and 1.5% annually during the past 5 and 10-year periods. Growth in oil demand therefore rose at 30% and 34% of the rate of GDP gains during the two timeframes. The amount of oil used per unit of GDP, which is known as oil intensity declined by 3.3% and 2.2% annually during the 5 and 10-year periods.

While oil is required to generate economic growth in all coun-tries, regional differences in oil intensity hold implications for future trends in oil demand. For instance, consumers in the U.S. demand seven and 20 times more oil per capita than faster growing countries like China and India. This implies that oil consumption will rise as GDP and living standards increase even though global oil intensity will decline. Factors driving this trend include the adoption of renewables, technological innovation, and the regulatory response to climate change. In essence, everyone in the world seeks to become more energy efficient every day.

The IEA, in conjunction with OPEC, provide the most dependable insights into oil fundamentals through the collective expertise of hundreds of analysts and forecasters within their respective organizations. Today, the IEA holds three scenarios: 1.) Stated Policies Scenario (STEPS) which shows the trajectory implied by today's policy settings, 2.) Announced Pledges Scenario (APS) which assumes that all aspirational targets announced by governments are met on time and in full and 3.) the Net Zero Emissions by 2050 (NZE) scenario which maps out a way to achieve a 1.5 °C stabilization in the rise in global average temperatures, alongside universal access to modern energy by 2030.

The IEA's STEP's scenario is the most realistic in our view. It indicates that sales of internal combustion engine (ICE) vehicles peaked in 2019 and that road transport will no longer be a source of oil demand growth by 2030. Gasoline appears to be most at risk with EVs likely to rise to 10% of the global vehicle fleet with fleet fuel efficiency increasing by 0.6% per year to 2030.

Key drivers include changing population effects, urbanization, automation, battery costs, and vehicle prices. While penetration of EVs will be significant, obstacles to EV growth include: 1.) cost (EV costs are higher without subsidies), 2.) home charging (35% of Americans and Europeans live in apartments, flats or condos), 3.) cold weather performance (battery performance falls in cold weather), 4.) charging infrastructure (more needed given long charge times), and

5.) environmental (at U.S. electrical grid CO_2 intensity EVs provides small decreases in lifetime CO_2 emissions versus hybrids). Overall, EVs appear to represent lower threats to oil demand than higher fuel economy and emissions standards especially with expectations for EV adoption rates declining.

Positive demand growth for diesel, aviation fuel, and petrochemicals will likely offset some of the declines from gasoline although the IEA envisions global oil demand peaking in 2029 or 2030 around 105 MMBPD. While possible, oil intensity would have to decline at a significantly faster rate than that of the past 10 years for their scenario to come to fruition. We will take the "over," as the effect of rising incomes on oil demand appears underestimated. We expect global oil demand to rise by around 1.0 MMMPD annually, reaching 110 MMBPD by 2030. We expect the IEA to eventually extend their projection for peak oil demand to the mid-2030s or maybe later. For perspective, OPEC envisions global oil demand at 110 MMBPD in 2028 and does not envision peak oil demand before 2045. With IEA considered to be consumer-oriented and OPEC being producer-oriented, it reasons that the truth will be somewhere in between.

Accordingly, while global growth in oil demand may decelerate, gains in oil supply will probably moderate too. Regionally, because all global growth in oil demand of 9.1 MMBPD was accommodated by gains in oil supply of 9.8 MMBPD from North America during the past decade, this means that supply growth was minimal from other countries. However, while U.S. oil supply growth peaked at 17% annually in 2014, this rate of gain will decline to 3% annually in 2024-2025, according to the U.S.'s EIA.

This deceleration is stark and holds important market implications since North America represents 25% of global oil supply. The new plateau is due to peaking capital efficiency in the major shale basins of the U.S., namely in the Anadarko, Appalachian, Delaware, Williston, and in the Gulf of Mexico. While gains appear likely in the Midland, and Powder River

Basins, these areas may also be in decline when adjusting capital efficiency for lateral length of oil wells. When considering productivity per acre which adjusts for the impact of up or down spacing, U.S. onshore productivity may have reached its peak as far back as 2017. This outcome is entirely consistent with the "Red Queen" sub-doctrine of the Pledge.

The reason that this is important for global oil market balances is that if output of crude oil from the U.S. slows significantly, higher supply will be needed from other countries to balance world oil markets.

In the rest of the world excluding OPEC+, which represents another 25% of global oil supply, production declined during both the past 10 and 20-year periods. This underscores resource, environmental, regulatory and investment constraints in these countries. While output gains look likely from Argentina, Brazil and Guyana they will be needed to offset declines elsewhere. Aggregate growth in oil production is not expected to be noticeably positive from this group of countries through 2030.

The remaining 50% of global oil supply emanates from countries within OPEC +, many of which have relationships with the U.S. that can be described as mediocre at best. These countries will be counted on to accommodate most global oil demand growth during the next decade and includes Iraq, Iran, Russia, Saudi Arabia, the UAE, and Venezuela.

In Iraq, Iran, Russia and Venezuela, access to capital and technology remain obstacles to investment as it has for decades. Constraints include geopolitical factors, internal conflicts, investment challenges, OPEC quotas, shifts to renewable energy, and the desire for economic diversification. Oil production in these four countries increased at less than a percent annually during the past 10 years.

With Russia's war in Ukraine and continued disorder in Iran and Iraq, future gains in oil and gas production are uncertain at best. In Iran, progress on nuclear activities could lead to sanctions relief and the same could be true in Venezuela if political progress unfolds. If so, the outlook for investment in oil supply would be enhanced, even though significant gains are unlikely from either country before 2028, in our view.

This leaves Saudi Arabia and the UAE which have historically been reliable partners—managing oil markets to the "fair price for producers and consumers," as former Saudi Arabian minister Ali al-Naimi would say. These countries also hold the majority of global spare oil production capacity enabling them to manage market balances under a variety of scenarios.

Of course, if growth in global oil demand becomes increasingly accommodated by a select group of countries outside of North America, new power dynamics will materialize. The list includes the rising influence of producing countries over consuming ones, shifts in geopolitical and economic power, changes to energy security, new regional alliances, and environmental policy effects. Another wildcard is the impact of AI on oil markets. While rising incomes should drive up demand, this could be counter-balanced by reduced oil supply costs due to improved logistics, better resource allocation, and increased petroleum reserves. The bottom line is that when considering most medium to longer-term fundamental and geopolitical scenarios, oil prices near $85/bbl seem most likely during the next five years.

The outlook in global refining is constructive too because of many of the same fundamental factors. Healthy demand growth, modest net gains in capacity, and increasingly stringent environmental regulations led to record high margins in recent years. Over the medium-term, demand growth of 5 MMBPD looks likely to exceed that of capacity of 4 MMBPD with profitability likely to remain robust through 2028. While the shares of industry R&M leaders Marathon Petroleum, Phillips 66 and Valero have doubled during the past five years, somewhat reflecting this positive outlook, further gains seem likely.

While Wall Street remains constructive on oil and gas equities, their potential might seem modest compared to the opportunities available from artificial intelligence and other technology related stocks. However, AI is highly energy intensive and the outlook for the power that fuels it is quite positive. According to the MIT Technology Review, "Training a single AI model can emit as much carbon as five cars in their lifetimes" and IEEE Spectrum notes that "AI chips require up to five times more power than traditional processors because of the complex computations involved in deep learning."

Although renewable energy is becoming more cost-effective and scalable, until storage technologies fully mature, fossil fuels like coal and natural gas will be needed to ensure stable and continuous power supply for the extensive data processing and computational tasks inherent in AI.

The investment implication is that while Wall Street firms cover crude oil, natural gas and refined products extensively, the same is not true for coal where governments, banks, and investors have shunned the sector in recent years. This is important because the IEA indicates that coal consumption will continue to rise. With coal currently making up 27% of global energy demand, IEA indicates that it will be difficult to dislodge from the energy mix. With only two to three Wall Street firms providing research on the coal sector, the ingredient for positive surprise seems likely. Leading coal companies boast ROCE near 50%, free cash flow yield of 15%, negligible debt and P/E ratios of only 8 (Fact Set). One major entity eliminated the dividend in 2023 to expedite share repurchases with 70% of free cash flow set for that purpose in coming years. Like R&M stocks in 2000, coal seems to be the most under-researched part of the energy sector on Wall Street today.

So, while oil and gas markets are likely to remain healthy, energy companies are also likely to remain judicious with shareholder capital, placing high value on surplus cash flow, balance sheet strength, and return of capital to shareholders—the intended outcomes of the Pledge. With industry reserve life declining by half during the past decade, a primary strategy will be for companies to replenish their inventory of development prospects in coming years through additional mergers and acquisitions.

While over 30 publicly traded U.S. E&P entities were acquired by larger entities since the Pledger phase commenced, activity will likely remain brisk during the next five years. Acquisitions will be beneficial if they add positions in new areas, increase integration with current positions, and combine skills and resources which lead to competitive advantage. Financial benefits are often significant too from economies of scale, technological and financial synergies, and better risk management.

While investors consider strategic benefits in transactions, changes in share prices are almost always explained by changes in economic value as defined by MVA and EVA, not to be confused with the myriads of partial profitability measures made popular by Wall Street.

That is, the value-based model informs companies as to whether prices being considered for acquisitions will be rewarded in the equity market beforehand and vice versa. Investors penetrate accounting fiction and are not fooled by partial profitability measures to justify transactions as has been repeatedly demonstrated in the market. The fact that the change in EVA explained around 80% of the change in share prices and MVA in the largest E&P transactions of the past cycle underscores investor emphasis on full-cycle valuation approaches.

A final strategic option that involves the Super-Majors is disintegration or separation of the key businesses, which is more controversial. That is, for the major integrated oil companies to split up their upstream and downstream businesses into standalone entities with separate financial statements, management teams, and boards of directors. The response to this idea from Super-Majors: BP, Chevron, ExxonMobil, Shell, and Total has been a resounding No on this topic in recent years. While some of their reasons are justified, others maybe not so much.

Typically, the Super-Majors indicate that vertical integration benefits, economies of scale, risk diversification, more efficient allocation of capital, and tax and legal considerations justify the integrated structure. If ROCE exceeds that of an entity in the same businesses and with the same business mix, the integrated model is probably adding value and serving shareholders.

The counterargument could be that increased focus on core competencies, more efficient capital allocation and risk management, and enhanced corporate governance could enhance value creation further.

While both views seem reasonable, the market is usually the best arbiter on matters such as these even though no two situations are the same. Because the E&P and R&M businesses of the Super-Majors exceed 85% of total profits and capital employed at these entities, examination of performance in both the integrated and "stand-alone" formats is insightful. The question is whether the Super-Majors in their integrated format have been able to post superior market results to the more focused "pure play" companies.

In relation to U.S. E&Ps, the stock market performance of the Super-Majors was mixed over 5, 10, 15, and 20 years, exceeding that of E&P indices during half of these periods. However, because the E&Ps and the Super-Majors underperformed S&P 500 during every period, results were not competitive with that which investors could attain in other sectors of the market i.e., alternative areas of investment for most major investors.

In relation to S&P R&M indices, each Super-Major substantially underperformed over 5, 10, 15, and 20 years. While industry conditions were weaker in E&P than R&M, capital management policy was superior at the leading R&M entities, Marathon Petroleum, Phillips 66, and Valero to that of the E&Ps and the Super-Majors during the past decade or so.

So far, ConocoPhillips has been the only former Super-Major to eschew the Super-Major model and split into upstream and downstream companies which it did in 2012. Marathon Oil and Marathon Petroleum were a smaller but significant integrated oil company and they split up in 2011.

Since these split offs, total market returns for companies

that abandoned the integrated model and focused their efforts in fewer areas have strongly surpassed those of the Super-Majors, lending credence to the counterpoint argument that the sum of the parts was greater than the whole in their formerly integrated model.

Total market returns including reinvested dividends for ConocoPhillips and Phillips66 was 260% which compares to Total at 150%, Chevron at 115%, ExxonMobil at 115%, Shell at 65% and BP at 50% since the ConocoPhillips split off in mid-2012.

For Marathon Oil and Marathon Petroleum, market outperformance versus the Super-Majors was even greater. Total market returns including reinvested dividends for Marathon Oil and Marathon Petroleum was 460% which compares to Chevron at 145%, ExxonMobil at 145%, Total at 125%, Shell at 85% and BP of 60% since their split off in mid-2011.

The performance of the separated companies was 11% and 15% per year for the ConocoPhillips and Marathon successors, which compares to 7% for Chevron and ExxonMobil, 8% for Total and 4% annually for BP and Shell. Not only did the "pure-play" entities double the annual performance of the SuperMajors since their split-offs over 10 years ago, but performance was also close to S&P 500, an outstanding result.

ConocoPhillips and Marathon indicated that they split up because in their former size: 1.) growth was difficult, 2.) that even when it did grow, gains were nominal in relation to smaller peers, and 3.) growth often came at the expense of returns and value creation. These are losing propositions which usually lead to corporate stagnation at best and outright deterioration in returns, valuation and share prices at worst.

These points and others remain relevant for consideration today.

First, business segment separation enhances focus on core competencies and deepens specialization, typically leading to better operational efficiency, improved resource allocation and expanded growth prospects. Bureaucracy is often reduced too, streamlining decision-making. Separation can also help attract and retain top energy sector talent by removing impediments to growth and offering more specialized career paths.

Corporate governance typically improves too as the focus of the management team and board of directors becomes spread over fewer functional and geographical areas. In the "pure play" structure, management incentives can be more effectively aligned with specific market objectives and individual performance, likely leading to more direct impacts on the value of the company in the equity market.

Finally, and maybe most importantly, is that separation usually creates opportunities for unlocking shareholder value by realizing the true worth of each segment. In R&M, Phillips 66 and Marathon Petroleum provide much more insightful information to investors today than in the previous integrated oil format and much more useful information than that the Super-Majors provide in R&M today as well. By providing investors with a clearer view of each segment's financials and prospects, better valuation and the recognition of untapped shareholder value is often the outcome.

While the decision to separate upstream and downstream businesses is complex and depends on many factors, including market conditions, company strategies, regulatory environments, and shareholder expectations—it ultimately must be justified by superior returns on capital. In other words, for separation to reward shareholders, the newly independent entities must deliver superior growth and returns compared to an integrated company with the same business mix. This is the ultimate test.

Because the Super-Majors are the most asset rich companies in the global energy sector, significant value creation opportunities are surely available from streamlining, reshaping, and focusing their portfolios. While these companies significantly contracted their global footprints in recent years, and much work has already been done, opportunities appear to remain given the quality and scope of their global asset bases. This is especially true if markets are truly shifting towards de-globalization.

This is not to say that the Super-Majors have not or could not employ the same strategies that delivered the superior performance of separated entities during the past decade or so. However, given their substantial underperformance over such an extended period, it is reasonable to question why they haven't, at least to the same degree.

It is also not to say that the Super-Majors are not set to thrive without separation of their upstream and downstream units in coming years. In fact, these entities are currently enjoying a heyday of sorts with ROCE above 15% and free cash flow yields near 10% during 2024-2025 according to the Wall Street consensus. These figures compare to ROCE of 3% and free cash flow yields of -5% before the Pledge commenced. Current levels of financial performance were last enjoyed near the end of the Era of the Super-Major in 2008. Results will remain strong over the longer term too, that is, if companies remain committed to the value-centric model that delivered their good fortune in the first place. Time will tell.

ACKNOWLEDGMENTS

This book is the culmination of countless contributions from individuals who have shaped my personal and professional journey.

I owe a debt of gratitude to my colleagues at Morgan Stanley, Evercore, the investment community and throughout the energy industry that are too numerous to mention. Their unwavering support and belief in the importance of these stories inspired me to document them.

I extend my thanks to Bethany McLean (*Enron: The Smartest Guys in the Room*), whose initial encouragement sparked the idea for this book.

I am especially indebted to Stephanie Glines, whose exceptional writing talent breathed life into these pages, masterfully weaving together the narrative threads. My appreciation also goes to Keith Glines for his guidance in bringing this book to market.

I am grateful for the wisdom provided by authors Andy Andrews and Watt Key. Their expertise has been instrumental in shaping this work.

I also want to acknowledge Rick Anderson, Mena Morgan, Miles Neumann, Juan Ronderos, and Amy Thompson for their candid perspectives and contributions.

A special note of thanks goes to Lewis Ropp for crafting the insightful foreword that sets the stage for the journey ahead.

To my family, your unwavering love and support have been my anchor throughout this process. Thank you to my parents for instilling in me the values of resilience, perseverance, and determination that have been crucial throughout my career and in the creation of this book.

Lastly, I extend my appreciation to you, the readers, for engaging with my story. It is my sincere hope that you find this book not only educational and entertaining but also inspiring, and that you may see reflections of your own journey within these pages.

With deepest gratitude,
Doug

ABOUT THE AUTHOR

Doug Terreson is the former Head of Energy Research at Evercore ISI and Morgan Stanley, where he covered the Integrated Oil, E&P, and R&M sectors. In this role, he was also responsible for the firm's global forecast for crude oil, refined product commodities, and Energy portfolio strategy. During his career, Doug was the #1 or #2 Integrated Oil analyst in the Institutional Investor poll a record 20 times and was a member of the All-America Research (II) team 24 times. He authored several notable reports, including "The Era of the Super-Major" (1998), "Higher for Longer" (Crude Oil, 2000), "The Golden Age of Refining" (R&M, 2003), "The Pledge for Greater Capital Discipline and Enhanced Corporate Governance" (2015), and "Time to Lean In" (2020). Doug was the lead analyst on some of the largest Energy IPOs in North America (Conoco), Europe (Statoil-Equinor), and Asia (Sinopec). He was also involved in major mergers, including BP-Amoco, BP-Arco, Chevron-Texaco, Phillips-TOSCO, Conoco-Phillips, Chevron-Unocal, Total-Fina, Total-Elf, and YPF-Repsol. Before leading the Global Energy Group at Evercore ISI and Morgan Stanley, Doug managed Putnam's energy mutual fund in Boston, which was one of the largest Energy funds globally. His early career began as an engineer with Schlumberger Limited on the US Gulf Coast. Doug holds a bachelor's degree in petroleum engineering from Mississippi State University, an MBA from Rollins College, and is a Chartered Financial Analyst (CFA). He currently serves as a Director at Phillips66, Third Gear Energy Fund, and chairs the Investment Committee on the Mississippi State University Board. Can't Deny It is his first book.

www.ingramcontent.com/pod-product-compliance
Lightning Source LLC
Chambersburg PA
CBHW040235110526
44582CB00020B/203/J